Affective Connections

Critical Perspectives on Theory, Culture and Politics

Series editors:

Critical Perspectives on Theory, Culture and Politics is an interdisciplinary series, developed in partnership with the Centre for Critical and Cultural Theory, which is based in the School of English, Communication and Philosophy at Cardiff University, UK. The series focuses on innovative research produced at the interface between critical theory and cultural studies. In recent years much work in cultural studies has increasingly moved away from directly critical-theoretical concerns. One of the aims of this series is to foster a renewed dialogue between cultural studies and critical and cultural theory in its rich, multiple dimensions.

Titles in the series:

Culture Control Critique: Allegories of Reading the Present,
Frida Beckman

Prometheanism: Technology, Digital Culture and Human Obsolescence,
Günther Anders and Christopher John Müller, translated
by Christopher John Müller

Creole in the Archive: Imagery, Presence and the Location of the Caribbean Figure,
Roshini Kempadoo

The Attention Economy: Labour, Time, and Power in Cognitive Capitalism,
Claudio Celis

Performative Contradiction and the Romanian Revolution,
Jolan Bogdan

Chinese Subjectivities and the Beijing Olympics,
Gladys Pak Lei Chong

The Extreme in Contemporary Culture: States of Vulnerability,
Pramod K. Nayar

Superpositions: Laruelle and the Humanities,
edited by Rocco Gangle and Julius Greve

Credo Credit Crisis: Speculations on Faith and Money,
edited by Laurent Milesi, Christopher John Müller and Aidan Tynan

Materialities of Sex in a Time of HIV: The Promise of Vaginal Microbicides,
Annette-Carina van der Zaag

From Shared Life to Co-Resistance in Historic Palestine,
Marcelo Svirsky and Ronnen Ben-Arie

Affective Connections: Towards a New Materialist Politics of Sympathy,
Dorota Golańska

Homemaking: Radical Nostalgia and the Construction of a South Asian Diaspora,
Anindya Raychaudhuri (forthcoming)

Partitions and Their Afterlives: Violence, Memories, Living,
edited by Radhika Mohanram and Anindya Raychaudhuri (forthcoming)

Contested Borders: Queer Politics and Cultural Translation in Contemporary Francophone Writing from the Maghreb,
William J. Spurlin (forthcoming)

Archaeologies of the Instant: Essays on Hypermodernity and Seeing,
edited by Peter R. Sedgwick and Damian Walford Davies (forthcoming)

Affective Connections

Towards a New Materialist Politics of Sympathy

By Dorota Golańska

ROWMAN & LITTLEFIELD
INTERNATIONAL
London • New York

Published by Rowman & Littlefield International Ltd
Unit A, Whitacre Mews, 26-34 Stannary Street, London SE11 4AB
www.rowmaninternational.com

Rowman & Littlefield International Ltd. is an affiliate of Rowman & Littlefield
4501 Forbes Boulevard, Suite 200, Lanham, Maryland 20706, USA
With additional offices in Boulder, New York, Toronto (Canada), and Plymouth (UK)
www.rowman.com

British Library Cataloguing in Publication Data Available
A catalogue record for this book is available from the British Library

ISBN: HB 978-1-78348-969-5
PB 978-1-78348-970-1

Library of Congress Cataloging-in-Publication Data Available
ISBN: 978-1-78348-969-5 (cloth : alk. paper)
ISBN: 978-1-78348-970-1 (pbk. : alk. paper)
ISBN: 978-1-78348-971-8 (electronic)

∞™ The paper used in this publication meets the minimum requirements of American National Standard for Information Sciences—Permanence of Paper for Printed Library Materials, ANSI/NISO Z39.48-1992.

Printed in the United States of America

Contents

Acknowledgments

This book results from a web of intense connections and inter-/intra-actions with many different people and bodies. It stems from an over four-year effort of doing research on memorial art, studying theories of new materialism, and investigating feminist knowledge production practices as well as from the various occasions for meeting people and exchanging ideas with them.

This work would have not been possible without the generous help from the National Science Center in Poland and an individual research grant that I received from this institution for running a project entitled *The Aesthetics of Trauma. Affective Perception vs. Representation of the Holocaust in Memory Sites* (grant number UMO-2012/05/B/HS2/04032, OPUS 3), hosted by the University of Łódź (Poland), the Faculty of International and Political Studies. This funding made my traveling to many sites and museums described in this volume possible. It also allowed me to meet scholars from different academic institutions worldwide (e.g., the US Holocaust Memorial Museum in Washington, DC, Yad Vashem—The World Holocaust Remembrance Center in Jerusalem, the University of Western Sydney in New South Wales, the Victorian College of the Arts in Melbourne, Columbia University in New York City) and discuss my thoughts and reflections with them. In all those places I met wonderful people willing to offer their help in the form of prolific discussions and critical insights that enabled making this book more comprehensible to readers. They also challenged my ideas forcing me to thoroughly think them through as well as suggested readings and concepts to be used in my argumentation. My special thanks go to Tvia Fried for teaching me how to navigate in the vast archives of Yad Vashem as well as for making my research stay in Jerusalem an absolutely rewarding experience. Similarly, I would like to thank Moti Fried for being my guide in the Israeli context. I am also extremely grateful to Marianne Hirsch for discussing with me my concepts and theoretical formulations to be further developed into this book as well as for inviting me (together with Susan Winett) to two conference events, which they coorganized. These were invaluable opportunities for sharing my research with others and for getting precious advice.

I owe a lot to Iris van der Tuin, a person whom I have known for many years now and who has always been willing to help. She invited me to join an outstanding network of researchers gathered within the COST European Cooperation in Science and Technology project on *New Materialism: Networking European Scholarship on "How Matter Comes to Matter"* (Action IS1307) wherein since 2014 I have served as an official representative of Poland. The researchers whom I met there as well as events in which I participated translated in a substantial broadening of my knowledge of new materialism as well as let me grasp the marvelous diversity of this philosophical ferment. This volume benefited a lot from my participation in this network and from the academic interactions with scholars from different geographical and disciplinary contexts that it enabled.

It is also absolutely necessary to appreciate the support and continuous encouragement that I received from my colleagues at the Department of American Studies and Mass Media as well as the Women's Studies Center at the University of Łódź, the two institutions where I am affiliated. On this occasion, I would like to thank the students enrolled in GEMMA program (run at the Women's Studies Center together with a bunch of other institutions from Europe), for their valuable contribution to my classes as well as for inspiring discussions, which provided me with a lot of new ideas and thoughts.

I would like to express my gratitude to the Rowman & Littlefield International team, especially Martina O'Sullivan, Michael Watson, and Holly Tyler, for making the whole publishing process nice and smooth. My thanks go as well to the editors of the book series Critical Perspectives on Theory, Culture and Politics—Chris Weedon, Glenn Jordan, Laurent Milesi, Radhika Mohanram, and Chris Norris—for being willing to host my volume within this marvelous series. I am grateful to Anna Catherine Hickey-Moody for suggesting this publishing house to me and for introducing me to Martina.

My special warm thanks go to my wonderful colleagues and friends Aleksandra M. Różalska, Monika Rogowska-Stangret, and Marek M. Wojtaszek, for their continuous encouragement, valuable comments on the previous drafts of this manuscript, patient readings, and challenging discussions. Finishing this book without their help would have never been possible. Finally, I would like to thank my loved ones for always being with me and giving me a lot of support and understanding.

Since the work on this book has been conducted for over four years, some ideas and concepts developed therein have already been published, yet in a different form. A discussion concerning a synaesthetic approach to memorial sites was included in the article "Affective Spaces, Sensuous Engagements: In Quest of a Synaesthetic Approach to 'Dark Memorials'" (published by *Interdisciplinary Journal of Heritage Studies* 8(21)(2015): 773–90). Remarks introducing affirmative approach to "dark installation art" as well as brief analyses of *The Garden of Exile* (by Daniel Libeskind), the installation *Shalekhet* (by Menashe Kadishman), and *Yad Layeled* (by Moshe Safdie) were published in "Terrifying Pleasures: In Quest of an Affirmative Approach to 'Dark Attractions'" (*Liminalities: A Journal of Performance Studies* 12(5): 1–17). Some comments on the material organization of the US Holocaust Memorial Museum in Washington, DC, together with remarks on the concept of affective aesthetics were included in the texts "Importing Trauma/Reclaiming the 'Wild': Holocaust Memory in the US" (published as a chapter of *American Wild Zones. Space, Experience, Consciousness*, edited by Jerzy Kamionkowski and Jacek Partyka. Frankfurt am Main: Peter Lang). Earlier, a cursory discussion on the concepts of affect and emotion was informing my argumentation in the chapter entitled "From Love to Hatred: Naming of Emotions in the 2010 United States National Security Strategy," published as a part of *Quilting Stories* (edited by Edyta Just and Marek Wojtaszek. Łódź: Łódź University Press). An analysis of paradigms of representation was a point of departure for ideas included in the text "Seeing Differently: Towards Affirmative Reading of Visual Culture" (a chapter in *Teaching Visual Culture in an Interdisciplinary Classroom: Feminist (Re)Interpretations of the Field*, edited by Elżbieta H. Oleksy and Dorota Golańska. Utrecht: Uithof Drukerijen), which I cowrote with Marek M. Wojtaszek. My reflections on the new materialist understanding of art related to trauma and on synaesthetic perception, illustrated with analyses of *The Garden of Exile* (by Daniel Libeskind) and *The Memorial to the Murdered Jews of Europe* (by Peter Eisenman), gathered in the article "Bodily Collisions: Toward a New Materialist Account of Memorial Art," are forthcoming in *Memory Studies* at the turn of 2017–2018. The volume is a more complete and longer version of these ideas and concepts, weaving them together into a coherent web of connections and experimental assemblages to offer a more comprehensive argumentation, informed thoroughly by my previous investigations and research.

Preface

Situated within the philosophical movement of feminist new materialism, the book fosters an affirmative perspective on art and positively approaches the process of nonrepresentational (or more-than-representational, where "more" should be read as "excess," rather than implying any kind of hierarchy) seeing, which makes an unconditional celebration of difference possible, beyond the negativist structures of dualism. The argumentation is inspired by Gilles Deleuze and Félix Guattari's philosophical framework, in particular, by their conceptualizations of "intensity" or "affect" (conceived of in terms of capability to affect and be affected) as well as by their formulation of the *process* of becoming (rather than the *state* of being). Accordingly, the general objective of the book is to disavow the oppositional system of thinking inscribed in the dominant renditions of the mechanism of representation and instead to offer an affirmative (as well as monistic) approach to perception, cognition, and experience, so vital—I argue—from the feminist point of view. Primarily theoretical in its construction, the book advances a new materialist concept of synaesthetic perception, where synesthesia is understood as a conjunctive and synthetic use of senses, or—quite simply—a union of senses. This idea is offered as a new figuration for approaching our cognitive (both intellectual and affective, or rather intellectual-affective as the two dimensions remain inseparable) faculties, away from taken-for-granted assumptions grounded in the negativist logic of the dominant systems of thinking. As such, my argumentation focuses on various intersections, or entanglements, of discourse and materiality, exploring the role of embodied experience as well as focusing on the agency of matter in the complex processes/events of producing knowledge.

Paradoxically (yet purposefully), although fostering an affirmative approach, the volume centers on the issue of trauma and traumatic memory as well as on the artistic production related to painful experiences, recollections, and occurrences. It critically approaches a number of memory museums, memorials, memory sites, and works of art related to the Holocaust. They, however, are located in three distinct culturo-political contexts, namely, Israel, Germany, and the United States, and—because of their different situatedness—function in dissimilar manners immensely affected by their singular material-semiotic settings. The decision to look at selected examples of memorial art and architecture from these three contexts is not accidental—my intention is to show various entanglements of discourse and materiality as related to the very different ways in which the events of the Shoah are remembered and made part of the public practices of commemoration in these distinct political contexts. I think these three culturo-political cases are particularly interesting, and different from each other, as far as the ways the memory of the Shoah operates as part of historical narratives present in the public discourse. This is especially relevant for the analysis of the so-called Holocaust museums, funded by governmental measures and offering "official" interpretations of these traumatic events. What concerns the more modest artistic installations—whose analyses I also include in my investigations—my choice of case studies was more determined by their specific constructions and workings. I focus on the illustrative aspects of these works of art with an aim of highlighting and explaining a number of theoretical and philosophical ideas offered within my argumentation.

As I also want to make clear, the practices of memorializing Holocaust have significantly changed over the past decades. Worth underlining is that the recently increased interest in and subsequent transition of the processes of memorialization of the Shoah must be related to the fact that witnesses of those events are passing away; hence, discernible is an urgent quest for keeping their stories and testimonies alive, and available for future generations. In a way, this phenomenon corresponds with a generally observable investment of contemporary societies in preservation of memory of the past. Taking into consideration the timeliness of this topic, and analyzing its broad theoretical context, the book—as mentioned earlier—focuses on a number of recently created Holocaust memorials, exhibitions, installations, and art objects, critically exploring the ways in which they operate and what kind of affective-intellectual experiences they offer. Importantly, in line with new materialist ideas, I approach them as *works of art* (cf. Bolt 2004a,b), acknowledging their active status as well as their multidimensional, incorporeal, and imperceptible workings within vibrant assemblages they form with other bodies.

Drawing on theoretical achievements of new materialism, the book aims to demonstrate that the new ways of interacting with the past/present/future and of encountering the lived experience of trauma—made available by contemporary artistic creation related thereto—can trigger a deeper understanding of these events and produce a more complex form of thoughtful and affective connections. As I want to demonstrate, this is vitally important from the feminist point of view and the nondiscriminatory politics connected therewith; however, the critical potential of such an approach still requires careful examination and theorization, especially in the context of current feminist epistemological debates and ethical deliberations. Bearing these diversified voices in mind, in this book, I propose a conceptual shift from the notion of "empathy" to one of "sympathy," as the latter connotes togetherness or assemblage rather than being in, or speaking from, the position of others. I also argue that such form of sympathy, which is not understood solely in terms of a purely sentimental response but rather itself constitutes a lived (affective) feeling/experience/event, is extremely useful in didactic terms as it allows for a more comprehensive grasp of experiences of discrimination, exclusion, suffering, or pain, so inscribed in our historicity.

The logic of the book is one of connections. First, this is effectuated by focusing on the intersectional, entangled coexistence and mutual co-constitution of the affective and the discursive, the past and the present, the social and the material, the movement and the stasis, the passive and the active, the learning and the unlearning, and so on. Second, the concepts that the book employs (especially *synaesthetic perception* and *sym*pathy) are themselves grounded in the new materialist philosophical paradigm, so they imply a dynamic assemblage-like connectivity. As such, the volume's objective is to redirect, or overcome, the binarized, oppositional logic, which always entails confrontation or conflict. By investing in the monistic approach, inspired by Deleuze and Guattari's philosophical ideas, my argumentation refuses participation in patriarchal structures of thinking, offering instead an affirmative and inclusive perspective. Such a theoretical framework focuses on machine-like creative continuities, flows, and becomings, and encourages a productive experimentation with novel figurations and inventive concepts. This serves the purpose of advancing timely nondiscriminatory politics.

The book is of interdisciplinary character and draws on academic insights from such disciplines as Holocaust studies, trauma studies, cultural studies, science studies, art theory and visual studies, memory studies, and tourism studies. Different from other publications related to this theme, the volume offers an affirmative conceptualization of trauma (practically nonexistent within the scholarship devoted to this topic). Consequently, it develops a new theoretical perspective on trauma and trauma sites (i.e., one grounded in radical empiricism that allows to explore the idea of memory from a bodily and materialist perspective) as well as a novel concept of aesthetic experience (i.e., one relying on the mobilization of affect rather than exclusively on cognitive mental processes). It also aims to offer a more concrete operationalization of affect theory within cultural studies by applying it in the analyses of cultural artifacts. By focusing on more-than-representational seeing, my intention is to emphasize that the synaesthetic, intersectional approach to perception is relevant for contemporary alliances based on equality and recognition of difference as well as for politics of solidarity. Consequently, in a truly Deleuzian spirit, the book signals the shift from arboreal representation to rhizomatic connectivity.

Introduction

Seeing Differently—Introducing a New Materialist Perspective

FROM NEGATION TO AFFIRMATION

Taking on new materialist lenses, the argumentation developed in this book offers a revision of the dominant ways of seeing, advocating instead for a more synaesthetic approach to the processes of generating knowledge, both scientific and not. The introductory section familiarizes readers with a new materialist philosophical strand, its roots and tendencies, and it points to certain novelties that this perspective advances, especially in the context of feminist critique. My objective here is to explain the potentials of this philosophical ferment with an emphasis on the post-representational (or more-than-representational) aspects of its ways of thinking, remaining in contrast with the dominant Western traditions of representational thought and the negativist logic inscribed therein. I proceed with explaining how in Western culture the processes of thinking and generating knowledge have always been intertwined and how this interconnectedness translated into certain criteria by which knowledge claims are judged, evaluated, and, subsequently, made universally valid. Since the ocularcentric paradigm has recently been challenged, I also comment on the historical circumstances that partially contributed to the crisis of the prevailing Western ways of thinking in terms of dualistic oppositions or binary pairs. In this context the book offers critical remarks on the dominant paradigms of approaching the visual, paying special attention to feminist investigations within this field. For this reason, the introduction briefly presents philosophical groundings of mimetic, intentional, and constructionist manners of conceptualizing representation in order to both sketch the most significant differences between them and expose their investment in the dominant dichotomous logic. Taking on a feminist point of view, the section explores uses and abuses of ideological renderings of visual culture and discusses both their theoretical assumptions and methodological shortcomings. It challenges the customary ways of reading art by dint of ideology, discourse, or semiotics advocated by theorists working within the methodological paradigm of the so-called "linguistic turn." By claiming that visual language is irreducible to conveyance, discovery, or construction of meaning (as these remain pertinent to representation), the book encourages a radical shift towards creational (i.e., affirmative) understanding of the visual.

There is a need for nonrepresentational or more-than-representational models to emerge that would allow to creatively approach visuality—as not reduced solely to seeing but rather understood as a complex phenomenon involving multisensual, synaesthetic, and affective dimensions. By underlining the ways in which traditional (i.e., dualistic) conceptualizations of the mechanism of representation have typically contributed to marginalization of women (and other "others"), I also focus on positive implications that affirmative perspective on the visual enables for feminist thinking. The turn to affect, I argue, advocated nowadays by many scholars and philosophers, offers a novel way of positively envisioning creative and pleasurable involvements with the visual and, importantly, facilitates approaching difference in affirmative manners. It also lets us overcome an impasse that feminism encounters when sticking to representational thinking as well as develops novel modes of critique—ones not grounded in confrontational, oppositional models but instead advocating for inventive alliances and fostering thinking in terms of continuities and connections. Consequently, the introduction outlines how this book implements a different (inspired by Deleuze and Guattari's philosophy) perspective on the processes of seeing and interacting with art/space/event, especially in the context of memorial art and artistic production related to traumatic occurrences, and how this can possibly translate into productive feminist politics.

In this part I also discuss the construction and logic of the book—I shortly present the content of each chapter, explaining critical links between the volume's different components and building connections between the concepts employed in my argumentation. My aim is also to make clear that it is of vital importance to work out vocabularies to critically and creatively approach these connectivities and alliances in order to provide such a conceptualization of the aesthetic experience that could offer novel, positive, and affirmative perspectives, important from a feminist point of view.

NEW MATERIALISM AND THE "MATERIAL TURN"

A new materialist perspective on broadly understood memorial art originates in a relatively recent philosophical trend, born partly out of dissatisfaction with purely constructivist tendencies dominating in cultural studies towards the end of the twentieth century. In literature one may encounter two terms that refer to this intellectual movement, namely, "new materialism" and "neo-materialism." They can be used interchangeably, although the former has become more common for the practitioners of this philosophical strand. Both these terms first entered the dictionary of cultural theory in the second half of the 1990s as a result of the theoretical developments offered by Manuel DeLanda (1996, 2006) and Rosi Braidotti (2000, 2002, 2006a). The two thinkers, although working independently, seem to have come to similar conclusions when diagnosing problems of cultural studies at that time and especially the field's continuous disregard for the issues of matter and materiality. New materialism aims at revising, or even reversing, this tendency. In Braidotti's words, it should be considered "a more radical sense of materialism" targeted at "rethinking the embodied structure of human subjectivity after Foucault" (2000, 158). Such a perspective necessarily takes into account its material dimension, that is, as Braidotti continues, it praises "the enfleshed Deleuzean subject," understood in terms of

> a folding-in of external influences and a simultaneous unfolding outwards of affects. A mobile entity, an enfleshed sort of memory that repeats and is capable of lasting through sets of discontinuous variations, while remaining faithful to itself. The Deleuzian body is ultimately an embodied memory. (2000, 159)

Such a conception assumes a constant dynamism and incessant transformation of subjectivity; it remains in flux, always a movement, never a stasis.

Even though both DeLanda and Braidotti are today considered pioneers of new materialism, typical for this strand interest in mutual co-constitution of matter and meaning has also been discernible in the 1990s in the oeuvres of other widely recognized scholars. Nevertheless, they have never referred to their concepts and theories applying the term "new materialism" (or "neo-materialism"). Groundbreaking has been the work of Bruno Latour (1993), in which he talks about "hybrids" and "collectives," that is, entities dwelling at the intersection of nature, culture, and discourse, which cannot be qualified as "purely" natural, cultural, or discursive. These hybrids, importantly, proliferate in the contemporary world. While looking critically at the ways in which knowledge is generated, Latour also notices the complex networks of agential interactions between human and nonhuman actors involved in these processes (1987). Offering a similar argumentation, Donna Haraway develops a concept of "natureculture" (2003) meant to capture inevitable entanglements of the material and the discursive, or of the natural and the cultural. These critical insights are aimed at disavowing the dualistic logic of thinking in terms of either/or, so typical for Western metaphysics. Going even further, yet taking important inspiration from performative approaches developed within the theoretical paradigm of the "linguistic turn," Karen Barad (1996, 2003, 2007)—working in the field of hard sciences or specifically quantum physics—proposes a philosophical approach that she names "agential realism," attempting at figuring out, in her words, "how matter comes to matter." This perspective rehabilitates matter, arguing that it is as active as our interpretative frameworks and meaning-generating structures. Accordingly, we do not simply equip matter with significations, but rather, she argues, matter is equally vigorous in the process of cognition—matter and meaning co-form each other. All these theories and concepts are of critical importance to new materialism.

Summing up, this philosophical tendency puts emphasis on what Haraway (1988) originally referred to as the "material-semiotic" and calls for a more detailed and critical examination of matter and materiality. Matter is then seen as lively, processual, transformative, and agential. For new materialists, matter's most significant quality is its capacity for "metamorphosis" (Braidotti 2002) or "morphogenesis" (DeLanda 1996, 2006), that is, its dynamic character. The increased interests in the vibrant operations of matter have been recently expressed by a growing number of scholars working from lots of scientific disciplines, ranging from philosophy of science and epistemology through biological, experimental, and hard sciences to social sciences, literary research, and art theory.[1] This phenomenon cannot be neglected as a symptom of more significant transformations of contemporary scientific ways of thinking discernible in the West.

Worth noticing is the fact that, although drawing critical attention to matter, by no means does the new materialism imply matter's independence from social contexts and cultural conditions. Admitting that meaning is important—and in that sense remaining in concord with the crucial assumptions of the "linguistic turn"—this approach nevertheless pays increased attention to matter, that is, to the element that has typically been crossed out from the dominant constructivist theorizations. Taking on a different perspective, it focuses on how the material and the social/discursive/cultural co-constitute each other and how this complexity is productive of singular events and knowledges. Rather than inert or brute, matter—in a new materialist account—is actively implicated in all complex processes of meaning production; therefore, its continuous dynamism has to be acknowledged. It means that this philosophical tendency's attitude towards social constructivism is more complex than it appears. Undoubtedly, as mentioned earlier, new materialism has emerged in the context of noticing shortcomings of the dominant approaches existing within the broadly understood cultural studies, a field having a propensity to reduce its analyses to ideological structures of power and meaning (see, e.g., Massumi 2002a). Nevertheless, it is far from claiming that poststructuralist investigations connected to discourse theory should be perceived as completely wrong or inadequate. New materialism does not argue that these critical developments should be trashed and disregarded. Rather, it draws quite heavily on the theoretical accomplishments of social constructivism, calling at the same time for more attention being paid to material processes and structures that coexist with the semiotic (or the discursive) and make the meaning/*mattering* possible.

Importantly, new materialism breaks up with the dominant Western ways of thinking in terms of binary oppositions. Taking on a monistic orientation, it is thoroughly suspicious towards any kind of dichotomous systems. Instead, it opts for—in Diana Coole and Samantha Frost's words—"a creative affirmation of a new ontology, a project that is consistent with the productive, inventive capacities they [new materialists] ascribe to materiality itself. The prevailing ethos of new materialist ontology is consequently more positive and constructive than critical or negative; it sees its task as creating new concepts and images of nature that affirm matter's immanent vitality" (2010b, 8). The nondualistic orientation of this philosophy also manifests itself in its refusal of the politics of sketching oppositional distinctions between mechanistic and vitalist, or inorganic and organic, understandings of matter. As such, it also draws a significant inspiration from the philosophical works of Gilles Deleuze, and especially from his readings of Baruch Spinoza, Friedrich Nietzsche, and Henri Bergson in which he accomplished what Dorothea Olkowski aptly calls "the ruin of representation" (1999).

An extended comment should be offered here on the theoretical and conceptual context in which new materialism emerged. This philosophical movement can be situated within what has started to be known as the "material turn." It has also undoubtedly provided a fresh impulse for (re)conceptualization of other relatively recent "turns" and—at least to a certain extent—paved the way for a creative integration of the humanities with other fields of scientific inquiry. Importantly, it offered a novel philosophical grounding for such significant shifts as "sensorial turn," "affective turn," "performative turn," "affirmative turn," "ecological/environmental turn," "spatial turn," "digital turn," or "post-secular turn."[2] Although some of these turns (e.g., the "sensorial" and the "performative") crystallized earlier, they have experienced considerable revival and have significantly reoriented under the impact of philosophical investigations conducted within the new materialist optics. These processes have opened the way for a more challenging research located at the intersection, or interference, of different academic fields. They also brought back the issues of knowledge production, epistemology, sources of cognition, or human-nonhuman cognitive and perceptual faculties to the fore of interdisciplinary humanities, in general, and philosophy of science, in particular. Except for offering new potentials for trans- and interdisciplinary studies, as well as for developing new epistemologies and theories of knowledge, new materialism—monistic in both its orientation and construction—also advances novel methodological approaches, that is, ones that are no longer grounded in the negativist, dualistic logic of thinking established within the dominant Western philosophical project (more on them will follow).

Obviously, the "material turn" has not been received uncritically. This onto-epistemological and methodological ferment has been contested by philosophers and epistemologists, especially those grounded in Anglo-Saxon empirical and analytical paradigms. The critique has mostly focused on such issues as the validity of thusly generated knowledges as well as their usefulness for a more generally defined scientific project. Yet potentials of these epistemological and methodological shifts to overcome the impasse discernible within the humanities since the late 1990s have also been acknowledged. As a result, although offering a refreshment, or refinement, of the humanities, the new materialist inquiry is still seen as consisting of a number of dispersed philosophical strands and epistemological tendencies, which—although resonating with each other—are not yet well integrated within a coherent and well-established paradigm. However, it must be noticed in this context that new materialists themselves, suspicious of any strategy of categorization and classification (or classi*fix*ation, as van der Tuin prefers 2014a), so typical for the positivist scientific project, are also critical of the very notion of a "paradigm" and perceive the suppleness and elasticity of this new epistemological tendency in terms of its significant potential rather than flaw.[3]

Taking the preceding discussion into consideration, this book experiments with new materialism as a perspective to approach issues of memory, perception, and knowledge production in the context of politics of relationality. As such, it postulates a shift from the logic of arboreal representation embodied in systems of oppositional classifications and hierarchies to the logic of Deleuze-inspired rhizomatic connectivity opting for unusual entanglements, surprising liaisons, singular knowledges, and creative experimentation. In order to fully recognize these potentials, it is, however, necessary to briefly go back to the rudiments of the dominant Western ways of thinking and the epistemological consequences this system produces. It is also indispensable to acknowledge symptoms of the crisis that this mode of thinking has been recently troubled with.

THE TWILIGHT OF OCULARCENTRISM

As explained in the previous section, new materialism is meant to grasp the necessary entanglements of the natural and the cultural (or the material and the discursive) in the examination of "practices of knowing in being," that is, the study of "onto-epistemology" (Barad 2003, 829)[4] or "science in the making" (Latour 1987). Undoubtedly, this tendency should be perceived as a creative response to the existing dominant philosophies of knowledge, especially since it questions their overestimation of the principle of vision. Post-ocularcentric in its construction, this philosophical ferment develops a rather skeptical attitude towards the mechanism of representation that has come to embody the dominant image of thought. In order to fully grasp the new materialist logic, it is, therefore, necessary to have at least a cursory look at the prevailing Western conceptions of the process of cognition as well as to briefly examine the contexts in which they consolidated.

In Western culture rational knowledge has typically been seen as a creation of an intellectual effort, a result of detached, objective, and unemotional observation effectuated by the means of vision. The reliance of the predominant Western philosophical systems on the sense of vision has been successfully grasped in Peter Sloterdijk's statement:

> The eyes are the organic prototype of philosophy. Their enigma is that they not only can see, but are also able to see themselves seeing. This gives them a prominence among the body's cognitive organs. A good part of philosophical thinking is actually only eye reflex, eye dialectic, seeing-oneself-see. (Quoted in Jay 1994, 21)

An eye has become the center of perception, the symbolic form, a metaphor for the self and knowledge (symbolically standing for logos, god, and wisdom, as well as different correlations thereof). The development of the most basic technologies, aimed at extending human capacities, has also been triggered by the principle of vision's primacy. Such fundamental inventions as artificial light, photography, magnifying glass, and print have been conceived as significant enhancements of human visual capacities, understood usually as a neutral and transparent means of generating knowledge. Consequently, as David Levin aptly notices, "Western culture has been dominated by an ocularcentric paradigm, a vision-generated, vision-centered interpretation of knowledge, truth, and reality" (1993, 2). Levin also points to the meaningful connections between vision and ontology, knowledge, power, and ethics (1993) so deeply embodied in the Western scientific project. The technological culture has further contributed to the separation and hierarchization of senses, with vision and hearing as the two most respected and reliable ones and smell, taste, and touch as the least privileged. The more "bodily" the sense, the lower position it occupies in the hierarchy. Not only does vision, the most "disembodied" of senses, operate from the distance, but also it potentially sees without being seen. This translates into the principles of objectivity in science, which fits well within the whole system of thinking. Certainly, such a classification of the human perceptual organs is derivative of the disrespectful attitude of Western philosophy towards the body. It also stems from the more general religious fundaments of Western culture with its contempt for a "sinful" human earthly form. In sum, this system, resting on the dichotomous logic of thinking (juxtaposing one against its other), ascribes special status to the mind, or the soul, at the expense of the "mere" body, or flesh.

Although the epistemological privileging of vision had been questioned by many philosophers historically, only recently observable has there been a more thorough and systematic challenging of the system of power implied in the primacy given to the viewing subject. Donna Haraway, for instance, writes that "the technologies of visualization recall the important cultural practice of hunting with the camera and the deeply predatory nature of a photographic consciousness" (1988, 169). And she continues that "vision in this technological feast becomes unregulated gluttony; all perspective gives way to infinitely mobile vision, which no longer seems just mythically about the god-trick of seeing everything from nowhere, but to have put the myth into ordinary practice" (1988, 189). This unrestricted quest for visual control (through representation) has transformed, especially in an academic context, into such ordering patterns as categorization, classification, and hierarchization (of species, phenomena, forces, societies, races, classes, etc.). These strategies allow for exercising jurisdiction over the object(s) of knowledge, to organize the field(s), and, eventually, to put the findings of academic inquiry into practice. Certainly, as postmodern and poststructuralist critiques (and especially deconstruction) have already made clear, such an organization of the processes of knowledge production should be seen as a by-product of the anthropocentric culture. The latter draws a clear division line between human beings and their environment and organizes the relationships between them in a hierarchical way (thanks to the dynamics inscribed in the mechanism of representation!—the active subject versus the passive object of vision/knowledge, the original versus the copy, culture versus nature, the human versus the nonhuman [the animal, the mineral, the technological, etc.]). As a consequence, the whole world becomes instrumentally put at the disposal of a human being, serving as a passive resource, a field of exercising power, an arena of control.

This practically oriented scientific project grounded in the assumptions of the anthropocentric culture has eventually led to the emergence of a new geological epoch—the Anthropocene. The term, whose accuracy is still being debated, was coined in 2000 by a chemist and a Nobel Prize winner, Paul Crutzen, to describe the circumstances and deep results of humankind's impact on the earth, taking especially into account the massive urbanization, excessive exploitation of natural resources, extinction of animal and plant species, pollution of the oceans, and the altered atmosphere. Although discussions on the Anthropocene have been triggered, on the one hand, by the selfish/narcissistic fear of the possible (perhaps impending) consequences these environmental changes would entail for the human beings and, on the other, by more attentive reflections on how humans are implicated in the world and the world is implicated in them, these new conditions also opened up novel paths of philosophical inquiry. The various complex entanglements of nature and culture, so crucial to the identity of the Anthropocene, have made evident that no longer can matter (both organic and inorganic) be approached as a passive object of scientific inquiry and control or a resource remaining at the humankind's disposal. Rather, it should be seen as a lively agent, actively participating in the hybrid natural-cultural-discursive processes (Latour 1993) proliferating in the contemporary world. In this context, as Latour prophesizes (1993), the long-established Western ontological divisions between nature and culture as well as the anthropocentric dominance of an active human over the passive world of things (exercised by means of vision/representation), which had paved the way for the Western scientific project, are about to collapse. Simultaneously, the issues of agency, plasticity, and liveliness of matter return to the fore of philosophical investigations. Such a situation signals the twilight of ocularcentrism and calls for a more-nuanced examination of these deep onto-epistemological entanglements.

Certainly, the undermining of the ocularcentric logic indicates at least a partial demise of the epistemological paradigms that it has produced. The dominance of (human) vision over other senses, inherent in this system of thinking, has obviously translated into the bias in cognition. As mentioned earlier, the latter relies on vision, preferably one that is intersubjective, decontextualized, and executed from the omniscient distanced position (which Haraway calls a "god-trick" [1988]). This strategy gives priority to the principle of noninterference, emotional detachment, and value neutrality, that is, all defining features of what has started to be known as positivist realism—a dominant paradigm of knowledge production. Importantly, in such an account, conceiving of *knowledge as representation* (i.e., representationalism) draws on the idea that language—defined as a neutral tool—can fully capture its referents or phenomena that preexist knowledge of them, objectively fixed "out there" and waiting to be "discovered." These procedures rely on a very obvious dynamics of cognition: an active subject of knowledge by means of rational reasoning produces knowledge about the passive object of knowledge, the latter remaining external to a transcendent consciousness of the former. Thusly construed, knowledge stands in fact for an accurate description of reality, that is, a set of truthful representations. As Karen Barad explains,

> Representationalism is a practice of bracketing out the significance of practices; that is, representationalism marks a failure to take account of the practices

> through which representations are produced. Images or representations are not snapshots or depictions of what awaits us but rather condensations or traces of multiple practices of engagement. (2007, 53)

As such, representationalism offers a rather simplistic, one-dimensional picture of how knowledge is produced, where the subject seems to be the only active agent capable of offering immaculate representations of the "immobile" external reality. Adopting an anthropocentric lens, this perspective conceives of a human being (proficient in producing images of the world) as the most important element of the whole system, without which its whole logic would inevitably collapse.

A most significant epistemological alternative to positivist realism is offered by social constructivism, and especially performativism, inspired mostly by works of Michel Foucault (1977, 1978, 1980) and Judith Butler (1990, 1993). Acknowledging that discourse is productive of our experiences of reality and taking into consideration the fact that it is historically changeable, constructivism fosters the view that facts do not preexist knowledge of them but rather are manufactured through the processes of representation. Hence, the proponents of this paradigm seem to argue that the matter of bodies/objects (both human and nonhuman), although historicized, is an effect of productive social or cultural field as well as of constitutive practices. Matter, accordingly, is turned into a cultural phenomenon, that is, the end result of human activity, ultimately derived from the agency of language and representational procedures, in general. Matter as such does not matter; what matters instead are the meanings that it conveys. For Barad, however, "to figure matter as merely an end product rather than an active factor in further materializations is to cheat matter out of the fullness of its capacity" (2007, 66). Although engaging with the social and cultural practices as constitutive of the material phenomena and offering a radically different account of how representation in science works, social constructivism is, therefore, equally anthropocentric as positivist realism, as it gives account of matter as brute, immobile, and a mere object of discursive inscription. Similarly, it crosses matter and materiality out of the realm of agency.

Unsatisfied with the existing approaches, Barad calls for "a robust account of the materialization of *all* bodies—'human' and 'nonhuman'—including the agential contributions of all material forces (both 'social' and 'natural')" (2007, 66), a "nonrepresentational form of realism that is based on an ontology that does not take for granted the existence of 'words' and 'things' and an epistemology that does not subscribe to a notion of truth based on their correct correspondence" (2007, 56). Summing up, Barad's new materialism assumes that "*experimenting and theorizing are dynamic practices that play a constitutive role in the production of objects and subjects and matter and meaning*" (2007, 56; original emphasis). Although active and agential in itself, matter is also dependent on productive social conditions. Hence, singular events result from the complex entanglements of the material and the discursive.

According to new materialism, paying detailed attention to practices lets us more comprehensively study their effects. As Barad clarifies, an inquiry of different relationalities involved in the process of knowledge production enables a study of how subject and object emerge as a result of "intra-activity" (2007). In physics—that is, a discipline within which Barad's work is located—this term refers to any relationship between organisms and matter (human or nonhuman) that are understood as not having any clear boundaries. For the proponents of this philosophical strand, any boundaries must be approached with suspicion, as they materialize only in social interaction, by mapping practices. The objects and subjects, in that sense, are the provisional products of drawing (often arbitrary) boundaries. The latter remain in motion, productive of meanings and bodies, and are never completely sedimented or consolidated. Boundaries are just temporary, fluid, and open to subsequent revisions. The same can be said about the distinctions that we usually assume. For instance, defining the human through possession of the agency and the nonhuman through dispossession of it should be seen as a legacy of (a rather obsolete) Western metaphysics. In Barad's account, agency does not belong exclusively to human, who exerts power and acts on the nonhuman; the nonhuman is equally agential and active. Yet such a conceptualization demands a novel rendition of the idea of agency. Latour underlines that we need to divorce the concept of agency from the one of intentionality, since otherwise it would remain embedded within the anthropocentric logic aiming at "humanizing" all matter (2005). It is therefore necessary to study human-nonhuman collectives focusing on the metamorphous, dynamic nature of these relationalities and their agencies. This often eludes the processes of conceptualization within the dominant linguistic and representational schemes and forces us to transcend the existing cognitive systems. The notion of intra-activity seems to grasp the complexity of these relationships; it is about interdependency and entanglement in a mutual liaison understood as a condition for existence of natural-cultural entities. As Barad explains, "Discursive practices and material phenomenon do not stand in a relationship of externality to each other; rather the material and the discursive are mutually implicated in the dynamics of intra-activity" (2007, 152); they are "entangled" (2007, 185). The prefix "intra" signals nonseparateness of this entanglement. It means that the entities do not precede the relation in which they enter. Rather, they constitute its provisional products, open to new transformations, constant becomings, and unexpected metamorphoses.

PROBLEMS WITH REPRESENTATION

Revising the ocularcentric logic, new materialism also aims at disavowing the representational system of thinking and points to the necessity of finding out novel ways of going beyond the traditional dualisms inscribed in the mechanism of representation regardless of how the latter is conceptualized. It is especially vital from a feminist point of view. As it can be concluded from the previous section, the mechanism of representation has come to be seen as a central issue in the study of knowledge and in approaching the processes of perception. It also belongs among the most celebrated yet simultaneously hotly debated technologies of self as well as serves as a means of exercising power and control. Vision is not a simple process or act. As described earlier, practices of looking and being looked at (or representing and being represented) organize and restrain processes of subjectification and objectification, translating into ordering, hierarchically organized patterns and, subsequently, shaping social and cultural structures. Vision, therefore, is not innocent. This applies to both the processes of seeing and the procedures of generating knowledge through observation. Noticeably, even though it may seem that the issue of representation has only recently acquired currency in the field of cultural studies, in fact we need to keep in mind that it has attracted attention of philosophers and theorists for an extremely long time. The mechanism of representation has been established as a prevailing paradigm of experiencing and theorizing (i.e., knowing!) the world since the Platonic inception of Western philosophy, giving eventually shape to the image of Western thought as well as contributing significantly to the formation of the concept of knowledge associated therewith.

Together with the flourishing development of feminist epistemologies and feminist critique of Western science, attention of many scholars has been drawn back to the mechanism of representation as well as to who represents and who (or what) is represented. This was not accidental as the processes of perception and knowledge production have started to be conceived as the dominant tools for establishing and sustaining social hierarchies (gendered, raced, classed, ethnicized, etc.). Derived from Western metaphysics, the conceptualizations of the mechanism of representation—although taking different forms—have always been dualistic and hierarchical in their construction. Nevertheless, they have varied in what concerns the relations of image/word vis-à-vis the real as well as the roles of the subject and the object in the process of both representing the world and being represented. It means that theorizing representation has never been a univocal practice. Quite the contrary—following Stuart Hall (1997), at least three dominant models of representational cognition can be identified. He distinguishes mimetic (reflective), intentional, and constructionist (constructivist) approaches to representation, each entailing different consequences for the understandings of the concept of image (and its relation to reality) and of the idea of subject(ivity). These paradigms serve to explain how representation of meaning is effectuated through image (or language), how meaning is constructed, where it comes from or how it is produced, whether or in which circumstances we can speak of meaning, and how to problematize its foundation in, or impact on, the "real" world. Taking into consideration their embeddedness in the patriarchal Western culture, it is crucially vital from a feminist standpoint to have a critical view on them with an aim to understand how they have typically worked to the disadvantage of women (and other "others").

Taking origins in the ancient notion of mimesis, and conceptualized by Plato, the reflective approach draws on the principle of reflection of reality in language (image), assuming fundamental similarity between the form and its appearance (or the original and its copy). Put differently, the copy always sends us back to the original, which is only knowable through and thanks to its various, yet partly deformed, appearances. Crucially, the copy would not exist without the original in the first place. Therefore, ontologically, the copy always remains secondary or imperfect. Even when it resembles the original in most miniscule details, when it literary mimics it, it can never be substituted for what it represents. The copy is what the original is not; it is other-than-original, or nonoriginal, expelled to the realm of negativity forever. As evident, the system draws on an asymmetrical opposition between the real and the represented, assuming that meaning (i.e., representation) is always wrested from the real, coming from the object for which it stands. The image is a mere appearance of the real to which it is ontologically subordinated. The gap between the object and its representation is practically unbridgeable. Since mimesis is never fully accomplished, the copy is deemed to always remain secondary, derivative, and as such devalued.

Similarly, binarized conceptualization of the mechanism of representation is offered by the intentional approach, yet this time the crucial elements of the system, as well as relations between them, are defined differently. This approach starts with Kantian philosophy of knowledge and his focus on the subject as the sine qua non of the mechanism of representation. The knowledge commences with the subject rather that the world of things—the world is knowable only through the subject's representations. Such a system demands that the object—in order to be known and experienced—has to be "other than the knower; it must be *given* to the knower. As *known*, things are only as they are re-presented to a subject" (Colebrook 2005, 2; original emphasis). The knowledge of the world is what is represented by the subject, to the subject, and for the subject. By stating this, Immanuel Kant introduces a strict distinction between who knows and what is known, that is, between the subject and the object of knowledge. He also organizes the relations between the two elements in a hierarchical way—the subject is active and agential; the object remains passive and deprived of agency. Importantly, the idea of subjectivity becomes itself a procedure of representation, as the system assumes the subject's capacities for self-representation. With Kant the object-derived theory of knowledge is replaced with one, which instead relies on the subject as the warrant of truth.

Only the twentieth-century theories of ideology, and especially the one offered by Karl Marx, have exposed the potentially oppressive character of the mechanism of representation. For Marx, representation is not immaculate. Rather, it becomes an intentional distortion of reality aimed at extending control of the dominant group over masses. An image falsifies the world and imposes a fictitious meaning on it. This critique has been taken further by feminists, who saw a villain of the perpetual oppression of women in the structures of capitalist patriarchy. Since then they have worked hard to unravel the ways in which the dominant representations of masculinity and femininity work to the disadvantage of women while presenting an inaccurate image of women's experiences and their involvement in the social sphere. Appended to the social critique was a feminist attack on the dominant (and seemingly neutral) concepts present in the realm of science. Feminists laid bare the false universality of the Western subject of knowledge, exposing its masculine construction and its embeddedness in patriarchal logic. The same can be said about the overall organization of the cognitive process and how it is institutionalized in the form of dominant methodologies, research techniques, and ways of asserting scientific "truths." Moreover, taking on a philosophical approach, Simone de Beauvoir (1953) emphasized the structurally discriminatory character of "difference," constituting the indispensable component of the patriarchal logic of domination. As she explains, femininity can emerge only via juxtaposition against masculinity. While the latter stands for sameness, the former must be conceptualized as otherness and forced out to the margins. Sameness can be asserted only by the exclusion of difference—a masculine subject, being the source of representation, constitutes himself by expelling his others (i.e., not-man, or *wo-man*) against whom he can get clearly defined. It is therefore salient for feminists to expose the discriminatory operations of dominant ideology in order to achieve social change by rendering the representation of femininity more accurate and just as well as by revealing how the realm of representations is constitutive of subjects' identities. This last aspect of the mechanism of representation has been thoroughly explored by Marxist thinker Louis Althusser (1971), who noticed its role as a necessary precondition of both subjectivity and sociality. Even though his approach still falls within the intentional paradigm, it already signals an important transition towards constructionist thinking.

Constructionism (or constructivism) argues for an immanent view of subjectivity and ideology. The emergence of such logic is marked by a shift from meaning to knowledge (still enmeshed, nonetheless, with ideology) and from language to discourse. Michel Foucault (1980, 1982) conceives of the discourse as instrumental in the process of constitution of subjectivity. The very procedure, however, is both productive and restrictive at the same time, as it makes subjectivity possible, yet only in already-premeditated ways. He describes the process as *assujettissement* (or subjectification), where, on the one hand, one becomes *the subject*, yet, on the other hand, this becoming translates into *being subjected* to the dominant rules. Thusly construed, power is not solely repressive vis-à-vis the subject, but it makes subjectivity possible in the first place. Discourse is a force in its own right—it does not express (accurately or not) any pregiven reality. Both subject and object are the effects of representation, spoken by the discourse, and as such, they are no longer sovereign or autonomous. Importantly, Foucault notices an instrumental function ideological representations play in the production of docile subjects and pinpoints the role of the imagined gaze in the structure of visual surveillance forcing a compliant behavior.

In the feminist context, performative functions of representation have been explored by Judith Butler in her influential work entitled *Bodies That Matter: On the Discursive Limits of "Sex"* (1993). As she explains, performance should be understood "not as the act by which a subject brings into being what she/he names, but, rather, as that reiterative power of discourse to produce the phenomena that it regulates and constrains" (1993, 2). Representation—a product of a normative system—impels itself on the everlasting processes of materialization of bodies. In such an account, representation comes first—"there is no subject prior to its construction," argues Butler (1999, 338). Since the performative process is never complete, subjectivity remains in flux. In order to last, it has to be rehearsed in a repetitive manner, as a form of theatrical act—it requires both a role to be performed and an actor to perform it. This is where Butler sees a significant potential for social change. The norm, in her account, can be repeated or reiterated in a disloyal fashion, hence subsequently reformulated and reworked.

Even though the constructionist/performative approaches do not establish an unbridgeable hierarchical gap between the original and the copy (as in the case of mimetism) nor differentiate between the subject and object of representation (as intentionalism proposes), they still enclose subjectivity within the realm of normative patriarchal ideology, aligning it with representation in the process of never-ending construction. Either compliance or resistance is possible alone from within the discourse. The three paradigms offer three different conceptualizations of representation: it may stand for a copy of an original, a subjectively distorted image of reality, or—as a force in its own right—it is a constant production of normative meaning. Representational is also the perception of the subject, framed as a natural and immaculate capacity for capturing and recognizing the experiences of the world and making them meaningful. The subject perceives, and in perceiving the world, it represents it to herself or himself. As evidenced earlier, dominant understandings of a subject's perception are rooted in dualistic Western philosophy that cannot do without the mechanism of representation, which is naturalized as a human capacity for cognition. This very mechanism is deeply grounded in the negativist structure of thinking. Perception is about recognition (of the already known), that is, about freezing the diversity of stimuli into a series of immobilized and ordered sequences, which are assumed to be derivative of the transcendent world. The power to represent belongs to the (masculine!) subject of knowledge, in whose image and from whose perspective the whole world (or, more precisely, its representation) is crafted. Consequently, the dominant culture is organized around masculinity, molded in its image, and represents its point of view. The perspective of the masculine subject of knowledge, figured as disembodied and genderless, falsely passes for a universal one and juxtaposes himself against the rest of the world, that is, his different "others."

Such an oppositional logic is deeply entrenched in the Western dualistic metaphysics against which feminist project has been targeted from its very commencement. As elucidated by Braidotti (2002), this framework juxtaposes *one* (e.g., man, human, the real, the original) against its *other* (woman, inhuman/technological, the virtual, the copy) and further expels the other for self-constitution. This logic thoroughly relies on the figure of the other—although excluded and marginalized, the other constitutes the necessary member of the entire system. Otherness is defined as difference (as opposed to sameness or similarity) and loaded with pejorative connotation (Braidotti 2002). Such rendition of difference allows for demonization of the other and, consequently, its expulsion to the margins. These margins, however, are crucial for reasserting of the center, since the latter exists only through its dialectic opposition to the former. Such a structure of thinking constitutes an important challenge for feminist critique, which—by definition—is always situated on the peripheries of the mainstream philosophical thought or, alternatively, occupies an ambivalent position of in-between-ness. After all, the strategy of situating itself on the margins implicitly assumes the existence of the center in the first place. The positions of resistance or opposition are therefore always connected to the dominant, albeit by negation. Such logic inevitably perpetuates the long-established negativist system of thinking.

Thus, by being resistant to the dominant, feminism is therefore essential for its constitution. A paradox is at play here—by contesting the center, feminists often even more radically assert its existence as well as its hegemonic position. Moreover, by opposing the dominant, feminists themselves often also rely on the dichotomous thinking, which runs the risk of replicating and sustaining the prevailing patriarchal status quo. This is obviously counterproductive as far as the more general feminist goals are concerned. Hence, there is a need for new approaches and new (affirmative) ways of formulating the critique.

"When we try to understand masculine domination we are . . . likely to resort to modes of thought that are the product of domination," writes Pierre Bourdieu (2001, 5). Hence, in order to eschew the enclosure that representation generates, we need to rely on a different logic, away from dualistic structures of thinking and negativist categorizations. It does not mean, however, that the hitherto critical achievements should be all trashed. Quite the contrary—as Rick Dolphijn and Iris van der Tuin rightly notice, "It is in the resonances between old and new readings and re-readings that a 'new metaphysics' might announce itself" (2012, 3). In their account, "A new metaphysics is not restricted to a here and now, nor does it merely project an image of the future for us. It announces what we may call a 'new tradition,' which simultaneously gives us a past, a present, and a future" (2012, 13). Therefore, the argumentation of this book is not oriented solely towards a critique of representation, but the idea is rather to inveigh against the origin of binaristic representational thinking with the ontological dualism and a figure of the thinking subject at its center. In line with feminist developments focusing on the corporeal forms of subjectivity, opening spaces for valuation of other senses (instead of prioritizing vision), the aim of my argumentation is to move beyond the dominant notion of everyday perception and the mechanism of recognition that it implies. In a new materialist fashion, the book subscribes to Gilles Deleuze's statement, that perception "is never conditioned by mechanisms peculiar to the subject; by escaping the mediation of the subject it becomes total, objective and diffuse" (1986, 24).

The poststructuralist approaches (mostly deconstruction), focusing on the performative powers of language/ideology and useful in grasping the assumed central status of the human in the world, as well as the different hierarchies associated thereto, are simply not enough if we want to understand the historicity of our times. Moreover, as new materialists argue, deconstruction in a way remains too modern, as it reasserts the Western oppositional logic of thinking in terms of either/or. Importantly, it is a negative strategy par excellence and as such perpetuates, rather than challenges, the oppressive, exclusionary structure of thought. Conversely, the "material turn" calls for a thoroughly novel perspective in cultural theory. Although drawing inspiration from the postmodernist, and especially poststructuralist, critique of the hierarchical binaries celebrated by the Western logic, it goes further in challenging the fundaments of modern thinking (understood in terms of an intellectual process effectuated by the mind) and aims at bringing nature, bodies, and objects (i.e., the matter!) back into humanities. Such a proposal is grounded in the recognition of matter's agency as well as its capacity to interact, change, transform, and move.

Undoubtedly, in order to disavow representationalism, and to do justice to the plastic, monist, and vitalist spirit of new materialism, it is necessary to experiment with novel methodologies and approaches that would, on the one hand, help us grasp the complexity of cognitive processes and, on the other hand, let us transcend the negativist mood hampering the creation of a more affirmative critique. In order to do so, we need to learn to *see differently*, that is, in a more-than-representational fashion, and in a more embodied, corporeal way. We also need to open ourselves to external influences or rather acknowledge the openness, which is an immanent part of our subjectivity. It is necessary to do justice to the complex relationalities in which we are involved and to recognize our susceptibility to the world as well as its susceptibility to our (non)actions. Hence, it is of crucial importance to unlearn the taken-for-granted schemes of thinking in terms of separation and negation and instead learn to think in terms of connectivities and entanglements. Such a shift enables new forms of critique and new manners of involvement, attachment, and commitment, translating into novel ways of situated and embodied knowledges, which are never fixed but remain fluid and metamorphous. This, undoubtedly, calls for a creative, intellectual effort, acknowledging embodied location, power relations, affects, emotions, situatedness, and particularity of each context in which one may found oneself *for* and *with* others.

SEEING DIFFERENTLY: NEW MATERIALISM'S METHODOLOGICAL ORIENTATION

Distancing itself from representational thinking, new materialism develops novel methodological approaches and strands of critique, enabling an overcoming of the negativist logic that representation generates. These methodologies are purposely not rigidly defined and encourage rather creative uses, which remain in concord with the overall spirit of this philosophical movement. This book draws significant inspiration from these approaches, developing an affirmative and nonconfrontational critique, transcending oppositional schemes of thinking so typical for Western metaphysics and hierarchical ordering patterns associated thereto. Let me briefly comment on these methodological developments, as this would shed important light on the argumentation that I present in this book.

Diffraction, for new materialism, seems to offer an alternative to purely representational thinking. The group of diffractive approaches has been inspired by works of Donna Haraway (1997, 2003) and Karen Barad (2007, 2014), for whom diffraction is a method for reading and writing based on physical phenomena. Haraway explains diffraction as an attempt to make differences while recording interactions, interferences, and reinforcements. It does not have a precise, well-defined origin or a straightforward history. It is heterogeneous and flexible. For Barad diffraction is about "marking differences from within and as part of an entangled state" (Barad 2007, 88), while Haraway describes diffractive methodology as "a narrative, graphic, psychological, spiritual, and political technology for making consequential meanings" (1997, 273). Diffraction refers to a principle from physics concerning "the way waves combine when they overlap and the apparent bending and spreading out of waves when they encounter an obstruction" (Barad 2007, 28). A methodology based on diffraction is an accounting attentive to detail, an inquiry of differences and relationalities, and a study of the phenomenon of how subject and object emerge as a result of intra-activity (Barad 2007). Haraway added diffraction to the dictionary of the semiotics—together with syntax, semantics, and pragmatics, diffraction could serve as a means of grasping and explaining how the patterns of interference emerge and how these productive encounters change the ways of generating and understanding meanings. Barad, likewise, considers diffraction as a metaphor for a methodological reading of texts stemming from different disciplinary contexts (e.g., in her case, quantum physics, poststructuralist theory, and feminist cultural studies) together or through each other. This process results in offering new senses and meanings as well as stimulates fresh trans- and interdisciplinary alliances.[5] Importantly, diffraction is a way of coping with epistemological problems of representation (e.g., the figure of an invisible knowledge maker, false sense of objectivity, and self-vision of reflexivity as totalizing and undermining knowledge claims). As Iris van der Tuin explains, "Diffraction is meant to disrupt linear and fixed causalities," and to work towards "more promising interference patterns" (2011, 26). This can be practiced by reading texts and theories in alliances and through one another. Such a strategy dislocates the temporality of a piece of writing, transverses disciplinary boundaries, and opens up established meanings to novel reconfigurations.

Cartographical methodology is similarly nonrepresentational. This technique has mostly been inspired by Rosi Braidotti's proposal of a cartographical approach for contemporary philosophical dialogue according to which "we think of power relations simultaneously as the most 'external,' collective, social phenomenon and also as the most intimate or 'internal' one" (Braidotti 2002, 6). As explained by Rick Dolphijn and Iris van der Tuin, new materialism "enacts a thinking about theory formation that is other than classificatory (new materialism sets in motion a non-dualistic epistemic practice)" and "enables us to understand the way in which theory formation used to be thought" (2012, 111). Whereas classification (a *territorializing* strategy) exemplifies the dualistic disciplinary logic of thinking, cartography (a *de-territorializing* strategy) is aimed at dismantling the binary oppositions and tends to replace the linear, chronological categorization or classification of tendencies and philosophical concepts with the process of working out of their cartography, which is about their constant rewriting in new contexts. As Dolphijn and van der Tuin continue,

> Classifying epistemic tendencies that are supposedly prevalent in cultural theory implies working along territorial lines, which is a transcendentalizing gesture along with invoking sequential negation and a narrative of progress (i.e., it is dualist). This does not allow for the (un)folding of cultural theory—the matter-energy flows of theory formation, the non-linear coding practices, the cutting across matter and signification—to be captured. New materialism de-territorializes the ways in which cultural theory has been classified. (2012, 111)

Such a strategy, which questions the scientific tendency to impose a fixed and determining grid on life, allows—in view of the two thinkers—"to see not only matter, but also language as a 'living force.' Questioning fixity thus opens up the possibility of thinking about theory formation in a non-linear, cartographical way" (2012, 112). Consequently, in a post-representational manner, cartographical methodology undermines the well-established divisions into the old and the new, the historical and the modern, and the modern and the postmodern. It challenges thinking in terms of separate generations as well as artificially sustained divisions of the research tendencies. Instead, it offers a parallel and diffractive reading of texts originating in different disciplines and produced in different historical moments or locations in such a way as to make them contemporary to each other, "translinear" or "transversal" with each other as far as their time and conceptual dimensions are concerned.

Another way of disavowing the confrontational, binarized logic of representational thinking has been offered by affirmative critique. Inspired by works of, among others, Rosi Braidotti (2000, 2002, 2006a), Elizabeth Grosz (2005, 2008, 2011), Bruno Latour (2004, 2005), and Brian Massumi (2002a, 2014), affirmative approaches transcend the negativist logic of thinking in terms of binary pairs so deeply embedded in representationalism. Massumi describes these methods as techniques by which an author adds or invents rather than as means for critiquing others. As he writes,

> It is simply that when you are busy critiquing you are less busy augmenting. . . . There are times when debunking is necessary. . . . Foster or debunk. It's a

> strategic question. Like all strategic questions, it is basically a question of timing and proportion. Nothing to do with morals or moralizing. Just pragmatic. (2002a, 13)

Therefore, although the traditional role of critique continues to be important, it is necessary to acknowledge new approaches that bypass critique and to explore the fruitfulness of engaging the indeterminacies that come with making connections in research. Rather than focusing on critical deconstruction and exposing the weaknesses of the work, affirmative methodologies explore the texts from their inside and are aimed at positive, productive analysis. They are distinguishable in that they depart not by merely critiquing representation but rather by offering something new. As I explain elsewhere (together with Marek M. Wojtaszek), affirmative approach "enlarges the critique by moving it way beyond everyday perception and the mechanism of recognition this implies. Rather than cling to . . . the various categorical classifications . . . one intuits . . . creative ontology" (2009, 184). As we also emphasize, affirmative methodologies in no sense amount to

> the mindless and uncritical affirmation of the dominant—undeniably oppressive status quo. On the contrary, [they] must be viewed and considered in keeping with the critical tradition as its deepening and enriching. It is essential, however, that the critique be thought of as unrestricted to the bounds of the established order of representation and its dualistic logic. . . . Therefore, this requires a sharpening of one's critical skill in that one needs to be cautious not to fall in a trap of affirmation of the oppressive, or negative, system. The affirmative reading entails shifting the emphasis away from separability and oppositionality to creativity. (2009, 195)

Such a perspective encourages us to broaden the scope and definition of critique by imaginatively engaging with concepts and approaches and aims to provide novel, positive (i.e., nonrepresentational or more-than-representational) ways of moving beyond negativity.

The earlier-described methodological tendencies typical for new materialist thinking serve as an inspiration for the argumentation that this book provides. Although not implemented in a strict, rigorous way—as they offer a lot of flexibility and suppleness—they constitute a methodological and conceptual framework of this book, aiming at offering productive, nonconfrontational analysis of a set of selected memorial artifacts.

ABOUT THE BOOK

In the context of recently increasing academic interest in the concepts of emotion and affect (especially visible among cultural studies scholars),[6] in chapter 1, entitled "Affect/Discourse: Towards a Synaesthetic Synthesis," I look into Gilles Deleuze and Félix Guattari's theorizations of "intensity" and "sensation" as a point of departure for developing an idea of *synaesthetic perception*. I also situate my approach within the body of existent scholarship in this field. In my analysis I turn both to original concepts developed by Deleuze and Guattari and to their more concrete operationalization for contemporary cultural studies effectuated by Brian Massumi (2002a, 2002b), who places emphasis on contemporaneous yet disjunctive workings of affect and emotion (or affect and discourse). Taking into consideration recent extensive criticism of Massumi's claims (e.g., Hemmings 2005, Leys 2011, Wetherell 2012), in this chapter I aim at clarifying my choice of theoretical framework as well as my uses of Massumi's theory. Furthermore, drawing heavily on Barbara Bolt's ideas, I focus on the concept of a *work of art* understood as a constant material-semiotic process generating effects in the world. Logically, in this context, I also turn to analyzing discussions of an aesthetic experience and the (problematic) location of memorial art within the body of art theory. After explaining the dominant modernist and postmodernist paradigms of critically understanding art, I point to Deleuze-inspired perspective, offering a different (i.e., affective and relational) conceptualization of both art and aesthetic experience. By doing so, I want to reveal how the standpoint grounded in "affective aesthetics" allows us for a more comprehensive grasping of singular events generated in an active and multidirectional encounter of the body and memorial space. From here my argumentation moves towards advancing a synthetic and synaesthetic approach to perception; I also offer a Deleuze-inspired definition of (memorial) art, on which I rest in the remaining parts of the book.

Since the volume focuses on diversified and multidimensional operations of memorial spaces and memorial art, which—at the same time—are often also conceived of as tourist destinations or attractions, chapter 2, entitled "Memory Sites: Remembering through Materiality," explores aspects of "heritage tourism," "dissonant heritage tourism," and "dark tourism" from critical perspectives of widely understood memory studies. As Sharon Macdonald clarifies, contemporary societies have become "obsessed with the disappearance of collective memory and its preservation," which is a tendency at the origin of erection of diverse heritage sites "designed to remind us of histories that might otherwise be lost" (2013, 1). These processes of materialization of memory are paradigmatic (and symptomatic) for shifts in formats that are currently observable in a number of contemporary museums, memorials, or artistic installations, and especially those commemorating past traumatic events. They tend to convey knowledges in not only intellectual but also corporeal manners, that is, affecting visitors on the most immediate, enfleshed level, leaving memorable traces on their bodies, and producing certain experiences.

This tendency is often at the origin of vigorous criticism of memory sites related to traumatic events, which are often conceptualized as "dark tourist attractions" and situated within an entirely negative theoretical framework. In this vein, it is also argued that they manufacture inauthentic experiences, usually by retraumatizing visitors. Therefore, the goal of this chapter is to overcome oppositional ways of thinking in terms of authenticity and inauthenticity of experiences with an aim of divorcing tourism connected to trauma from its typical negative valance. My analysis centers on the so-called Holocaust memorial museums located in different geographical and cultural contexts, away from the sites (crime scenes) where the actual trauma of the Shoah took place. My aim is to critically approach the ways in which these institutions operate as they stay in a constant and dynamic interaction with the social and the cultural as well as with the bodily and the physical, which remains in line with new materialist thinking. In this way the chapter aims at transcending the dichotomies of the social and the material as well as of the past and the present, pointing instead to their multiple entanglements in the processes of their mutual co-constitution. This refers both to contemporary memorial artifacts immersed in the complex meaning-making practices and to the ways they affectively and intellectually relate to and interact with the visitors' bodies. Logically, such a conceptualization implies a specific understanding of memory as intermediality of connections produced within these interactions, which seems to correspond with the multimedia nature of our memories.

Chapter 3—"Memory and Trauma: The Unspeakable"—continues explorations of the concept of memory, especially as related to trauma. It establishes links between affective *synaesthetic perception*, materialization of memory, and difficult experiences. As evidenced in this chapter, on the one hand, memory is currently regarded as social or collective rather than as purely individualized, while processes of remembering—or not forgetting—are assumed to take place in particular contexts (be they social, national, racial, etc.). Yet, on the other hand, an approach to memory—no longer conceiving of it as a purely mental procedure—clearly reveals that memory should be also considered as a bodily process of incorporating practices. Moreover, extensive research on trauma—to which most of the commemorative institutional practices are connected nowadays—has made explicit that we should think of memory in corporeal terms and that trauma, in that sense, could be considered a bout of embodied experiences eluding processes of signification. Such a perspective demands a more-than-representational approach to (traumatic) memory. While elaborating on Marianne Hirsch's concept of *postmemory*, in this chapter I explore how we invest in the past personally and how the past lives in us in constant, sometimes violent and vibrating, flows of memories and affects. If considered inclusively, Hirsch's concept can be useful in grasping different (i.e., narrative and affective) operations both of remembrance sites and of memory (either personal or collective) and how memories can be transmitted to others. This issue is analyzed in reference to a number of selected artistic installations related to the Holocaust trauma. Yet, since I am mostly interested in how in these particular situations the mat(t)er(iality) comes to matter, I discuss the possible application of a new materialist approach to memory sites. This refers both to the functioning of these (material/discursive) places/art objects and to the very process of their (affective/intellectual) interaction with visitors. This results in producing memorable bodily experiences/knowledges or, better, imprints and impressions. My theoretical argumentation in this chapter concludes with a number of short analyses of memorial *works of art*, approached from new materialist perspective of (post)memory studies.

Rhythm and movement are chapter 4's two leading concepts through which a number of memorial artifacts are approached. Here, they are also combined with notions of *synaesthetic perception* and bodily (traumatic) memory, elaborated on in previous parts of the volume. As discussed on a few examples, the interaction with a memorial space/work/installation is not a purely visual experience but rather one that recruits from other senses and sensations, and eventually translates into a synaesthetic event. The aim of the chapter is to point to the complexity of the procedure of *seeing*, understood in terms of a set of multidimensional, embodied, and sensual dynamic processes. The chapter opens with a discussion of the concepts of rhythm and movement, inspired especially by the works of Elizabeth Grosz (2008, 2011) and Erin Manning (2006 2009, 2013, 2014), and explores their relevance to artistic/aesthetic/affective experience. Through such a conceptual framework, I subsequently approach a number of memorial works of art, focusing especially on different sensual dimensions of experiences they generate in the vibrant and dynamic encounter with our bodies. I explore, for example, acoustic, proprioceptive, kinaesthetic, olfactory, and haptic aspects of the material, affective, and bodily experience in order to point out how they creatively coexist within a (memorial) work of art, actively taking part in the process of conveying meanings and sensations. I also explain how these vibrant and dynamic processes both rely on and are productive of bodily memories and embodied knowledges. The chapter offers a transition from the concept of synaesthetic perception elaborated on in chapter 1, through dynamic concepts of subjectivity-as-becoming exposed in encounters with memorial works of art and posing the challenge of *un/learning*, to the formulation of an ethico-onto-epistemological position of *sym*pathy, developed in chapter 5 and constituting a comment to the more general concept of politics of experience.

Drawing on the synaesthetic operations of a number of memory sites and memorial artworks that I explored in the previous chapters, my aim in the closing chapter, entitled "Affective Connections: Feminist Politics of

Sympathy," is to focus on how lived, affective, embodied experiences or events offered to visitors/spectators of these sites/installations can be considered useful in feminist terms. I perceive the analyzed memorial art objects as active material/semiotic agents, works of art, which—when encountered bodily—can produce a deeper and more complex form of connection. The latter can be creatively employed for an advancement of feminist politics and feminist knowledge production. Reviewing the recent feminist scholarship on concepts of sympathy, empathy, and compassion, I point to the usefulness of the first term, even though it has been thoroughly critiqued, and argue for its inventive reformulation in new materialist terms. My conceptualization of *sym*pathy relies on the application of the idea of active and passive syntheses, developed by Gilles Deleuze in *Empiricism and Subjectivity* (2001) and *Difference and Repetition* (2011). Consequently, my argumentation here is again grounded in radical transcendental empiricism, that is, a framework allowing for exploration of the concept of memory from bodily, new materialist perspective. It offers, I believe, a dynamic understanding of subjectivity as constant becoming, where subjects speak the patterns of multiple and serial syntheses that fold in on themselves. The concept of passive syntheses is applied to the process of *synaesthetic* interacting with memorial works of art, which produce memorable bodily-intellectual imprints and impressions. I situate this argumentation within the framework of feminist politics of affect and embodied becomings. The new materialist concept of *sym*pathy (implying a particular ethical, political, and epistemological position) serves as a way of referring to or, better, connecting with others, understood in terms of "thinking/feeling" *with* them.

In the concluding part of the book I underline the multiple connections between the chapters and issues explored therein. Importantly, I also return to the more general aim of this volume, that is, pointing to the relevance of the synaesthetic, new materialist approach to perception for feminist politics. Furthermore, I emphasize the necessity of overcoming negativist ways of thinking (explored in the introductory section as contributing to the constant perpetuation of exclusionary, dualistic logic), arguing instead for a more affirmative approach. I insist that, philosophically, affect is always positive; it is about production, generation, and movement. Importantly, I do not want to argue that the experiences produced in the encounter of the so-called trauma sites or trauma-related works of art are purely aesthetic/affective and therefore asocial. Neither do I claim that affect and representation are not linked to each other. Quite the contrary, they are intertwined in complex ways and often harnessed for political purposes. Hence, it is vital to work out vocabularies to critically and creatively approach these connections. Yet, at the same time, such a conceptualization of aesthetic experience can offer novel, positive, and affirmative perspectives, important from a feminist point of view.

NOTES

1. See, for instance, works by Elizabeth Grosz (2005, 2008, 2011), Brian Massumi (2002a, 2011), Erin Manning (2006, 2009, 2013), Stacey Alaimo and Susan Hekman (2008), Jane Bennett (2010), Diana Coole and Samantha Frost (2010a), Rick Dolphijn and Iris van der Tuin (2010, 2012), and Estelle Barrett and Barbara Bolt (2013).

2. The unprecedented preoccupation with matter and materiality, increasingly present within a number of academic disciplines (including cultural studies), itself deserves an insightful scrutiny, especially in the context of matter having been almost completely absent from critical investigations undertaken within what has come to be called the "linguistic turn" (see, e.g., Grosz 1994, 2008, Massumi 2002a, 2011). Yet the return of the issue of active matter as implicated in the material-semiotic processes has also been discernible in the discussions and reconceptualizations conducted within other intellectual turns. These include the "sensorial turn," developed (also in the context of the "material turn") by, for example, David Howes (1991, 2003, 2004), Constance Classen (1993, 1998), or Jim Drobnick (2004). These scholars focus on the natural-cultural onto-epistemology of the senses in the context of relations between different objects and bodies and investigate the bodily-intellectual aspects of cognition. The "affective turn" (e.g., Braidotti 2002, 2006a, Massumi 2002a, Thrift 2007) focuses on the material dimensions of perception and different entanglements of affect and language, body and intellect in the process of sensing, experiencing, and *becoming* with the world. The "performative turn" (e.g., Butler 1993, 1997, 2010) underlines the different ways in which materiality performs and is performed, and aims to conceptualize how human practices are grounded in their contexts. In a similar manner, "spatial turn" (e.g., Cosgrove 1999, Thrift 2007, Warf and Arias 2014) focuses on the landscape and place as they materially and semiotically inter-/intra-act with human behaviors and cultural development. The "ecological/environmental turn" (e.g., Alaimo 2010, Buell et al. 2011, Kerridge 2012, 2014, Domańska 2013) underlines pan-humanity, sensitivity towards the environment, and investigates how different forms of matter entangle and co-constitute each other (these include environmental criticism, cultural green studies, material environmentalism, indigenous knowledges), offering a more democratic and connective idea of being/*becoming*. Related to it, in a sense, is the "post-secular turn" (e.g., Shiva 1997, Braidotti 2008) focusing on transversal neohumanism, posthumanism, and neovitalism as well as earth-based spirituality, affinity of cult and culture, and post-anthropocentric ethics. The "digital turn" (e.g., Parikka 2007, 2010, Westera 2012, Colman 2013) investigates the impact of contemporary technologized and digitalized historicity on (not only human) life while focusing on the materiality of the digital. The "affirmative turn" (e.g., Braidotti 2000, 2002, 2006b, Massumi 2002a, 2011, Latour 2004, 2005, Grosz 2005, 2008, 2011, Domańska 2014a,b) offers a relational, rather than confrontational, epistemology and ethics, centering on the creative and productive powers of the critique as well as fostering alliances among different agents, social groups, species, and substances. These intellectual tendencies develop novel methodological tools, grounded in *post-representational*, *post-anthropocentric*, *posthuman*, and

post-ocularcentric affirmative philosophical ideas. Hence, noticeable has been a recent development of interdisciplinary investigations joining artistic research, action research, practice-related research, sensorial research with animal (e.g., Parikka 2010, Massumi 2014) and plant methodologies (e.g., Marder 2014a, 2014b), ecological, environmental, and sustainable humanities (e.g., Buell et al. 2011, Kerridge 2012, 2014, Domańska 2013), historio-/cartographies (e.g., Dolphijn and van der Tuin 2010, 2012), digital material methodologies (e.g., Parikka 2007 Colman 2013), and different variants of self-reflexive situated knowledges. Undoubtedly, this conceptual ferment has to be approached in the context of contemporary metamorphous historicity and with the methodological tools that would resonate with its plastic, affirmative, monist, and vitalist spirit.

3. Recently, there have been attempts to clarify the "material turn" as well as to explain its basic concepts or ethical/onto-epistemological implications (see, e.g., Alaimo and Hekman 2008, Coole and Frost 2010a, Dolphijn and van der Tuin 2012, Barrett and Bolt 2013). This strategy has been aimed at introducing new materialism to broader academic and nonacademic audiences. These fascinating works have typically focused on the selected fields of research (e.g., philosophy, biology, physics, and the arts) and their interferences, rather than offering a more comprehensive and detailed map, or cartography, of new materialism and its scope. Interestingly, because of its diversity and democratic orientation, the term has increasingly been used in plural (i.e., "new materialisms") to mark the situatedness and partiality of thusly generated knowledges. Consequently, new materialism is still rather diffused and vague; its relationships to other currently observable turns in the humanities remain unclear. The latter are typically considered as separate and relatively independent theoretical phenomena; they are usually seen as isolated tendencies, focusing on their specific fields of interests and developing their own vocabularies and concepts, rather than constituting a part of a more general and overwhelming philosophical movement. A more precise map, or cartography, of the philosophical interactions between and within these turns has not yet been drawn. This results in an overall skepticism towards and hesitation about the "material turn" as well as indecision about its broader applicability in the academic inquiry. This situation is further complicated by the haziness of methodological approaches and research techniques developed within the "material turn"—they are still not yet gathered in a more practical toolkit or manual and, consequently, often used just intuitively or even incoherently. This translates into difficulties with their more concrete operationalization as well as triggers a vigorous critique of the overall turn. Consequently, the theoretical and methodological vagueness of the "material turn," together with its contested location at the intersection, or interference, of a number of research fields, poses a serious challenge for contemporary humanities.

4. Karen Barad herself does not use the term "new materialism" in her original theorizations, yet she has become one of the most important inspirations for scholars working within the new materialist philosophical strand.

5. Diffraction has been recently becoming increasingly popular within the new humanities and posthumanities. Innovative explanations and uses of diffraction have been recently offered by many theorists and authors (see, e.g., van der Tuin 2011,

2014b, Geerts and van der Tuin 2013, Barad 2014, Edmond 2014, Kaiser and Thiele 2014, Thiele 2014).

6. See, for instance, the works of Federica Giardini (1999), Brian Massumi (2002a), Eve Kosofsky Sedgwick (2003), Teresa Brennan (2004), Sianne Ngai (2005), Elspeth Probyn (2005), Denise Riley (2005), Patricia Clough and Jean Halley (2007), and Mike Featherstone (2010).

Chapter 1

Affect/Discourse: Towards a Synaesthetic Synthesis

ILLOGICAL PERCEPTION: AN INTRODUCTION

In *Essays Critical and Clinical* (1998), Gilles Deleuze deliberates on the nature of cognitive processes, offering a description of T. C. Lawrence's experience of being gang-raped in the dessert. In this context he especially comments on the relative autonomy of the body in its unpredictable, or even illogical, responses to "an event," pointing out that Lawrence's story reactivates Spinoza's formula—"We do not know what our body can do!" (1998, 123). Continues Deleuze: "In the midst of his tortures, an erection; even in the state of sludge, there are convulsions that jolt the body . . . in its normal state, the body never ceases to act and react *before the mind moves it*" (1998, 123; original emphasis). The way the body autonomously responds to the event gives rise to shame, which means, as Deleuze explains, "that the mind is ashamed *for* the body. It is as if it were saying to the body: You make me ashamed, You ought to be ashamed." This relies on a very particular understanding of the body as having "autonomous external reactions," signaling the fact that "the body is an animal. What the body does it does alone" (1998, 123; original emphasis). Clarifying the complexity of the processes of knowing, Deleuze identifies the following order:

> I am in an exhausting situation: my body "crouches down and crawls"; my mind is ashamed. The mind begins by coldly and curiously regarding what the body does, it is first of all a witness; then it is affected, it becomes an impassioned witness, that is, it experiences for itself affects that are not simply effects of the body, but veritable *critical entities* that hover over the body and judge it. . . . Entities rise up and act on the mind when it contemplates the body. These are acts of subjectivity. (1998, 124; original emphasis)

As evidenced, what is involved in the encounter with the other, or what an event generates, is of compound nature—both intellectual and bodily, emotional and affective. Such an understanding of perception, in terms of a multidimensional and composite process, will be a guiding principle of my further argumentation resting on radical monism inscribed in Deleuze's philosophy.

Yet, in the context of recently increasing academic interest in the issues of emotion and affect (visible especially among feminist and cultural studies scholars),[1] my approach as well as my use of the terms "affect" and "emotion" need to be situated within the body of existent scholarship in this field. As signaled earlier, my argumentation primarily draws inspiration both from original concepts developed by Gilles Deleuze and Félix Guattari and from more concrete operationalization of these ideas for contemporary cultural studies effectuated by Brian Massumi. These formulations place emphasis on contemporaneous yet disjunctive operations of affect and emotion (or affect and discourse). Such a theoretical framework offers an interesting approach to the functioning of many memorial artifacts, *to some extent* divorcing the aesthetic experiences they offer from their political and commemorative character or ideological contexts. Nevertheless, agreeing in this regard with many critics (e.g., Blackman 2012, Hemmings 2005, Laurier and Philo 2006, Leys 2011, Papoulias and Callard 2010, Pile 2010, Wetherell 2012, 2013), I do not intend to claim that affect and discourse are completely separate from or independent of each other. Neither, in my opinion, is this Massumi's intention. I totally subscribe to the idea that the lack of dialogue between affect and discourse research is theoretically counterproductive and, therefore, I think it is of critical importance for cultural studies to search for constructive manners to invent novel ways and new vocabularies to do justice to the entanglement of the affective and the discursive. Such formulation is, I believe, offered by new materialism. Yet, at the same time, it must be kept in mind that we need to learn how to think of affect, also in order to thoroughly grasp the operations and effects of discourse. It is obviously true that the attempts at separating between affect and language prove to be artificial, sometimes even pretentious, or that the only way to "operationalize" the concept of affect for cultural theory is through language (Laurier and Philo 2006, Pile 2010, Wetherell 2013). It does not mean, however, that affect itself does not exist *beyond* representation. Consequently, my intention in this chapter is to elaborate on how affect and discourse overlap and entangle, with an aim to advance a more synthetic (and synaesthetic) approach to perception.

The majority of affect theories underline that affect is what relates us to the other, a potential residing in matter that, in case of individuals, often provides them with an impulse for narrating their lives. Yet, in this context, it is often stressed that the concept of affect, as it is problematized by Deleuze and further explored by Massumi, is very different from and should not be confused with its more psychological renditions, where it stands for subjectively experienced feeling or observable emotion, that is, its biological portion.[2] I am aware of the fact that different meanings of such terms as "emotion," "affect," "sensation," "cognition," and "perception" are widely discussed both within and between different disciplines. The debate about the relation between the bodily sensation, emotion, and cognition has been present across diverse fields of research, including psychology, sociology, anthropology, philosophy, neuroscience, and, more recently, cultural studies.[3] Hence, in order to clarify my approach to affect, and my understanding of "affective aesthetics," I first need to briefly explain the differences between various theoretical renditions of affect and emotion, that is, the two central concepts in my argumentation developed in this chapter. Afterward I turn to Deleuze and Guattari's theorization of intensity in order to clarify their approach to bodily affectivity, which serves as a point of departure for the analyses of aesthetic experiences that I offer in the subsequent chapters of the book. Also for this reason, in this part, I elaborate on the problems with defining aesthetic experience, especially in relation to memorial art, whose problematic status within the art theory has been contested for a long time. Then I explain the new materialist account of art, which focuses on its material-semiotic processual nature as well as on its agential capacities. This serves as a context for sketching a synaesthetic approach to both the aesthetics and the processes of perception on which I rely in my further theoretical investigations as well as in analyses of selected case studies.

EMOTIONS AND AFFECTS

A brief overview of the voices present in the debate on the nature and status of emotions lets us broadly identify two dominant perspectives on the issue: one linking emotions to immediate bodily sensation, affect, or feeling and one conceiving of emotions in cognitive terms. The development of the former approach was stimulated by William James's work wherein he argued that bodily changes (sensations) are excited by particular environmental stimuli (1884, 189). For James, emotion should be defined as a feeling of bodily changes, immediate and not demanding interpretation. Although drawing heavily on James's insights, Antonio Demasio (1999) claims that we should distinguish between feeling (which is private and inwardly directed) and emotion (which is public and outwardly directed). Conceptualizing feelings in terms of variants of the experience of pain or pleasure leads Demasio to argue that emotions both precede and engender feelings (2003, 28), the latter being derived from perceptions of pain and pleasure elicited by bodily responses (i.e., emotions). The differences in their approaches notwithstanding, both

James and Demasio understand emotion as immediate, that is, not demanding any intellectual effort (which, actually, means that they do not differentiate between basic emotion and affect).

Conversely, the cognitive approach offers a different rendition of emotion. For cognitivists, emotions should rather be understood as "intelligent responses to the perception of value" (Nussbaum 2003, 1) and, as such, they at least involve (Spelman 1989, Krause 2008) or even are (Solomon 1995) value judgments, appraisals, attitudes, and evaluations. The cognitive approach also quite clearly differentiates between feeling (bodily sensation, physiological change) and emotion, the latter being defined by reference to ethical thought or deliberation.

Another line of theorizing emotions focuses on their "direction"; in this case, again, two paradigms of thinking can be discerned. Psychological model assumes that emotion is centered internally in a subjective feeling and therefore is expressed from inside out (see, e.g., Strongman 2003, Denzin 1984). In a different vein, sociological and anthropological approaches point to the social and cultural construction of emotions and understand them in terms of practices rather than self-present states that might be expressed towards the others (see Lutz 1988, Abu-Lughod and Lutz 1990, White 1993). Such conceptualization, however, assumes the existence of the inside (i.e., an individual subjectivity) and the outside (i.e., the social or the cultural) as two different and separate realms.

Apart from these somewhat extremely different strands of theorizing emotion, there is a large scholarship in this field that should be classified as hybrid in the sense that these theories tend to, on the one hand, combine affective and cognitive components and, on the other hand, revise dichotomous categorizations implied in both individualistic and social/cultural approaches.[4] Falling into this category, Sara Ahmed's definition of emotion is grounded in the assumption about its sociality, which means that emotions are not in subjects or in objects of emotions but rather are effects of contacts between the two. To put it another way, "feelings take the 'shape' of the contact we have with objects" (Ahmed 2004b, 5); they depend on how we are affected by something and "this dependence opens up a gap in the determination of feeling: whether something is beneficial or harmful involves thought and evaluation, at the same time that it is 'felt' by the body" (2004b, 6). Importantly, this contact is not innocent or immaculate in nature, but rather it involves processes of reading and signification as well as draws on histories and narratives that are already there (Ahmed 2004b, 6). Such an approach is to some extent consonant with what Denise Riley says about the structures of everyday language, which—in her opinion—are responsible for the production of affective selves. The words are, for Riley, injurious and "vampirically" lodge themselves inside their victim (2005, 9); they—upon their falling on "some kind of linguistic soil"—take root in memories these words conjure and evoke (2005, 11). She claims that not only are people willing to accept the formulations effectuated within the emotional language as well as the effects it has caused on their lives but also they often desperately need these formulations to be correct (to justify the language's detrimental effects) as much as they repudiate them (as, e.g., derogatory or humiliating) (2005, 14). Yet the effects are not just produced by the words but rather should be seen as processual.

For Ahmed, "Emotions are both about objects, which they hence shape, and are also shaped by contact with objects. . . . [These] objects . . . can also be imagined" (2004a, 7). As she argues, "The circulation of objects of emotion involves the transformation of others into objects of feelings" (2004b, 11). Emotions shape our contacts with others and produce "the surfaces and boundaries that allow all kinds of objects to be delineated" (Ahmed 2004b, 10). In other words, "the outside" and "the inside" actually emerge as effects of emotions because through emotions, or through our responses to (broadly defined) others, surfaces and boundaries are made. All discourses name or perform emotions. Logically, we can also talk about the performativity of emotions, which make use of discourse depending on past histories and narratives. More important, however, "these emotions generate effects" (2004b, 13). This is also achieved by the circulation of words. Interestingly, Ahmed offers a theory of emotions as economy, which partly draws on Marxist critique of capitalism. She argues that "emotions work as a form of capital: affect does not reside positively in the sign of commodity, but is produced only as an effect of its circulation" (2004b, 120). As she further explains, "Affective economies need to be seen as social and material, as well as psychic" (2004b, 121), meaning that any distinction between sensation/affect and emotion can be solely analytical.

Importantly, in her creative analysis, Ahmed is more concerned with what emotions can do rather than with what they are. This is also my position, yet, I believe, it is vital to critically problematize the (analytical) distinction between affect and emotion (which Ahmed somewhat skips) as shedding light on, first, the (embodied) process of cognition and, second, the composite workings of a conglomerate of the material and the discursive in the procedure of perception. Yet, in order to explore that, I first have to turn to the concept of affect to explain its meaning and importance for my approach. In fulfilling this goal, I will proceed in a somewhat unconventional way by first sketching different paradigms in thinking of affect, then turning to recent criticism of the approach I take inspiration from, and, finally, elaborating in more detail on the position offered in this book. I feel that such a trajectory will let me focus on the intersection, or entanglement, of affect and discourse, that is, an approach not only vitally important for my analysis but also imperative for the goals on the agenda of feminist criticism.

Like emotion, the conceptualization of "affect" has never been a univocal and universally shared practice. In order to briefly sketch the most important differences (and similarities) in approaches to affect, I will partly, and succinctly, refer to the brilliant discussion by Ruth Leys (2011; see also Leys 2007), who clearly explains (and critiques) the dominant paradigms in affect theory.[5] As she reveals, what is called the Basic Emotions paradigm (which still continues to dominate the research field) dates back to the works of Silvan S. Tomkins and Paul Ekman and assumes that "affective processes occur independently of intention and meaning" (Leys 2011, 437). Basic emotions (i.e., affects according to this approach!) are "rapid, phylogenetically old, automatic responses of the organism that have evolved for survival purposes and lack the cognitive characteristics of the higher-order mental processes" (Leys 2011, 437). Although affects combine with the cognitive processing of the brain, they are essentially separate; they are nonintentional, bodily reactions, and crucially there is a gap between the causes of affect/emotion and human interpretation of these causes (Leys 2011, 437; she also quotes Tomkins 1962, 1963, 248).[6]

In a slightly different approach, inspired primarily by works of Gilles Deleuze and Félix Guattari, another group of scholars[7] emphasizes analytical distinction between affect and emotion, defining affects as "a non-signifying, nonconscious 'intensity' disconnected from the subjective, signifying, functional-meaning axis to which the more familiar categories of emotion belong" (Leys 2011, 441). What binds the new (i.e., Deleuze-inspired) affect theorists with those representing Basic Emotions paradigm is "their *shared anti-intentionalism*" (Leys 2011, 443; original emphasis) as well as a "belief that affect is independent of signification and meaning" (2011, 443). This, for Leys, means that, in spite of many differences, there is in fact a deep coherence between the views of the two groups as they both assume that "affect is a matter of autonomic responses that are held to occur below the threshold of consciousness and cognition and to be rooted in the body" (2011, 443). Although different from the proponents of the Basic Emotions paradigm but to the same end, Massumi and other scholars subscribing to the Deleuze-inspired paradigm are committed to the idea that, as Leys asserts,

> there is a disjunction or gap between the subject's affective processes and her cognition or knowledge of the objects that caused them. The result is that the body not only "senses" and performs a kind of "thinking" below the threshold of conscious recognition and meaning but . . . because of the *speed* with which the autonomic, affective processes are said to occur, it does all this before mind has time to intervene. (2011, 450; original emphasis)

Leys thus points to the fact that according to these theories, affect and cognition separate chronologically, with affect first. This position, critical towards the Deleuze-inspired scholarship, is also shared by Margaret Wetherell (2013). For Leys, however, the distinction made by Massumi and his followers translates into the fact that they subscribe to the idea of a radical body/mind dualism, which they want to critique in the first place.[8] As I make clear in the course of this chapter, although I admire Leys's brilliant and systematic discussion, at the same time I disagree with the points she makes about alleged dualism of Deleuze-inspired theorization of affect and the assumed time chronology of affect and emotion. Let me explain this position in a more detailed way.

It was predominantly Massumi's famous assertion about autonomy of affect (more on which will follow) that has provoked most vigorous critique. As Wetherell points out, for many scholars (including Massumi), it seems that "what is most exciting about affect is that it is not *discourse*. Affect seems to index a realm beyond talk, words and texts, beyond epistemic regimes, and beyond conscious representation and cognition" (2013, 19; original emphasis). She continues by underlining the distinction being made by many affect scholars where "discourse is identified with the *conscious*, the *planned* and the *deliberate* while affect is understood as the *automatic*, the *involuntary* and the *non-representational*. Discourse and affect are seen as having an almost antagonistic relationship" (2013, 52; original emphasis). In a similar vein, and in response to the claim on affect's autonomy, Leys indicates that the distinction between affect and emotion or affect and signification, problematized by Massumi (among others), simply cannot be sustained. As she writes,

> The whole point of the turn to affect by Massumi and like-minded cultural critics is . . . to shift attention away from considerations of meaning or "ideology" or indeed representation to the subject's subpersonal material-affective responses, where, it is claimed, political and other influences do their real work. (2011, 451)

As she further explains, "The discontent between 'ideology' and affect produces as one of its consequences a relative indifference to the role of ideas and beliefs in politics, culture, and art in favor of an 'ontological' concern with different people's corporeal-affective reactions" (2011, 451). I am reluctant to accept such a reading of Massumi's ideas. In the introduction to his *Parables for the Virtual*, he pays attention to the fact that within the past decades cultural theory has tended to bracket such terms as "movement" and "sensation" and their unmediated connection (2002a, 1) in favor of a " 'discursive' body: one with its signifying gestures" which can make and unmake sense (2002a, 2). Such an approach "catches the body in cultural freeze-frame" (2002a, 3). As he further writes,

> Also lacking is the notion that if there is a qualitative movement of the body, it as directly concerns sensings as significations. Add to this the fact that matter,

> bodily or otherwise, never figures into the account as such . . . matter can only enter in indirectly: as mediated. Matter, movement, body, sensation. Multiple mediated miss. (2002a, 4)

Consequently, Massumi's project is not aimed at contradicting poststructuralist theory but rather to "put matter unmediatedly back into cultural materialism, along with what seemed most directly corporeal back into the body," and to "find a semiotics willing to engage with continuity" (2002a, 4). This argumentation, therefore, builds on the accomplishments of poststructuralist cultural theory, while refreshing its vocabulary with infusions from neglected or underappreciated sources (see also hoogland 2009). A somewhat similar concern is expressed by Margaret Wetherell, who agrees with Massumi (but also with Thrift and Stewart) that the operations of affect are not well captured in poststructuralist discourse theory and that "it is time to take the effervescent, the mobile, the concrete, and ordinary social action seriously," yet adding that it cannot be achieved "without sustained attention to discourse" (2013, 56). I do not think that Massumi actually argues for an ultimate divorce of affect and discourse. Rather, I believe, his claims do not stand in strict opposition to discourse research, but he focuses instead more vigorously on what it has subsequently excluded. Hence, I argue (agreeing with Wetherell 2013, 56), we need an eclectic approach, which would allow us to overcome a dualistic system that tends to always juxtapose one against another. As I will also make clear in the course of this book, such a synthetic/monistic approach has major consequences for feminist critique, as it tends to disavow a binarized logic of thinking being at the origins of patriarchal system of domination from its very inception. It also offers a point of departure for formulating a novel, nondualistic account of (embodied) perception, which—again—is a strategy vital from a feminist point of view.

Echoing Deleuze, in his work Massumi urges to transcend our taken-for-granted routines and perceptual habits and try to open ourselves to new ways of thinking, beyond the linear logic and binarized hierarchical systems. Writes Massumi:

> Social and cultural determinations feed back into the process from which they arose. Indeterminacy and determination, change and freeze-framing, go together. They are inseparable and always actually coincide while remaining disjunctive in their modes of reality. To say that passage and indeterminacy "come first" or "are primary" is more a statement of ontological priority than the assertion of a time sequence. They have ontological privilege in the sense that they constitute the field of emergence, while positionings are what emerge. The trick is to express that priority in a way that respects the inseparability and contemporaneousness of the disjunct dimensions: their ontogenetic difference. (2002a, 8)

Thusly explained, Massumi's argumentation avoids a chronological ordering of the flow of experience, assuming instead (as does Deleuze) a radical monism beyond dualistic structures of thought. Certainly, affect and thought cannot be experienced as distinct realms; in an event they are always already assembled. As Wetherell observes, "The flow of affect is located in the body but it is located, too, within the flow of ordinary life. It becomes part of social interaction" (2013, 77).

Being aware of the difficulties involved in the process of singling out pure affect from discourse or social practice as well as of methodological or practical problems involved in applying affect theory to particular case studies, nevertheless I want to stress once more that the fact that affect cannot be clearly separated from meaning does not imply that affect itself cannot be theorized or approached critically. Consequently, in the remaining part of this chapter, I pay more attention to affect rather than discourse, yet bearing in mind that perceptual experience is in fact a combination of both. My singling out of affect is therefore solely *analytical* rather than *factual*. Certainly, there is a goal that I want to pursue by establishing this provisional distinction—what I intend to make clear is that some aspects of operations of a(n) (artistically arranged) memory site and the experiences it generates cannot be entirely grasped if analyzed exclusively through discursive lenses; hence, they need a more encompassing approach.

EMBODIED AFFECTIVITY

Taking on an inspiration from Baruch Spinoza's writing on affectivity, and with an aim to extend our thinking on experience, Deleuze and Guattari (1997) conceptualize affect as incorporeal or imperceptible bodily quality that has a potential capacity to confound social logic and pierce cultural interpretation. Initially, for Deleuze (1968) and Deleuze and Guattari (1987), an "affection" (*affectio*) indicates the state of a body affected by another body; "affect" (*affectus*), conversely, signals the passage from one state to another, an inexorable duration and a relentless intensity that can increase or decrease in volume and amplify or reduce the power of acting. In Spinoza's words, affects are "the modifications of the body by which the power of action on the body is increased or diminished" (1959, 85). Although an affect implies an affection, it is confined to it since it is "purely transitive, and not indicative or representative" in nature and experienced as "lived duration that involves difference between the two states" (Deleuze 1988b, 49). In his later works, Deleuze (1986 [1983]; see also Deleuze and Guattari 1997) replaces *affectio* and *affectus* with "perception" and "affection," respectively, while the term "affect" stands for autonomous pure qualities and potentials extracted from affections (cf. Smith 1997, 181, note 77). Perceptions (i.e., what we *receive*) and affections (i.e., what *happens* to us) are produced in an encounter with other body and are irreducible to perceptions and affections *of a subject*. They are born out of the rhythm of bodily perception, or within the process of constant becoming-other, where—as Daniel Smith explains—"becoming is something between the two, outside the two" (1997, xxx). The percept and the affect, for Deleuze and Guattari, are "autonomous and sufficient beings that no longer owe anything to those who experience or have experienced them" (1997, 168). As such, they have to be understood as singular, sensible events, freed from actual bodies that experience them and unconstrained by well-established representational structures and meaning-making schemes.

It goes without saying that focusing on affect implies, in the first place, coming to terms with the body; it is about an interest in the lively sensual realm of perception, yet this is not about thinking of the body as of a fixed entity. An interest in affect means, as Deleuze argues, that "you will not define a body (or a mind) by its form, nor by its organs or functions, and neither will you define it as a substance or a subject" (1992, 626). A focus on affect conceived in this manner entails thinking about the different changes, modes, and relations (speeds and slownesses) that the body might possibly pass through. This also leads to conceptualizing the body not in terms of subjectivity but rather in terms of effects of which it is capable.

Inspired by Deleuze's thinking about the body and its becomings, Brian Massumi defines affect as the *capacity* to affect or be affected (2002a, 23–45), that is, as a faculty to enter into virtual relations with other bodies, or to become-other(s). Bodies' affectivity, in such an account, implies dynamism and potential for continuous transformations. As Patricia Clough explains, affect is not an action. Rather, it signals a "*capacity for activation*" (2009, 49; original emphasis), pointing to the various potentials of the body—to what it can do and not to what it is. In ontological terms, Clough observes, affect is an "implicit form"—a movement, virtuality, prospective power, or a self-informing immanent to all matter. Subsisting in matter, it stands for an always-present "incorporeal potential" (2009, 48).

As Massumi's examples of empirical studies on media effects show, there is no necessary logical correspondence, or straightforward connection, between the immediate affective response to an image and the conscious, emotional perception or understanding of it. As measured physiological reactions and subsequent verbal responses of research subjects to selected visual material suggest, there is "a gap between content and effect" of the event of image reception implying the "bi-level" character of this process (2002a, 24). The immediate intensity of the experience is therefore qualitatively different from its content determined by social context, although they both are, as Massumi underlines, "immediately embodied." As he explains, whereas "intensity is embodied in purely autonomic reactions most directly manifested in the skin," other embodied functions are "depth reactions" (e.g., heartbeat or breathing) that "belong more to the form/content (qualification) level" of response, marking a "reflux of consciousness into the autonomic depths, coterminous with a rise of the autonomic into consciousness" (2002a, 25). Intensity remains "beside this loop, non-conscious, never to be conscious autonomic remainder" of primary affect. It does not mean, however, that language and affect are opposed to each other. Rather, they get entangled in various possible ways—language can interfere with an image's effect or may enhance its intensity (2002a, 25). The analysis effectuated by Massumi leads him to the conclusion that we need to differentiate between affect and emotion. Whereas affect cannot be understood in any linear terms nor recognized in sociolinguistic categories, emotion stands for an intensity captured in language or equipped with meanings. Affect and emotion are relatively autonomous from each other—affect eludes theories of signification and representational structures of language or emotion signaling instead a nonconscious and immediate process of visceral perception, offering a plane for conscious, intentional reading. The latter, on the other hand, limits affective events, rendering them meaningful and interpreted in signifying terms. As Massumi observes, "Visceral sensibility immediately registers excitations gathered by the five 'exteroceptive' senses even before they are fully processed by the brain" (2002a, 60). This signals that the very processing—grounded in representation—is ontologically a secondary procedure, animated by bodily perceptual experiences.

This, however, does not mean that these two realms of perception—the bodily and the semiotic—operate independently of one another. Conversely, they are entwined and constantly inform each other. As Clough clarifies, "Affect and emotion are in a virtual-actual circuit. . . . The temporality of affect is to be understood in terms of thresholds, bifurcation, and emergence—the temporality of the virtual" (2008, 3). Any perceptual event is in fact a combination, or a singular assemblage, of the affective and the emotional, or the material and the semiotic. Writes Massumi,

> Sensation is never simple. It is always doubled by the feeling of having a feeling. It is self-referential. This is not necessarily the same as "self-reflexive." The doubling of sensation does not assume a subjective splitting and does not of itself constitute a distancing. It is an immediate self-complication. It is best to think of it as a resonation, or interference pattern. (2002a, 13)

In such an account, the process could best be understood in terms of a material-semiotic continuum, where affects and emotions are distributed, combined, and reconfigured in constant movement and transformation into and through each other, a “dynamic unity of reciprocal variation” and “under varying modes of operation, in various phases of separation and regrouping,” in “reciprocal becomings; together they ally in process. They are tinged with event” (Massumi 2002a, 11).

Although Massumi does not explicitly and extensively elaborate on the overlap of the affective/material and the emotional/semiotic, focusing instead on the possibilities of bifurcations between the two, he—in my opinion—clearly assumes that the two are simultaneously yet disjunctively appearing aspects of the same event, that is, they coexist within an assemblage. Yet, as mentioned before, this lack of attention to the discursive or social aspects of the bodily perceptions is at the origin of criticism developed by other scholars vis-à-vis his claims. For Wetherell (who follows Barrett 2009 and Russell 2003 and speaks exclusively of human affect), it is more accurate to conceive of affect and discourse in terms of a constructive feedback process, as core affects are “simultaneously perceived, organized, categorized, labeled and communicated becoming socially recognizable ‘emotions’ ” (2013, 355). As she further argues, “Any initial bodily hit . . . is always already occurring within an ongoing stream of meaning-making or semiosis”; therefore, “we cannot . . . ignore the meaning-making contexts and histories that so decisively shape the encounters between bodies and events” (2013, 355). It means that, in her words, “the moment of ‘intensity’ is indissolubly linked to the history of ‘quality’ (in Massumi’s terminology)” (2013, 355). Taking into consideration Massumi’s discussion on perception (e.g., the aforementioned focus on a feeling accompanied with a feeling of having a feeling), I do not think that Wetherell’s criticism of affect/discourse split—arguing that “an obvious entanglement for human social actors occurs *routinely* between embodied states and the semiotic” (2012, 353; my emphasis)—really contradicts Massumi’s ideas. Evidently, he conceives of (also perceptual) “routine” or “habit” as of a nature-culture hybrid: “Habit is an acquired automatic self-regulation. It resides in the flesh. Some say in matter. As acquired, it can be said to be ‘cultural.’ As automatic and material, it can pass for ‘natural’ ” (Massumi 2002a, 11).

Crucial in Massumi’s theory, at least in the context of my argumentation, is that his understanding of perception acknowledges the possibility of seemingly unexpected, or better *singular*, combination of the material/bodily and the semiotic/intellectual within an event, which might pierce the taken-for-granted cultural assumptions and social logic.[9] He also exposes that deterministic tendencies in poststructuralist discourse theory do not allow us to entirely grasp the complex cognitive processes at work in an assemblage. Similar concerns are raised by other critics of purely discursive research,[10] arguing instead for a more relational approach. It does not mean, however, that the “traditional” discourse research should be rejected, but rather, as

Massumi makes it clear, we need to acknowledge that its "sphere of applicability must be recognized as limited to a particular mode of existence, or a particular dimension of the real (the degree to which things coincide with their own arrest)" (2002a, 7). In his account, to which I subscribe in this book, perception is a far more complex process, involving a conjunctive use of senses and aesthetic bodily and incorporeal interactions. They—in an assemblage-like fashion—produce a field of possibility of emergence for thought and translate into singular knowledges. This kind of perception, I argue, is also at work in many contemporary memory sites and memorial artworks, whose analyses I present in the subsequent chapters of this book. Yet, before clarifying the assets of the process of synaesthetic "seeing," on which my further argumentation rests, I first turn to the contested status of memorial work within the art history discourse on aesthetics and to the concept of aesthetic experience.

MEMORIAL ART

Sites of remembrance and memorial artifacts hold a relatively uncertain aesthetic position. This is derived, at least to a certain extent, from the dominant understanding of the notion of "aesthetic experience," whose meaning—nonetheless—has never been precisely established. As Adele Tomlin explains, the concept has already been defined in a number of, sometimes openly contradictory, ways—it has been described, she notices, "as an experience that imparts knowledge, as one that does not impart knowledge, as will-less, as disinterested, as active, as passive, as cathartic, as contemplative . . . [as] an experience not essentially unlike other experiences . . . [or as] a type of experience that is uniquely different from others" (2008, 1). Such a cacophony of voices might owe much to the imprecise indication of the referent of this notion. As Noël Carroll (1986) aptly states, *the aesthetic* within the philosophy of art has at least a twofold meaning. First, it denotes a way of our experiential or perceptual responding to or interacting with art (as opposed to reasoning or application of concepts); second, the notion of aesthetics is instrumental for theories dealing with the nature of art objects understood as artifacts designed to afford aesthetic experiences. Combined together (although ostensibly independent), they make up a "commonsensical approach that holds that what an object is can be captured through an account of its function" (1986, 57). It is partly due to such conceptualizations of *the aesthetic* that the place of memorial art within art theory is deeply problematic. Carroll suggests that this is also directly connected to the fact that memorial artworks are designed to perform social (or, more specifically, memorial) functions rather than provide a disinterested aesthetic experience (2005, 1), the latter—according to many traditional views—being the domain of fine art. Such an approach obviously owns much to the more general tendencies of contemporary art theory as well as to their (often-futile) efforts aimed at precisely defining what the notion of aesthetic experience actually stands for.

Richard Shusterman appropriately notices that the term "aesthetic" in its contemporary meaning was established in modernity, whose philosophy "typically identified the aesthetic not only *through*, but also *with* subjective experience" (1997, 29; original emphasis). Such an intentional approach, which assumes that experience is dependent on the existence of a transcendental subject and guaranteed therewith, led to the formulation of two broad concepts of aesthetic experience. Consequently, as Gary Iseminger explains, we can conceive of it as an "experience of something characterized primarily by 'what it is like' to undergo it . . . [or] as involving direct or non-inferential knowledge" (2003, 100). Whereas in the former case we can talk about a *phenomenological* concept of the aesthetic experience, in the latter one, we should understand it in *epistemic* terms (2003, 100). Iseminger also notices, that "most recent attempts to defend the notion of aesthetic experience within this tradition, while not in general incompatible with the idea of a phenomenologically distinctive aesthetic experience, see it in fundamentally epistemic terms" (2003, 100; see also Iseminger 2008).[11] As Shusterman clarifies, phenomenological renditions of the aesthetic experience tend to approach it as an experience that is distinctly felt by the experiencing subject (i.e., this kind of experience is never registered in an inattentive way but rather consciously savored); it is also always intentional as it presupposes some object of experience (i.e., the "what" of the experience) as well as it assumes it is experienced in a particular way (i.e., the "how" of the experience). As such, it is a meaningful perception rather than a "mere" sensation, although the latter is always included. Cognitive understandings, in a different way, focus exclusively on "a special mental state of perceiving and appreciating certain features of an object for their own sake but without any need for subjective affect to be present or felt" (2008, 82–83); yet, also in such an account, "a subject's state of mind nonetheless remains central" (2008, 83). Importantly, both these formulations assume (although in different manners) that the process of engaging with art is quintessentially intentional and as such rests on the concept of (active) subject of knowledge/perception who experiences, evaluates these experiences, and, eventually, makes them meaningful.

Whether phenomenological or epistemic (or a combination of the two), aesthetic experience—as viewed within classical art theory—usually refers to an *artwork* and does not extend to experiences that are not in that sense "artistic." As Carroll writes, aesthetic theory defends the view that "something is an artwork *if and only if* it is designed with the primary intention of affording or having the capacity to afford experiences valuable for their own sakes"

(2005, 1; my emphasis). In a similar vein, Monroe Beardsley offers definition of an artwork as "*either* an arrangement of conditions intended to be capable of affording an experience with marked aesthetic character *or* (incidentally) an arrangement belonging to a class or type of such arrangements" (1982, 299; original emphasis). In such a context, aesthetic experience is seen within the tradition of art theory as one distinctively pertaining to art and therefore dramatically different from experiences of other kind or generated in the encounters with other objects, spaces, or bodies.

Shusterman highlights four historical and intellectual assumptions central to the Western twentieth-century tradition of aesthetic experience.

> First, aesthetic experience is essentially valuable and enjoyable; call this evaluative dimension. Second, it is something vividly felt and subjectively savored, affectively absorbing us and focusing our attention on its immediate presence and thus standing out from the ordinary flow of routine experience; call this its phenomenological dimension. . . . Third, it is meaningful experience, not mere sensation; call this its semantic dimension. . . . Fourth, it is a distinctive experience closely identified with the distinction of fine arts and *representing art's essential aim*; call this the demarcational-definitional dimension. (1997, 30; my emphasis)

In his argumentation, Shusterman evidences how John Dewey's (1934) original rendition of the concept of the aesthetic experience—evaluative, phenomenological, and transformational—has been increasingly substituted in analytical aesthetics with its purely descriptive semantic understanding, which serves as a criterion for distinguishing art from other human activities or products.[12] Importantly, the last characteristic outlined by Shusterman, that is, the claim that art by its very definition should be intended primarily to deliver aesthetic experience, is, according to Carroll, a clear reflection of modernism and, as he underlines, "both high modernism and the aesthetic theory of art appear constitutionally inhospitable to memorial art" (2005, 2). In modern aesthetics there is, as Carroll suggests, a "strong tendency to withhold the title of art . . . from works noteworthy for their social utility" (2005, 1). This corresponds well with the construal of the modern notion of aesthetic experience (as valued for its own sake), which was introduced precisely with the purpose "to mark a contrast with social or religious utility" (Carroll 2005, 3). Similar distinction also stands at the heart of a modern division between the fine arts and practical arts, that is, between the aesthetic and the nonaesthetic. As explained in the introduction to this book, such a representational structure, resting on an oppositional organization of ideas and aiming to deliver precise definitions as well as clearly outlined concepts and notions, seems to have been the underlying principle for modern Western development of philosophy and science.

Noticeably, yet rather predictably in light of the preceding discussion, the definitional ambiguity of the concept of aesthetic experience has translated, as Shusterman argues, into its significant demise as well as it has produced growing resistance against it (1997). As he explains, a combination of the two very ambiguous terms ("aesthetic" and "experience")[13] into one concept will necessarily lack clarity and precision. Therefore, it should come as no surprise that analytical philosophy has never been "particularly friendly to the notion of aesthetic experience, questioning its theoretical value and sometimes even challenging its very existence" (Shusterman 2008, 80). At the same time, many Continental and Asian philosophers[14] have pointed out that the depreciation of *the aesthetic*[15] (as well as of *experience*) in the Anglo-American philosophical tradition has stemmed from the aforementioned Western insistence on a dualistic model of thinking in terms of hierarchically structured concepts and categories, as well as from a similarly organized construction of scientific thought and method connected therewith (privileging the mind and the intellect over the body and the senses). Such formulation, dominating within the Western tradition, owes much to original distinctions pertaining to human perception introduced already by Immanuel Kant. The oppositions between reason and sense, or interest and disinterest, have paved the way for the modernist structure of perception, grounded in a dichotomized logic. This model, nevertheless, has recently been questioned by philosophical developments offered by, among others, existential phenomenology, deconstruction, and hermeneutics, as well as postmodernism, which all have substantially undermined the hitherto dominance of the modernist understanding of the aesthetic experience, as well as of the binaristic distinctions on which the concept is premised.

Postmodernism (especially as discussed within the cultural studies scholarship)—skeptical towards any kind of straightforward distinctions between popular and fine arts—claims that art should be included within a broader context of representational practices. The idea of art having some kind of autonomy apart from its social, historical, and cultural context has been thoroughly contested, if not entirely discredited, among postmodern scholars focusing on art theory and visual culture education. Such rendition of the concept of an artwork entails a necessary contextualization of any piece of art, that is, an obligatory need to situate it within cultural history; otherwise any interpretation of artwork would run a risk of being deemed superficial, fictional, or even naïve (Lankford 1998, 23). These assumptions produced at least two contemporary powerful explanatory critiques of art, that is—as Simon O'Sullivan outlines—one having its origins in Marxism and one stemming from deconstruction (2001, 125). They both privilege the interpretative approach to aesthetics: whereas Marxism aims at explaining art historically by focusing on circumstances of its production, deconstruction conceives of it as an outcome of more general discursive practices and thus a product demanding explanation or decoding. Consequently, we deal with two different ways of understanding art, that is, as O'Sullivan clarifies, "art as representation, and then . . . art as being in the crisis of representation; appealing to origins as final explanation, and then putting the notion of origin under erasure" (2001, 125).

It is worth stressing here that deconstruction has become the dominant cultural studies approach applied in the analysis of visual culture products (note that a shift from art theory to visual culture or visual studies is remarkable for postmodernism), which to a certain extent contributed to a relative marginalization of approaches originating in Marxism. This was partly due to the fact that deconstruction—turning the aesthetics into *discourse on/of representation*—itself also constituted a critique of both Marxism and cultural materialism based on critical theory (O'Sullivan 2001). Although cultural studies critiques, in general, and deconstruction, in particular, are still thoroughly grounded in negativity, they shed an altogether different light on the operating of an artwork, which no longer works in isolation from the social or the cultural, but instead is seen as a product of discourse, yet one itself reproducing the social order, or performatively reenacting it. Consequently, what has come to be known as the "linguistic turn" was drawing heavily on Lacanian psychoanalysis on the one hand and on Derridian deconstruction on the other. These poststructuralist inventions significantly redefined the "content" of art theory, both its objects and its practices, reducing them in fact to the effects of representation and practically stymieing, or at least significantly constraining, any thinking of them beyond textuality or signifiers.

The aesthetic position of memorial art is therefore dramatically different when situated within modern or postmodern context. As explained earlier, within modern theory of aesthetics, it was precisely on account of their instillment within the social (i.e., within interested rather than disinterested practices) that memorial artworks' status *as artworks* remained widely unacknowledged among fine art critics. Such a perspective on memorial art, that is, an approach grounded in modern theory of art that argues that art's definitional function is its capacity to afford aesthetic experience, obviously seems to be deeply problematic if we take into consideration the fact that historically a great lot of artworks had memorial character and, as such, performed also other functions that were at least rival to or even surpassing the aesthetic one (Carroll 2005). These, as Carroll (2005) explains, include enculturation as well as therapeutic functions, both being effectively engendered in and accomplished by contemporary memorials or memorial artworks. In a radically different manner, postmodern critiques would rather underline that the fact that memorial art engages us aesthetically *while* fulfilling other aforementioned functions makes it a privileged object of cultural analysis and in-depth critical investigations, yet ones away from the traditional art criticism.

This claim is in concord with a postmodern call—contra modernism—to include all artworks (also those previously defined as fine art or, alternatively, high culture) within more general (yet not innocent) representational practices of signification, institutional regimes, and ideological discourses.

Its negativity notwithstanding, I am far from necessarily conceiving of deconstruction as a wrong or useless strategy. Instead, what I argue in this book is that deconstructionist interpretations of (memorial) art are simply not sufficient, since after revealing of its entanglement within particular noninnocent discursive formations, art (whether memorial or not) remains transformatively dynamic in a sense that it still affects us and mobilizes our (creative) responses. We do not become entirely immune to the workings of an already-deconstructed artwork and—even adopting the position of resistance vis-à-vis ideological meanings conveyed thereby—we still actively and productively engage in its *affective* operations. The deconstructed artwork is still dynamic in all its complexity, yet this fact remains largely unacknowledged (or partly ignored) within the poststructuralist theoretical paradigm. Such an approach does not fully account for the vibrancy of an artwork, focusing instead solely on its representational layer. A more encompassing understanding of how a work of art functions (affectively and discursively, or materially and semiotically) is in line with Jean-François Lyotard's claim that an artwork "is not merely a cultural object, although it is that too. It harbours within it an excess, a rapture, a potential of associations that overflows all the determinations of its 'reception' and 'production' " (1991, 93). Thus, in order to capture these nonlinear processes, that is, to realize how art (memorial or not) absorbs and transforms us, a novel approach is necessary—one that takes into consideration the complex "entanglements" (Barad 2003, 2007) of meaning and matter as contributing to the emergence of an aesthetic experience. This, I believe, is offered by the new materialist account of art. Consequently, my argumentation developed in this chapter aims to (re)affirm the vitally transformational role of aesthetic experience, also through returning to the notion's etymological origins and meanings. Defined in new materialist terms (and inspired by Deleuze and Guattari's philosophical developments), no longer does the concept pertain exclusively to art, but rather it extends to experiential "material-semiotic" aspects of life, in general. By offering a nonrepresentational, or more-than-representational, rendition of the aesthetic experience in terms of "synaesthetic perception," I want to undo the limitative fetters imposed on it within the dominant Western philosophical tradition (and representationalism!), hence opening it to the undetermined (and unpredictable) flow of potentialities and metamorphoses. Before I do that, however, I first need to turn to new materialist renditions of art to explain how this approach is different from the more traditional ones and what kind of new possibilities for conceptualizing both art and aesthetic experience it offers.

BEYOND REPRESENTATION—NEW MATERIALISM AND THE ARTS

If we focus on art through new materialist lenses,[16] we have to acknowledge that the experience of art is one of both matter and meaning—the materiality of art creates and gives form to the discursive and vice versa—the discursive makes sense of matter, that is, it makes it *matter*. Such an understanding of art and how it operates serves as one of the guiding principles for my argumentation. It owes much to both the philosophical ideas developed within new materialism and the nonrepresentational philosophy (of art) worked out by Gilles Deleuze and Félix Guattari. This formulation enables approaching art in terms of its forces, its provocations and incitements, its intensities and flows, rather than focusing exclusively on meanings it conveys. It also does away with those philosophical and phenomenological understandings of art that stress the dynamics of intentionality inscribed in the (dualistic) interactions of the subject and the object in artworks and aesthetic experience (as briefly outlined in the previous section). Art, as a dynamic assemblage of vibrating movements, generates affects and intensifies sensations. It is a way of addressing problems, a creative becoming of the brain, an embodied knowing, which produces effects and transformations. Aesthetic experience, in such an understanding, is a form of thought.

In their influential book *What Is Philosophy?* Deleuze and Guattari postulate that the thought should be understood as a heterogenesis (1997, 199). Chaos has for them three daughters. They are the *Chaoids*, "the forms of thought and creation" or "the realities produced on the planes that cut through the chaos in different ways" (1997, 208). The three routes the thought could follow are art, science, and philosophy. They can be distinguished by what occupies them—thinking, accordingly, may take place through generation of concepts (the domain of philosophy), production of functions (the faculty of science), or intensification of sensations (through art). Yet—as the two thinkers notice—"no one of these thoughts is better than another, or more fully, completely, or synthetically 'thought' " (1997, 198). In that sense, "*The brain is the junction*—not the unity—*of the three planes*" (1997, 208; original emphasis), as thought might take various forms and simultaneously follow different enmeshing trajectories; it is heterogeneous by its very nature. Write Deleuze and Guattari,

> What defines thought in its three great forms—art, science, and philosophy—is always confronting chaos, laying out a plane, throwing a plane over chaos. But philosophy wants to save the infinite by giving it consistency: it lays out a plane of immanence that, through the action of conceptual personae, takes events or consistent concepts to infinity. Science, on the other hand, relinquishes

> the infinite in order to gain reference: it lays out a plane of simply undefined coordinates that each time, through the action of partial observers, defines the states of affairs, functions, or referential propositions. Art wants to create the finite that restores the infinite: it lays out a plane of composition that, in turn, through the action of aesthetic figures, bears monuments or composite sensations. (1997, 197)

What the three forms of thought have in common is the fact that they are vibrantly generative. As for the potential of art (which is an issue this chapter tackles), it produces affects and intensities, that is, generates immanent and intimate knowledge. Art monumentalizes sensation, which, as Elizabeth Grosz notices, "is nothing but a vibratory difference capable of resonating bodily organs and the nervous system" (2008, 62); it is a material unfolding, a constant becoming, a knowledge process. Since affects are profoundly material, if not biological phenomena, the processual character of art must remain material-semiotic. As Grosz continues,

> There can be no art without the materials of art, but the artistic is an eruption, a leap out of materiality, the kick of virtuality now put into and extracted from matter to make it function unpredictably. Sensations, artworks, do not signify or represent . . . they assemble, they make, they do, they produce. (2008, 75)

Not only does such an account of art rely on art's material dimension, but it also underlines its productive potential, that is, its ability to generate transformative outcomes, which forces understanding of arts in agential terms (such conceptualization, as evidenced in the introductory part of this book, is consistent with a new materialist philosophical thinking). Thanks to its agential capabilities, the artistic object (or experience) could produce *meaningful* effects in the world, triggering its metamorphoses.

In a similar vein, and with an aim of underlining both the importance and agency of matter in art, Barbara Bolt (2004a, 2004b, 2009)—drawing partly on Martin Heidegger's ideas—offers a concept of a *work of art* that she differentiates from that of an *artwork*. Significantly, she claims that whereas a more traditional notion of an *artwork* is a noun, that is, denotes a passive object or a medium for artist's ideas, the term "work of art" clearly refers to a verb, that is, to the *work* of art. Such a distinction enables a more-nuanced thinking about the agential character of an aesthetic object or experience. Bolt pays attention to the processual and active character of a *work of art* and points to its so-called "work-being" (2004a, 8) as opposed to the "instrumental-being" of an *artwork* (which suggests that art is solely a vehicle for conveying of the already-existing representations and meanings). The *artwork*, she explains, "can be defined as production—the novel, poem, screenplay, performance, painting, film, installation, drawing, or event that has emerged in and through practice—it is what is published or exhibited or performed" (Bolt 2014, 30). The *work of art*, on the other hand, "is the work that the artwork *does*; it is the *movement* in concepts, understandings, methodologies, material practice, affect and sensorial experience that arises in and through the vehicle of art and the artwork" (Bolt 2014, 30; original emphasis). In other words, "the work that art *does* is its performative quality" (2014, 30; original emphasis), which—as Bolt clarifies—"can relate to the process of making the artwork and the effect for the artist and for the field, and/or to the effect that the artwork may generate in the world" (2014, 30). Such a formulation conceives of the *work of art* in agential or active manners, recognizing its capacities for forming dynamic assemblages (with other bodies) and fueling significant transformations.

Focusing on what art is capable of doing, that is, on the agency of art, allows us to approach *a work of art* in material terms, as a fundamentally material process and to appreciate matter as movement capable of creation. This lets us shift attention away from art's solely representational functions (i.e., its symbolic or semiotic dimension) and zoom in on art's creative potentials as well as its constant material becomings. The fact that art is seen as productive offers an opportunity for its affirmative renditions, which is a logic consonant with new materialist thinking. This fuels new positive politics, so alien to those of representation. As Bolt explains elsewhere, representation is a concept and practice that always signals an absence or a gap. Something represented is *not* here and not *now* (2004a, 171); representation denotes nonpresence and is therefore an entirely negative concept; it stands for the lack of the represented object/phenomenon. Differently from that, and acknowledging an active status of materiality, Gilles Deleuze and Félix Guattari (1997) offer a nonrepresentational theory of art (on which Bolt occasionally draws), where art is defined—as mentioned earlier—in terms of sensations rather than of what it represents. Sensation, in such an account, makes the thought possible. As explained earlier, from this perspective art should be understood as a creation of impersonal affects and percepts rather than as purely representational activity. It is therefore about an assemblage that introduces a singular state (i.e., affect) independent of the participating bodies. Art is about immediacy, or an aesthetic encounter, a product of a relation between bodies. For Deleuze and Guattari, art is

> a zone of indetermination, of indiscernibility, as if things, beasts, and persons . . . endlessly reach that point that immediately precedes their natural differentiation. This is what is called an *affect*. . . . Life alone creates such zones where living beings whirl around, and only art can reach and penetrate them in its enterprise of cocreation. (Deleuze and Guattari 1997, 173; original emphasis)

Claire Colebrook explains this approach with the following words: "Art is not about knowledge, conveying 'meanings' or providing information. Art is not just an ornament or style used to make data more palatable or consumable" (2007, 24). It does not mean, however, that art cannot be approached in representational terms, yet the symbolic dimension does not testify to its nature *as* art. Although, as Colebrook continues, "art may well have meanings or messages . . . what makes it *art* is not its content but its *affect*, a sensible force or style through which it produces content" (2007, 24; original emphasis). In that sense, "no art and no sensation have ever been representational," Deleuze and Guattari underline (1997, 193). So understood, the function of art is not to reflect, represent, or reproduce the world, but it rather works to evoke *affect* (not as opposed to thought but as a set of means by which understanding is generated). Hence, the operation of art is relational, as it emerges in the process of material-semiotic collision or assemblage, which animates further thoughtful becomings and generates conceptual movements, a force that triggers intellectual unfolding. As Deleuze writes, "Something in the world forces us to think. This something is not an object of recognition, but a fundamental *encounter*" (2011, 176; original emphasis). This encounter may function as a catalyst for a critical and profound inquiry, or as a plane on which thought rises and develops. He advises,

> Do not count upon thought to ensure the relative necessity of what it thinks. Rather, count upon the contingency of an encounter with that which forces thought to rise up and educate the absolute necessity of an act of thought or a passion to think. (2011, 176)

For Deleuze,

> what is encountered . . . may be grasped in a range of affective tones: wonder, love, hatred, suffering. In whichever tone, its primary characteristic is that it can only be *sensed*. In this sense it is opposed to recognition. . . . The object of encounter . . . really gives rise to sensibility with regard to a given sense. (2011, 176; my emphasis)

Such an understanding of the thinking process relies on the aesthetic dimension of the experience, or sensation that is produced within an assemblage of bodies (actual, virtual, physical, symbolic, animal, technological, etc.). Although situated within a different philosophical paradigm, Maurice Merleau-Ponty offers a somewhat similar understanding of art when he rhetorically asks: "How would the painter or poet express anything other than his *encounter* with the world?" (quoted in Kearney 1994, 82; my emphasis). The artistic process is—in such account—an effect of a relation or an encounter. Therefore, drawing inspiration from philosophies primarily concerned with the body and its multiple and complex entanglements with the world, new materialism is not principally interested in representation or signification but is rather fascinated by affect, force, sensation, and movement. This is also due to the fact that whereas the object of recognition (i.e., representation) offers the already-known meanings or symbols, the object of a fundamental encounter invites the new and encourages a serious reconsideration of our perceptual routines. As Simon O'Sullivan aptly explains, "An object of recognition is . . . precisely a *re*presentation of something always already in place . . . representation . . . stymies thought" (O'Sullivan 2006, 1; original emphasis). Conversely, by the object of a genuine encounter "we are forced to thought. . . . It produces a cut, a crack . . . the rupturing encounter also contains a moment of affirmation . . . of a new world, in fact a way of seeing and thinking this world differently" (O'Sullivan 2006, 1). Accordingly, art is not about conveying meanings and representations, but it is rather about sustaining sensations. And "sensation requires no mediation or translation. It is not representation, sign, symbol, but force, energy, rhythm, resonance" (Grosz 2008, 73).

Art is about an affective assemblage that involves immediate (although sometimes imperceptible) material interactions. This invites a processual material-semiotic understanding of art. As a result, no longer is art considered a set of determined objects, but rather it is defined in terms of a constant material unfolding and becoming. For Grosz, one of the thinkers whose work reveals a new materialist spirit, art emerges "when sensation can detach itself and gain an autonomy from its creator and its perceiver, when something of the chaos from which it is drawn can breathe and have a life of its own" (2008, 7). Art is "about transforming the lived body in an unlivable power, an unleashed force that transforms the body with the world" (Grosz 2008, 22). It engenders "material becomings . . . in which life folds over itself to embrace its contact with materiality, in which each exchanges some elements or particles with other to become more and other" (Grosz 2008, 23). There are a lot of material processes involved in the operation of art, as well as in its onto-epistemology. And there is a lot of materiality involved in the aesthetic encounters. Hence, if we want to grasp the way art absorbs us, we need to approach it in terms of its material-semiotic becomings.

Certainly, as mentioned earlier, art is not *solely* about sensations; it does also have symbolic and semiotic dimensions. Crucially, in art, both the material and semiotic processes interweave. Art simultaneously affects us indirectly (through its symbolic means, producing emotions) and directly (through its active materialities, evoking affects). These two levels, however, are always entangled and cannot be approached in isolation from each other. Hence, it is necessary to look at the material world with its flows, movements, and forces in a more detailed way. This is especially vital due to the fact that although materiality has always constituted an important dimension of art, it has been to a large extent missing from mainstream investigations within the field of art theory (and history).

Focusing on materiality and affectivity of art lets us acknowledge that in fact matter never simply *is*, but rather it creates and produces, that is, it *does* or it *becomes*. It is, therefore, not a *mere* matter but rather, as Diana Coole and Samantha Frost notice, "an excess, force, vitality, relationality or difference that renders matter active, self-creative, productive, unpredictable" (2010b, 28). For Deleuze and Guattari, "Matter is a molecular material, not dead, brute, homogenous matter, but a matter-movement" (1987, 512). Matter is active and entirely relational (i.e., affective!) for it relates bodies to each other. Its generative movement is productive of assemblages as it bears in its folds singularities and their encounters with other singularities. Matter's affectivity, as clarified earlier, stands for its faculty to enter into lively relations with other bodies. In such a context, however, the term "body" has to be understood in entirely inclusive ways. For Deleuze, "A body can be anything; it can be an animal, a body of sounds, a mind, or idea; it can be a linguistic corpus, a social body, a collectivity" (1988a, 127). They all have some sort of material existence. As such, the body is defined in dynamic terms, through its potentials, so—again—in reference to what it *can do* or what it can *become* rather than, statically, to what it *is*. This approach does not privilege any specific bodies (e.g., human). Instead, it argues that all bodies evince certain capacities and agencies to enter into affective relations with others. Consequently, in a new materialist account, the function of art is not to reflect, represent, or reproduce the world, but it rather works to evoke affects. Art is not defined through its capacity to signify. Instead, what truly matters is the sensation arising from the affective *encounter* with it (see Bennett 2005), a movement of becoming and a transformation that this encounter triggers. In O'Sullivan's words,

> Art then is the name of the object of an encounter, but also the name of the encounter itself, and indeed of that which is produced by the encounter. Art is this complex event that brings about the possibility of something new. (2006, 2)

Affect, however, is not central exclusively to the work of art. It is a quality of *all matter*. For Deleuze and Guattari, matter is extremely heterogeneous, dynamic, and supple. It is about relations—affects and intensities—which are often imperceptible or happen on the micro-level. Affects are then about the capacity of bodies *to collide*, that is, to engage, connect, and dash with each other; they are the imperceptible forces of transformation, or potentialities, opening onto the world. In such an account, the whole life is about affects and relations, that is, about constant becomings and vibrant metamorphoses.

SYNAESTHETIC PERCEPTION

The understanding of matter in terms of relations, assemblages, and collisions relies on an enlarged idea of perception or on—what I call—"seeing differently," in a more-than-representational fashion. Such a formulation disavows the well-established assumptions that perception pertains to the knowing subject and is guaranteed therewith. In a new materialist spirit the perceptual procedure has to be conceived of as a nonlinear, immediate, and extended process of seeing that synaesthetically enlists other bodily senses and sensibilities. Thusly conceptualized, perception is embodied and relational—it is not solely about recognition of the already known (i.e., perceiving in solely representational manners) but also about bodily, affective assemblages and sensuous intra-actions in which the body enters physically and virtually. Perception is an enfleshed process in which simultaneous and conjunctive work of all senses is engaged; it is therefore synaesthetic by its very nature. As Merleau-Ponty explains (in phenomenological terms), "My perception is not a sum of visual, tactile and audible givens: I perceive in a total way with my whole being. I grasp a unique structure of the thing, a unique way of being, which speaks to all my senses at once" (1968, 48). Such a rendition of the concept of perception is partly in line with what Juhani Pallasmaa, an architect and theorist, writes about our engagement with space. His theorization, again, rests on the phenomenological conceptualization of the body and its sensuous engagement with the surroundings. Writes Pallasmaa,

> Every touching experience of architecture is multi-sensory; qualities of space, matter and scale are measured equally by the eye, ear, nose, skin, tongue, skeleton and muscle. . . . Instead of mere vision, or of classical five senses, architecture involves several realms of sensory experience that interact and fuse into each other. (2005, 41)

This has serious consequences for the reconsideration of the structures of power inscribed into the traditional dynamics involving the relations between the subject and the object of knowledge (vision) that I briefly outlined in the introduction to this book. Whereas, for Pallasmaa, "the eye is an organ of distance and separation . . . touch is the sense of nearness, intimacy and affection. . . . The eye surveys, controls and investigates, [the] touch approaches and caresses" (2005, 46). The eye sees, but "the skin reads the texture, weight, density and temperature of matter" (2005, 56). Therefore, the eye would be nothing without the former bodily memory of how textures feel. The procedures of seeing and knowing are thoroughly embodied and happen in the context of encounter with other bodies (physical, virtual, symbolic, imaginary, etc.).

Considering the relations of power that the execution of vision implies, and in a feminist fashion, Pallasmaa introduces the distinction between the "focused vision" (which "confronts us with the world," "pushes us out of space, making us mere spectators") and "unfocused peripheral vision" (which "envelops us in the flesh of the world" and "integrates us with space") (2005, 10). The two ways of seeing shape the two very different manners in which we experience the world as well as how we relate to it. While the focused vision embodies the anthropocentric quest for power and domination or an unrestrained pursuit of might and control, the peripheral vision is more dispersed and relies on multiple horizontal connections and democratic relationalities. In other words, the unfocused vision for which Pallasmaa advocates is about withness and connectivity rather than about separation and distance. He also argues that this kind of vision as well as hapticity molds "the very essence of the lived experience" (2005, 10). This stands for a way of synaesthetically seeing with the whole body, an affective involvement in and a relation with the milieu. What has to be discerned in this context is the potentially emancipatory faculties of such sensitive, sensual, and connective seeing, so important for the logic that this book fosters: "Perhaps, freed of the implicit desire of the eye for control and power, it is precisely the unfocused vision . . . that is . . . capable of opening up new realms of vision and thought" (2005, 35). Such an argumentation might add to the existing feminist critiques of how the traditionally conceived process of seeing operates and how it structures sociocultural relations. "The loss of focus brought about by the stream of images," Pallasmaa claims, "may emancipate the eye from its patriarchal domination and give rise to a participatory and empathetic gaze" (2005, 35), the way of seeing that is involved with the world and assumes a deep intimate relationality or a machine-like interconnectedness of different bodies. In his opinion, the distinction between the focused and unfocused vision corresponds to a certain extent with the one made by David Levin, who speaks of "the assertoric gaze" ("narrow, dogmatic, intolerant, rigid, fixed, inflexible, exclusionary and unmoved") and "the aletheic gaze" (one that "tends to see from a multiplicity of standpoints and perspectives, and is multiple, pluralistic, democratic, contextual, inclusionary, horizontal and caring") (Pallasmaa 2005, 36; see also Levin 1988, 440). This latter manner of gazing might be loosely related to what Donna Haraway (1988) calls a "situated knowledge" or "partial perspective"—an embodied way of seeing, which acknowledges the location (both the most immediate bodily one and the larger sociocultural context) from which the vision is performed and knowledge generated. Hence, what Haraway proposes constitutes an alternative to the traditionally conceived visual quest (with its predatory nature or practices of visual "hunting"), which can be compared to the process of plundering and/or subordinating the "seen" others to the gaze of the "seer" (1988). Located, bodily seeing constitutes, in this context, a disavowal of such relations of power and is based stronger in politics of connective relationality (more on this in chapters 4 and 5).

In a Deleuzian account, which is an optic to which this book thoroughly subscribes, an understanding of perception in bodily terms offers a departure from what Massumi calls a "mirror-vision" (where eyes tend to freeze movement to produce extended static images) towards a "movement-vision," that is, "sight turned proprioceptive" (2002a, 59). Proprioception stands here for the "sensibility proper to the muscles and ligaments as contrasted with tactile sensibility (which is 'exteroceptive') and visceral sensibility (which is 'interoceptive')" (Massumi 2002a, 58). It is a way of sensing with the body; an enfleshed, carnal form of perception, or a "gut feeling" (as Mike Featherstone calls it [2010, 209]). Consequently, proprioception is the mode of perception that "opens exclusively onto the space and registers qualities directly and continuously as movement" (Massumi 2002a, 59); it is a way of seeing or sensing movement, an affective bodily-spatial assemblage. An affect, from this perspective, is what results from a coupling together of visceral and proprioceptive sensibilities, although, as Massumi points out, "the dimension of viscerality is adjacent to that of proprioception, but they do not overlap" (2002a, 61). Henceforth, the synaesthetic perception should be understood in terms of "thinking-feeling" (Massumi 2008) rather than as a production of purely rational knowledge based on representational procedures and meaning-generating structures. Perception is a bodily, sensuous process that animates an intellectual becoming, an assemblage that entangles the physical sensing and the symbolic deciphering, a material-semiotic production or thoughtful creativity.

"What forces us to think is the sign" (Deleuze 2008, 10).[17] Yet, as Deleuze elaborates, the sign cannot be understood in purely symbolic ways: "The sign is the object of an encounter, but it is precisely the contingency of the encounter that guarantees the necessity of what it leads us to think" (2008, 62). Signs, therefore, cannot be perceived solely in representational terms (i.e., recognized), but rather they can be experienced and felt. The affective encounter with a sign is what triggers critical thought. To put it differently, for Deleuze, sensation—which grasps us (sometimes involuntarily) through senses—does not constitute an end in itself but rather mobilizes and animates the process of thinking or bodily-intellectual becoming. Yet, as Deleuze keeps repeating, more important than thought is what leads to it—"impressions which force us to look, encounters which force us to interpret, expressions that force us to think" (2008, 61). Accordingly, what is indispensable for thinking to take place is what Massumi terms "a shock to thought": a jolt that does not so much reveal the truth as thrusts us involuntarily into a mode of critical inquiry. Hence, if conceived in a Deleuzian fashion, the act of thinking does not stem from a natural possibility—it is "the only true creation" (Massumi

2002b, 62), a "genesis of the act of thinking within thought itself," which "implicates something that does violence to thought, which wrests it from its natural stupor and its merely abstract possibilities" (Massumi 2002b, 62). In that sense the synaesthetic perception involves an entanglement of an affective encounter and an intellectual cognition. Such thinking-feeling is a series of assemblages of sensuous-intellectual nature. It forces thought, but—as explained earlier—the thought is not born out of nothing. There are things that force us to think: "no longer *recognizable* objects, but things that do violence, *encountered* signs" (Deleuze 2008, 64; original emphasis). By doing us violence, the sensuous sign "mobilizes memory, it sets the soul in motion; but the soul in its turn excites thought, transmits to it the constraint of the sensibility, forces it to conceive essence, as the only thing that must be conceived" (2008, 64). Such encounters necessarily demand openness and susceptibility—"one must be endowed for the signs, one must open oneself to their violence," as Deleuze explains. And he continues by stating that "the intelligence always comes after; it is good when it comes after; it is good only when it comes after" (2008, 63). This chronology, however, can be conceived of only in ontological manners, where the openness within the encounter is seen as a plane for emergence of thought.

Consequently, the process of bodily-intellectual thinking-feeling constitutes a conjunction of cognition and affect and is based on the dynamic entanglement of the semiotic and the material dimensions of experience as well as how this assemblage translates into knowledge. It is also a more practical form of knowing, as it emerges from an active engagement of the body (with)in the world as well as from passive exposure. It is, therefore, *knowledge as (non)action*. What matters here is not the fact, or a series of facts, but rather the *aesthetic* process, which has relevance both for an encounter with art and for life itself. Considering the conceptualization of the aesthetic experience on which I elaborated earlier, such an assumption is already present in the accounts of philosophers and art critics. Both John Dewey (1934) and Richard Shusterman (2000b) argue that what counts in the encounter with the art is not the actual artistic object but rather the aesthetic experience that the encounter generates. This approach does not prioritize the final product of the artistic process, but rather it pays attention to the activity, or action, that generates it. As Shusterman argues, "With this privileging of aesthetic process over product, art is redefined as 'a quality of experience' rather than a collection of objects; the aesthetic experience thus becomes the cornerstone of the philosophy of art" (2000b, 25). This has further important implications for the conceptualization of the process of perception.

The emphasis on immediate perception (where immediacy stands for no detour of the subject) necessarily implies reworking of the concept of aesthetics towards an affective engagement with the other, a pure experience, a multiplicity of virtual-actual becomings. Henceforth, what I refer to in this book as a notion of *affective aesthetics* returns to the original meaning of the term *aisthetos* (derived from Greek), which denotes "perceptible to the senses," "sensitive," and "sentient," and implies immediacy as well as a far broader field of applicability than subjective judgment allows. Affective perception is never purely visual but rather mobilizes a synaesthetic use of senses. They work together to produce the ways we *sense* the world (or other bodies) in a creative and vibrant encounter. Pure experience refers to a bodily process; a vital, rapid, and intense movement that triggers the subject's passionate becoming-other, where "becoming" stands for an intensive flow of affective (micro)perceptions. Immediate (or pure) perception does not grant time for secure recognition, as Deleuze writes, it "is never conditioned by mechanisms peculiar to the subject" (1986, 64). Accordingly, even if a conscious perception is to be understood as a narration or qualification of affect, there is nonetheless always "a never-to-be-conscious autonomic reminder" of affect (Massumi 2002a, 25). Or, in other words, there always is a reflux back from conscious experience to affect, which is registered and nonconsciously reactivated as affect, so that "past action and contexts are conserved and autonomically repeated" (Massumi 2002a, 30).

Logically, the emphasis on thusly understood immediate perception implies reworking of the concept of aesthetics, or aesthetic experience, towards an affective engagement with the other, a pure experience, a multiplicity of becomings. This introduces a synaesthetic interaction, where the milieu—understood as *Umwelt* or an "island of senses" (Uexküll 2001, 107)—constitutes an ongoing provocation to the organism to utilize its randomly emergent qualities. By using its organs, an organism becomes a provisional response to the *Umwelt*, a sense-bubble carrying fragments of its milieu, or of broadly defined "bodies" (biological, technological, material, cultural, symbolic, linguistic, organic, inorganic, etc.) and how they productively, sometimes unexpectedly, assemble within an event of encounter.

As mentioned earlier, such a revision of perception obviously bears an aesthetic dimension. The logic, according to which *works of art* operate, is one of a bodily, sensuous, and tactile encounter rather than a purely intellectual or emotional visual interpretation. As Pallasmaa writes,

> All the senses, including vision, are extensions of the tactile sense; the senses are specializations of skin tissue, and all sensory experiences are modes of touching and thus related to tactility. Our contact with the world takes place . . . through specialized parts of our enveloping membrane. (2005, 10)

Affect (or sensation), therefore, is born out of a bodily collision and necessarily involves a sensuous (material) dimension of the encounter. This collision, however, is always already material-semiotic; it is about a corporeal material sensing, that is, physicality of the encounter, as well as about a semiotic procedure where materiality becomes equipped with meaning that, at the same time, it makes possible. This is how *matter matters* (Barad 2003, 2007). Importantly, sensing is also individual-collective, a singular event that is forever different, yet always situated in specific material-semiotic contexts. As David Howes aptly notices, "'The facts of sense' are always a product of *con-sensus*—that is, of sensing along with others. Perception is a social activity in that it is conditioned by culture" (2013, 9; my emphasis). Hence, the sensorium also needs to be historicized (Classen et al. 1994, Classen 2012). It does not mean, however, that it is grounded in always the same conceptual schemes and meaning-making structures, as proponents of "sensory studies" would like to see it. Within the new materialist framework, the "new" might emerge performatively through reiterative practices, yet—as I want to underline—performativity should not necessarily be here conceived exclusively as a repetition (and henceforth [re]production) of the same. Rather, I would propose to approach it via Deleuze's understanding, where "repetition produces only the same of that which differs" (1990, 289). This means that each repetition produces new flows, new connections, and new intensities. Each repetition is singular—it is a differing of difference.

The aesthetic encounter affects and transforms all entities involved, although it must be remembered that the entities themselves do not preexist the relations into which they enter. Rather, they are constantly produced and reconfigured within the encounters in which they participate; they are in the process of becoming, or constant differing. As Deleuze and Guattari remark, "We are not in the world, we become with the world; we become by contemplating it. Everything is vision, becoming. We become universes. Becoming animal, plant, molecular, becoming zero" (1997, 169). The sensuous becoming is a process of life itself—a combination, and constant variation, of the actual and the virtual, of the bodily and the intellectual, of the affective and the emotional. It is also a becoming *with*, that is, a process in which different others are involved by coproducing (or codestroying) each other. Perception, therefore, is not about a distant or detached observation, but rather it is itself productive of the various entanglements of the perceivers and the perceived. In perceiving in a synaesthetic manner, we make ourselves exposed, vulnerable, and fragile to the others. To put it differently, it is about making ourselves open to new metamorphoses, violent transformations, or (unexpected) becomings (I will come back to this theme in chapters 4 and 5).

In a new materialist spirit, a synaesthetic perception can be seen as a series of *intra-actions* (to borrow the term from Barad 2003, 2007). In sensing, the cultural/social and the material/bodily coincide and co-constitute each other. A synesthetic perception is both a conjunctive, *syn*thetic use of senses and a process involving a *syn*thesis of the material and the semiotic. Consequently, this new materialist concept favors relationality and connectivity while referring to a multidimensional and multiaxial encounter of differently understood bodies, a collision that never leaves them completely unchanged. This compound process of perception is not biased in favor of any single modality but rather, as Walter Ong suggests, focuses on their interplay, or dynamic coexistence (1991). It means that, in Howes's words, "the essence of the aesthetic experience lies in the union and/or transposition of sensations, rather than their separation" (2013, 15). "The senses communicate with each other" (Merleau-Ponty 1968, 232)—they connect and provide confirmations or contradictions to each other; they are also transposable onto each other's domains as well as combine their effects. It also refers to the process of constant material-semiotic metamorphoses affecting all bodies involved and never leaving them unchanged—it is about touching while being touched, a mutual coproduction of becoming. Perception, accordingly, operates simultaneously on different levels and engages various dimensions. As Félix Guattari explains,

> The same semiotic material can be functioning in different registers. A material can be both caught in paradigmatic chains of production, chains of signification [under the cardologic], but at the same time can function in an a-signifying register [the ordologic]. So what determines the difference? In one case, a signifier functions in what one might call a logic of discursive aggregates, that is, a logic of representation. In the other case, it functions in something that isn't entirely a logic, what I've called an existential machinic, a logic of bodies without organs, a machinic of bodies without organs. (Guattari in Strivale 1998, 219–20)

THE WORK OF (MEMORIAL) ART: CONCLUDING REMARKS

If, following Barbara Bolt's distinction (and in a new materialist spirit), we approach memorial art in terms of "productivity" rather than "production," we will be able to focus on what it *does* and not on what it *is* (2014, 29). Whereas "artwork can be defined as production . . . [the] work of art is the work that the artwork does; it is the movement . . . that arises in and through the vehicle of art and the artworks" (Bolt 2014, 30). As Bolt further explains, "The work that art *does* is its performative quality. . . . This can relate . . . to the effects that the artwork may generate in the world" (Bolt 2014, 30; original emphasis). The close examination of the culturo-materiality of a *work of art* as well as of how it inter-/intra-acts with the culturo-materiality of the visitor/spectator clearly exposes both the agency and the constant (yet often imperceptible) transformation of matter as well as its generative potentials.

Such a perspective, logically, underlines connectivity of the bodies (rather than their separateness) as well as their constant dynamic movement (rather than stasis). This corresponds well with Merleau-Ponty's joyous claim: "My body is made from the same flesh as the world . . . and moreover this flesh of my body is shared by the world, the world . . . encroaches upon it and it encroaches upon the world" (1968, 248). Discernible is here an assumption about the interweaving of the world and the self, that is, their intra-active entanglement, or creative assemblage. Consequently, the *work* of the art is about conjunctive, synthetic, and synaesthetic production of *new* knowledges, *new* qualities, and *new* subjectivities emerging from the creative encounters. This newness is generated without resorting to solely representational means. Yet the knowledge is not simply given to visitors/spectators, but it rather arises from the plentitude of material-semiotic micro-encounters; hence, it is always different and always moving.

As I wanted to point out in my argumentation fostering a new materialist approach to art, sticking to the preconceived, traditional understandings of aesthetic experience and the processes of representational seeing may preclude recognition of other, more creative possibilities of thinking of experience and the procedures of generating knowledge. Differently, acknowledging the intellectual-affective nature of cognition can stimulate a critical reflection on how we are entangled with the world as well as how art—that registers and embodies affects—can help us think about the processes of cognition. This is especially vital in the context of trauma art, as it enables approaching it beyond textuality, yet not through the return to traditional aesthetic theory or artist-centered models. Conversely, such a strategy signals a turn to matter and its expressive potentials, which corresponds well with the bodily affective, or indeed unspeakable, nature of traumatic memory. Thusly conceptualized, the new materialist approach to the generative encounters with memorial art allows us to more fully grasp the ways in which it operates. In such an account, the "reading" of its organization and symbolic meanings is simply not enough. Instead, we need to focus on the aesthetic aspects of the *works of art*, that is, on such their qualities that are perceptible to senses and that actually emerge in the direct, bodily contact. The aesthetic, therefore, is not a matter of representation but of a material-semiotic assemblage. Such an approach is employed in the following chapters of this book.

NOTES

1. See, for instance, works by Patricia Clough and Jean Halley (2007), Brian Massumi (2002a, 2002b), Eve Kosofsky Sedgwick (2003), Mike Featherstone (2010), Federica Giardini (1999), Teresa Brennan (2004), Sianne Ngai (2005), Elspeth Probyn (2005), and Denise Riley (2005).

2. Such an account was theorized by Silvan Tomkins (1962, 1963), the founder of affect theory in psychology.

3. A comprehensive discussion of psychological approaches to emotions is offered by Kenneth Strongman (2003). The psychological perspective is also developed in Norman Denzin (1984). Theodore Kemper (1990) and Gillian Bendelow and Simon Williams (1998), for example, discuss emotions from sociological perspective, whereas Catherine Lutz (1988) conceives of emotions from an anthropological standpoint. For a historical approach, see William Reddy (2001), and for a philosophical account, see, for instance, Robert Solomon (2003). An interdisciplinary perspective can be found in, for example, Michael Lewis and Jeannette Haviland (1993) and Deborah Lupton (1998).

4. Yet, in such an account, as Alison Jaggar argues, these two tend to be presented as different aspects of emotion (1996, 170).

5. My discussion of affect in this chapter is just cursory, as it is not my aim in this book to offer a detailed overview of approaches to affect. My intention is just to situate my argumentation in the broader context of inter-, cross-, and transdisciplinary debates on this concept. Except for Ruth Leys's work (2011), an excellent and critical review of existing approaches to affect is offered by Margaret Wetherell (2012), who discusses both its psychological renditions and more recent cultural studies conceptualizations, and taking into considerations a number of current perspectives, shifts, and turns in theorizing affect and emotion.

6. This paradigm is fostered by, among others, Donald Nathanson (1992), Paul Griffiths (1997), Joseph LeDoux (1996), Antonio Demasio (1995), Eve Kosofsky Sedgwick (2003) (also with Adam Frank 1995), and Daniel Smail (2004), yet it is extensively critiqued by, for instance, Alan Fridlund (1994), James Russell and José-Miguel Fernandez-Dols (1997), Lise Barrett (2009), and Ruth Leys (2007, 2011). In her 2007 book, Leys offers an excellent critical discussion questioning the validity of claims developed by Basic Emotions paradigm scholars.

7. This group of scholars includes, for instance, Brian Massumi (2002a, 2002b), Nigel Thrift (2004), Patricia Clough (2009), and Eric Shouse (2005).

8. Paradoxically, Ruth Leys illustrates this point with critical discussion of Brian Massumi's empirical evidence, which I also briefly evoke in this part of the book.

9. Yet the solely analytical character of the distinction between affect and discourse should be kept in mind. In other words, there are no events that are *purely* affective nor are there events that are *purely* discursive; they are always combined and conjunctive.

10. See, for instance, works by Eve Kosofsky Sedgwick (2003), Margaret Wetherell (1998, 2012), Michael Billig (1999), John Cromby (2007), and Lisa Blackman and Couze Venn (2010). Some of these accounts are equally critical of Brian Massumi's ideas.

11. It must be noted here that the assertion made by Gary Iseminger is not shared by, for instance, Richard Shusterman, who opts for a more transformational (rather than demarcational) concept of aesthetic experience (see Shusterman 2008).

12. Shusterman himself argues for a more inclusive understanding of aesthetic experience as not exclusively pertaining to interactions with artistic objects but rather extending to other interactions as well (e.g., sexual). See, for instance, works by Richard Shusterman (1999, 2000a,b, 2008).

13. Hans-Georg Gadamer, for example, described the concept of experience as "one of the most obscure we have" (1982, 319).

14. For a more detailed account of the more up-to-date critical renditions of the concept of "aesthetic experience," see Shusterman and Tomlin (2008).

15. The term "aesthetic," originally derived from Greek where it stood for sensory perception, has been popularized in its current meaning by Alexander Baumgarten (2013) to depict what he regarded as lower, sensory (i.e., bodily) faculties of cognition and as such always subordinated to more valued intellectual cognitive capacities.

16. New materialist theories of art have emerged relatively recently, with the pioneering works of such scholars as Barbara Bolt (2004a, 2004b, 2006), Elizabeth Grosz (2005, 2008, 2011), Jill Bennett (2005), and Simon O'Sullivan (2001, 2006).

17. In his thorough and complex discussion on signs, presented in the work *Proust and Signs*, Deleuze writes about different sorts of signs. Signs constitute different worlds: worldly signs, empty signs, deceptive signs of love, sensuous material signs, and finally the essential signs of art (which transforms all the others) (Deleuze 2008, 10).

Chapter 2

Memory Sites: Remembering through Materiality

MATERIAL MEMORIES OF MATERIAL PLACES: AN INTRODUCTION

In 1987 some 400 color slides depicting the life in the Litzmannstadt Ghetto were discovered in one of the Viennese antique bookstores. Then they served as a basis for a documentary entitled *Photographer* (1998) directed by Dariusz Jabłoński.

> It was a real shock when I saw these pictures developed from some of the historically first color slides taken by Walter Genewein, a Nazi official employed in the ghetto. These photographs represented the Łódź Ghetto but it was not the ghetto whose recollections I have had so deeply engraved in my memory, even though they pictured the same people, the same buildings, the same streets. Where then shall we search for the truth? Shall we look into my memory or is the truth to be found in the color photographs taken by Walter Genewein?

This reflection belongs to Alfred Mostowicz, a Jewish medical doctor working in the Litzmannstadt Ghetto during World War II. In the movie his testimonial account is confronted with the story produced out of the Genewein's pictures and letters. These two perspectives offer very different views on life in the ghetto, or two different forms of remembering it. Preoccupied with the reddish color that the slides adopt after the film would have been developed, Genewein's story is unemotional and offers a rationalized account of the life of the ghetto, appended with numbers illustrating the size of production enabled by the slave labor of the Jews inhabiting the district. Unlike Genewein's color pictures offering a one-dimensional visual description, Mostowicz remembers sounds and odors, which still pervade his memory making these recollections difficult to forget. This synaesthetic complexity of

Mostowicz's memories is what makes them lively, infused with emotions and sensations, and vividly present today. The two accounts offer two different stories or two different truths. They clash. Anxious about documentary qualities of the color photography enabling a meticulous visual recording, Genewein's work focuses on the technical details of both the color pictures and the life in the ghetto turned into numbers of manufactured goods and levels of generated incomes. Mostowicz's story focuses on the lives of people inhabiting the ghetto or, more specifically, on the inevitability of their apocalyptic fate and their everyday struggle for survival. Thus, the focus of each of these stories is on different dimensions of the historical events.

When I first watched the documentary, I was appalled by the shocking contradiction of the two narratives as well as by the dry, emotionless style of Genewein's account. Yet most striking for me was one of Mostowicz's memories wherein he recalls a scene of the noise of thousands of feet clashing against the pavement of the streets of Litzmannstadt Ghetto, made by a crowd of people going at dawn to the factories where they performed slavery work. Although he did not remember where it exactly happened, he mentioned Młynarska Street. This name gave me sudden chills, a material impression evoked by its sound and connected to my own memories of the site it stood for. 8 Młynarska St. This is the place where I spent early years of my childhood—with my parents, family, and first friends from the neighborhood. I remember with great detail how the site looked like, how it smelled, and what sounds it produced. At the turn of the 1970s and 1980s the site was my home as well as a place where I spent most joyous and untroubled moments of my life. Even though I know exactly where the borders of the Litzmannstadt Ghetto were drawn, this was the moment I suddenly realized that I had spent the most serene days of my life on the site of an actual crime scene. I felt material connection with the physicality of the place: the terrain of imprisonment of so many, which later on turned to be my home. The material persuasiveness of the memory of this material space activated by the documentary's narrative was astounding. The atemporal nature of the *matter* and *mattering* of the site was striking.

This chapter tackles the issue of materiality, especially in the context of contemporary practices of commemorating the Shoah, offering an important starting point for investigations of the materiality of (traumatic) memory developed in chapter 3. In this context I start my deliberations by looking at the processes of materialization of memory as well as how this materiality translates into material impressions left on visitors' bodies. This, however, cannot be divorced from complex, often politically informed, operations of discourse. Such an analysis makes clear that the past frequently gets instrumentalized and mobilized for advancing very present interests and pursuing current political objectives. Focusing on diversified and multidimensional operations of memorial spaces, which—at the same time—are often conceived of as tourist destinations or attractions, this chapter also explores aspects of "heritage tourism," "dissonant heritage tourism," and "dark tourism" from critical perspectives of widely understood memory studies.

As Sharon Macdonald clarifies, contemporary societies have become "obsessed with the disappearance of collective memory and its preservation," that is, with a tendency that sits at the origin of erection of diverse heritage sites "designed to remind us of histories that might otherwise be lost" (2013, 1). The discourse surrounding "dark attractions" is, however, quite controversial. I critically comment on different classifications and categorizations applied in connection to the dark tourism trope pointing to their immersion into more general scientific discourses and Western epistemological paradigms. From there I continue by illustrating my theoretical investigations with analyses of case studies of memorial museums commemorating the Shoah. Looking at their complex narrative-discursive, or material-symbolic, operations, I want to reveal how their impact and educational functions rely on their multidimensional character shaped by both the political discourses of the present and the materiality of artifacts from the past. Moreover, as I make clear, these sites operate through offering certain narratives as well as through their material organization. These two dimensions, nevertheless, constitute each other and can never be separated.

By presenting such investigations, the chapter aims at overcoming the dichotomies of the social and the material as well as of the past and the present, pointing instead to their multiple intersections and overlaps in the processes of their mutual co-constitution. This refers both to contemporary memorial material artifacts immersed in the complex meaning-making practices and to the ways they affectively and intellectually relate to and interact with our bodies. Consequently, on the one hand, their material-semiotic nature leaves memorable material-semiotic traces on the encountered bodies that, on the other hand, bear "memories" of these encounters. Analyses of the three Holocaust museums included in this chapter serve as illustrative examples of these entangled processes.

REMEMBERING TODAY: MATERIALIZATION OF MEMORY

In contemporary culture the practices of memorialization of traumatic past proliferate with an unprecedented intensity. What we currently deal with as far as the processes of remembrance are concerned is, as Sharon Macdonald underlines, "materialisation of memory in heritage," that is, "the complex and particular coming together of a mix of agents (human and non-human)" as well as its "unpredictable—though not unpatterned and random—effects" (2013, 6). This should be approached as a compound, multidimensional phenomenon, to which Macdonald refers in terms of a "memory complex," that is, "an assemblage of practices, affects and physical things, which includes such parts as memorial services, nostalgia and historical artefacts" (2013, 6). Operations of none of these agents can be properly explored in isolation from the others. If singled out, each element's analysis remains incomplete and cannot do justice to the complexity of both memorialization and materialization. Hence, crucial is elaboration of a more encompassing approach to this dynamic assemblage of sundry processes. Such a perspective should take into consideration the intricacy of relations between miscellaneous agents as well as how they come together to form particular and multidimensional material-semiotic "events."

This is remarkably important if we pay attention to a number of recent theoretical trends emerging within the research fields focusing on different aspects of memorialization practices. Noticeably, what surfaces in latest investigations stemming from such areas as trauma studies, memory studies, heritage studies, and cultural studies is an increased attention to diversely problematized issues of materiality and matter. Let me offer a couple of relevant examples testifying to this meaningful shift of focus: mnemonic and commemoration practices are considered to be about materialization of memories in forms of, for instance, memorials, museums, artistic installations, which all have some sort of material existence; traumatic memory is seen as a corporeal form of memory inscribed in the organic matter/flesh of our bodies (more on this in chapter 3); the encounter with art is framed in terms of a physical, bodily transaction engaging senses and sensibilities and producing feelings, sensations, and affects, which fosters a novel conceptualization of the processes of both perception and knowledge production (which I explored in chapter 1). Obviously, this preoccupation with materiality deserves a more insightful examination, especially in the context of matter having been almost completely crossed out from critical investigations undertaken within the theoretical paradigm of the "linguistic turn" (see, e.g., Grosz 1994, 2008, Massumi 2002a, 2011).

Another important aspect of how contemporary sites of remembrance operate and how they are encountered by audiences is their immersion in political and cultural landscape of their present, which structures interpretation and perception of the past. It is vital to acknowledge and critically reflect on how some material artifacts, sites belonging to the past, as well as artistic production related to traumatic occurrences are oftentimes turned into significant resources of the present—in a cultural, political, and economic sense. Therefore, what counts as heritage is more about the meanings and representations created in the present and ascribed to the material objects and practices, rather than about tangible and intangible artifacts or forms from the past. The complex nature of the heritage cannot be fully accounted for if we do not take into consideration how the materiality of these objects becomes equipped with and emerges from particular meanings as well as how it makes these meanings possible.

Heritage works according to the demands of the present. Consequently, the study of it does not necessarily involve any direct engagement with the past, but it rather requires a critical attitude and an in-depth examination of the current political, cultural, and social discourses (see Graham et al. 2000, Graham 2002, Smith 2004, Ashworth et al. 2007). This complex entanglement of the past and the present is partly discernible in many contemporary theorizations and analyses. As James E. Young underlines, "Remembrance as a vital human activity shapes our links to the past, and the ways we remember define us in the present" (1993, 9). Similarly, although focusing on a more immediate and personal level, Gilles Deleuze and Félix Guattari aptly notice that

> the monument is not something commemorating a past, it is a bloc of present sensations that owe their preservation only to themselves and that provide the event with the compound that celebrates it. The monument's action is not memory but fabulation. We write not with childhood memories but through blocs of childhood that are the becoming-child of the present. (1997, 167)

This entanglement of heritage (allegedly belonging to the past) with the present is an important context for approaching a number of contemporary memory sites, memorials, and museums. Worth noticing is that these spaces currently work as institutions whose task is not exclusively *to remember* past events (also taking into account contradictory historical narratives and context-informed accounts) but also to induce experiences *to be remembered* by visitors (i.e., to inscribe them with certain knowledges). It is so due to the fact that the role of these places, side by side with commemoration and therapeutic coming to terms with trauma, still remains deeply intertwined with education or enculturation. It therefore seems crucial to analyze the ways in which these institutions operate and how they remain in a constant, dynamic interaction with the social and cultural as well as with the bodily and corporeal. In this regard, as Silke Arnold de Simine emphasizes, contemporary memorial sites rely on specific strategies and "can be described as a multimedia platform on which different medial practices can be combined: an exhibition works with objects, but increasingly also with texts, images and audiovisual representations in a spatial arrangement," often adopting a mode of (re)presentation that so far has been reserved for art (2012, 16–17), and not exclusively for a narrative or figurative art. Consequently, the emotional-affective impact of what is currently referred to as a "narrative museum"

(Pieper 2006, 28; more on this will follow) resembles that of "novels, plays or motion pictures" (Weinberg and Elieli 1995, 17).

Moreover, it must be kept in mind that the practices of remembering the past oftentimes work as a means of fulfilling current political and cultural interests (most frequently, yet not exclusively, ones of dominant groups). Yet, in order to more comprehensively grasp how memory sites operate, we need to—as I made clear earlier—move beyond purely representational thinking, so typical for the majority of the (discourse) analyses effectuated within the poststructuralist paradigm. A critical attention being paid to their material-semiotic ontology, enabled by the new materialist theoretical framework, lets us engage more thoroughly with the question *how* these operations happen and what kind of consequences they might possibly entail.

Certainly, sites of remembrance work in a number of diversified ways. In this regard, a provisional distinction could be drawn between monuments and memorials, since their tasks and modes of interacting with, or engaging, viewers/visitors seem to differ in a significant manner. Arthur C. Danto explains that whereas monuments aim at presenting a triumphalist reference to past events, memorials rather seek to encourage a process of coming to terms with or negotiating the past traumatic experiences, that is, they initiate a process of reconciliation and, eventually, of healing (Danto, quoted in Rowlands 1999, 130). Monuments and memorials are situated within different codes of remembrance and serve distinctive purposes. Whereas, as Danto explicates, "we erect monuments so that we shall always remember . . . [we] build memorials so that we shall never forget" (1985, 152). This means that these two kinds of cultural artifacts seem to refer to different sorts of events—monuments connote victory and triumph, while memorials commemorate defeats, tragedies, or sacrifices. Noteworthy, what counts as success and what passes for a defeat remain defined within the dominant cultural, social, and political discourses and rely on the structures of what Foucault calls power/knowledge (1980, 1982). Another characteristic differentiating the two types of sites of remembrance is highlighted by Marita Sturken: "Monuments tend to use less explanation, while memorials tend to emphasize texts or lists of the dead. Therefore, while monuments . . . are usually anonymous, the irony of lives lost for an unattained goal . . . in a memorial seems to demand the naming of the individual" (1991, 121). These differences obviously tend to translate into different designs and formats that monuments and memorials currently adopt.

Bearing the aforementioned ideas in mind, the sizable dissimilarity between these two types of cultural artifacts can be discerned by pointing to different functions they are assigned. Monuments are primarily concerned with transmission of the dominant cultural assumptions and national(istic) narratives, on account of their being first and foremost celebrations of past heroic deeds or sacrifices. As such, they must be seen as important tools of displaying national values or constructing coherent and widely approved historical discourses. They offer sequences of events always already interpreted, narrativized, and officially sanctioned, that is, turned into institutionalized forms of collective memory. Along with the deconstructionist arguments, it must be noted, however, that the meanings conveyed by such cultural artifacts do not rely on the process of mimetic recording of the past. Rather, they interpret and construct the history from very concrete points of view and, therefore, their modes of operating are to be understood in performative, or productive of reality, terms. Monuments' function is therefore to sustain rather than contest the existing social order. This task is closely connected with enculturation, which—as Nöel Carroll explains—is an apparent function of most of the memorial art, in general, "whether in the form of statues, monuments, murals, pageants, processions, paintings, dances, songs, poems, films, etc." (2005, 7). This argument is in line with what Alain Badiou calls a "didactic" function of art (2005, 2). Memorials, on the other hand, seem to work in a therapeutic mode and aim at giving, in Carroll's words, an "articulate focus on the unease the loss has caused and allow[ing] for the reassessment of the event in retrospect; this enables mourners to manage their emotions, to move from shock to healing" (2005, 9). From such a perspective, memorials' tasks should be defined in terms of catharsis. Such conceptualization clearly corresponds with another rendition of arts' function as identified by Badiou (2005, 2), that is, art as providing means for curative coming to terms with horrific experiences, whether collective or not. This is obviously connected to the fact that in recent times the practices of communal remembrance have almost exclusively been referring to trauma and, logically, involved complex commemorative practices of victimization.[1] Henceforth, such an interpretation of memorials' functions bears explicitly a therapeutic dimension.

Recently, noticeable has been a significant transformation in the ways memory sites are preconceived, designed, and arranged. Nowadays, they tend to adopt a format that, as James E. Young suggests, invites multiple, or even contradictory, meaning-making practices as well as creative experiential uses (1993). This novel trend also allows for different forms of participatory practices being developed and performed by visitors, inviting them to interact with the material aspects of the site, to explore its physicality, and to experience it in different individualized manners. To put it another way, the transformation of contemporary sites of remembrance into spaces of negotiation or even contestation of the past events or of how framed and recounted they are in the dominant culture seems to grant visitors a possibility of a more singular response to the past as well as creates opportunities for personal rewriting of the "official" accounts of historical events. Ideally, if such an open format is to be successful in achieving its goals, the architectural arrangements of these spaces should not be intended for conveying predetermined meanings, reenacted in a form of stabilized and naturalized narratives; instead, it should rather enable, or even encourage, a creative, sensible, material-semiotic engagement.

As mentioned earlier, current practices of memorialization are predominantly related to the commemoration of the collective (or, rarely, individual) traumas: events of death, genocide, catastrophes, massive killings, violence (institutionalized or not), or other atrocities. As such, they are often referred to in terms of a "difficult past" (Logan and Reeves 2009), "undesirable heritage" (Macdonald 2006), "dissonant heritage" (Tunbridge and Ashworth 1996), or "heritage that hurts" (Uzzell and Ballantyne 1998). These labels are meant to signal—in Macdonald's words—"a heritage that the majority of the population would prefer not to have" (2006, 9). Since many of these sites have recently become important destinations for lots of pilgrims and tourists, the concept of "difficult heritage tourism" has been coined (Macdonald 2006, 9) to refer to visitations to the commemoration sites that appeared in the aftermath of slavery, Nazism, totalitarian regimes, genocide, terrorism, extreme poverty, and so on. This obviously includes what is usually called "genocide tourism" (Beech 2000), constituting a meaningful niche of what is more generally termed "dark tourism," of which Holocaust tourism is seen as an important subcategory.

Unsurprisingly, conceptualization of the Holocaust memory sites in terms of "dark attractions" is not unproblematic. This is mostly because of the fact that the latter term often evokes pejorative connotations, pointing to the commercialized and commodified aspects of tourist activities performed in the sites commemorating atrocities and traumas. Objections are raised against both the label "dark" (signaling a negative valance; the adjective "dark" necessarily refers to "dark deeds," "dark moods," or "morose tones" [Bowman and Pezzullo 2010]) and the terms "attraction" and "tourism" (both indicating association with recreational pleasure, entertainment, or amusement). The combination of the two notions generates a rather peculiar mixture, which seems to be completely unfit for describing such tremendous and overwhelming genocidal disasters as, for instance, the trauma of the Shoah. As clarified in the introduction, one of my aims in this chapter is to approach "dark attractions" through new materialist lenses in order to divorce the term "dark tourism" from its typically negative connotations, focusing instead—in an affirmative manner—on generative, aesthetic aspects of such memory sites. Looking closer at their sensuous, material, aesthetic dimension (which obviously combines with their narrative and symbolic facets) as well as acknowledging the intensity of their synaesthetic operations sheds an altogether different light on Holocaust sites and lets us more fully comprehend their material-semiotic nature as well as how they productively assemble with the (bodies of) visitors. Later in this chapter I will specifically look at the Holocaust memorial museums functioning in three different geographical, political, and cultural settings and operating through a synthetic combination of narrative and affective means. Yet, before I turn to their more detailed analyses, it is necessary to locate them more precisely within the broader context of dark tourism as well as to reflect on the diverse motivations of people visiting such places. As I want to make clear, it is not enough to approach such sites by looking at their discursive workings, even though the term "narrative museum" often applied to describe these institutions might suggest so. Arguing in a new materialist spirit, it must be highlighted that this dimension would not be operative without the material aspects that sustain and make meanings possible in the first place. As Nicole Boivin (2008) underlines, the material facets of the place not only provide a medium through which social values become encoded, expressed, and transmitted but also act as a significant tool enabling understanding and provoking feeling through both its physical features and the ways in which visitors engage with and use these features. My aim, therefore, is to place emphasis on their aesthetic operations. And, as I clarified in the previous chapter, the aesthetic, after all, is about a material encounter.

APPROACHING "DARK ATTRACTIONS": MOTIVATIONS, PERCEPTIONS, EXPERIENCES

Although the history of traveling to places where death, suffering, genocide, or atrocity occurred, or to places that refer to horrible, dreadful events, is long and complex, dark tourism is often seen as a relatively recent but, at the same time, one of the most important types of contemporary tourist activities as far as both demand for and supply of dark sites are concerned (Timothy and Boyd 2006, 2). The term itself has been forged by Malcolm Foley and John Lennon (1996) to describe a "visitation to any site associated with death, disaster and tragedy in the twentieth century for remembrance, education or entertainment" (Lennon and Foley 2010, 155), and "the phenomenon which encompasses the presentation and consumption (by visitors) of real and commodified death and disaster sites" (Foley and Lennon 1996, 198). Chronologically, however, one of the first labels used to describe tours of the abject, the macabre, or the disgusting was the term "negative sightseeing" (MacCannell 1989), which originally referred to experience of "real poverty" and dicey situations. The use of the expression "dark attraction" was initiated by Chris Rojek (1993), who in his analysis of several sites of deaths, assassinations, and catastrophes proposed the concept of "Black Spots" or "fatal attractions" (1993, 85), which he further developed in his subsequent studies (see Rojek

1994, 1995, 1997).[2] Similar concepts to describe pretty much the same set of processes are proposed by other scholars—these include "milking the macabre" (Dann 1994), "thanatourism" (Seaton 1996), "tragic tourism" (Lippard 1999), "morbid tourism" (Blom 2000),[3] and "grief tourism" (O'Neill 2002, West 2004, Trotta 2006). Although often referring to slightly different types of destinations, motives, and contexts for visiting, all these terms are linked to the phenomenon of traveling to "sites associated with death, disaster, and depravity and sites of death, disaster, and depravity" (note the distinction, which has been clearly underlined by William Miles 2002, 1175). Philip Stone, in a slightly different manner, while defining dark tourism as "the act of travel to sites associated with death, suffering or the seemingly macabre" (2006, 146) points to the fundamental difference between "sensation tourism" (i.e., traveling to sites of contemporary death and suffering) and "premeditated visits to structured and organized attractions or exhibitions which portray recent and/or distant historical occurrences." He also differentiates between the sites that were constructed with an aim to interpret dark events and those which accidentally became "dark attractions" (2006).[4]

Whereas some scholars conceive of dark tourism as a relatively recent occurrence (Rojek 1993, 1997, Blom 2000, Williams 2004, Slayton 2006, Lennon and Foley 2010),[5] others (Seaton 1996, Beech 2000, Ryan and Kohli 2006) offer a more historically informed view of tourist practices associated with death and atrocity. Let me briefly sketch these two lines of conceptualizing this phenomenon.[6] Lennon and Foley think of this type of tourism as specifically connected to the context of the twentieth and twenty-first centuries and associate the emergence of dark tourist practices with the end of World War I, arguing that it "is both product of circumstances of the late modern world and a significant influence upon those circumstances" (2010, 3). Emerging of dark tourism is, according to these two scholars, inevitably linked to such conditions as growing popularity and use of communication technologies (which both play a major role in invoking the initial interest in places associated with death and make journeys to these places available for many), the more general "anxiety and doubt about the project of modernity"[7] that are clearly alluded to by-products of dark tourism and, eventually, the peculiar combination of educative functions of these places with "elements of commodification" and "commercial ethic" (2010, 11–12). Henceforth, dark tourism is seen in this view as derivative of the postmodern condition and relates to the events that took place within the "memories of those still alive to validate them" (2010, 12). However, what introduces dark tourism for the two authors is "this peculiar element of commodification of anxiety and doubt within interpretations offered and the design of the sites as both products and experiences (including merchandising and revenue generation)" (2010, 12).

Conversely, A. V. Seaton (1996) in his elaboration of the concept of thanatourism reflects on a long tradition of traveling to sites of atrocity and death dating back to the Middle Ages and exceptionally widespread in the period of Romanticism. Accordingly, thanatourism should be considered "a travel dimension of thanatopsis" and defined in terms of "travel to a location wholly, or partially, motivated by the desire for actual or symbolic encounters with death, particularly, but not exclusively, violent death" (1996, 1). Although for Seaton this type of tourist activity cannot be bound exclusively to postmodernity, he acknowledges that the great role of the media as well as the impact of global communication technologies and their availability to an increased number of people in the world translate into an augmented popularity of this type of travels.

As evidenced in the wide spectrum of definitions of the concept of dark tourism, it might encompass—depending on an adopted perspective—a whole variety of attractions, tourist destinations, and memory sites, ranging from fun factory sites and entertainment theme parks through sites of catastrophes and famous people's deaths, museums, memorials, and cemeteries to the actual crime scenes, sites of extermination, and mass death. This pursuit of formulating straightforward definitions and precise classifications as far as the demand for and supply of "dark attractions" is concerned exemplifies, as Michael Bowman and Phaedra Pezzullo (following Löfgren 1999) notice, a positivist tendency towards systematic labeling (2010, 199), which seemingly converts into a sense of control and power over "scientific data." This inclination to categorize or systematize is undoubtedly a part of a more general quest observable within some areas of social sciences (and notably tourism studies) towards delineating a clear-cut boundary between different concepts, diverse phenomena, or specific sociocultural processes. More important, however, Bowman and Pezzullo rightly point out that the conceptualization of "dark attractions" in terms of commodification and "commercialization as a 'tourist' product" is not accurate as "there is ample evidence to suggest that the various technological and commercial factors involved in reshaping tourists' encounters with death also shape tourists encounters with relaxation and pleasure" (2010, 190).

Similar tendencies are discernible in the scholarship aiming at drawing a precise classification of dark tourism's demand on the one hand and its supply on the other. These efforts are aimed at a more thorough understanding of motivations for traveling to these places as well as of behaviors and experiences of sightseers.[8] In this context what surfaces in most of the existent literature tacking these issues is an important distinction—alluded to earlier—between sites of atrocity and those that are *merely* associated with atrocity (cf. Dann 1998, Miles 2002, Sharpley 2005, Lennon and Foley 2010), that is, a distinction between authentic and inauthentic sites. This division becomes often further complicated through the imposition of another classification, that is, one referring to (behavioral) motives for visiting dark sites (cf. Seaton 1996, Uzzell 1998, Ashworth 2004, Preece and Price 2005, Sharpley 2005, Poria et al. 2006, Timothy and Boyd 2006).

As far as the supply of "dark attractions" is concerned, they are usually ordered in a form of continuum from the lightest to the darkest. Adopting such a perspective, and tackling the issue of Holocaust tourism, William Miles (2002) notices the important difference between visits to the United States Holocaust Memorial Museum (USHMM) in Washington, DC (which counts as "dark exhibition"), and to former concentration camps (such as Auschwitz-Birkenau), arguing that "if visitation to the former is rightfully characterized as dark tourism, then journey/excursion/pilgrimage to the latter constitutes a further degree of empathetic travel: darker tourism" (2002, 1175). Perceived as more authentic, sites of death are usually classified as conceivably darker that those "merely" associated with death. Important is for Miles's classification also temporal proximity—sites in which tragic events that can be validated by those still alive (like witnesses or survivors) occurred are assigned a "darker" position, as they trigger visitors' passionate identification and amplify their feelings of empathy. This is, for Miles, definitely the case of Nazi concentration camps (2002). Similar classification is developed by Philip Stone (2006, 152–57), who identifies "dark tourism spectrum" encompassing seven categories of sites based on their temporal, spatial, and ideological product features.[9] Graham Dann (1998), in a descriptive manner, lists the following categories of "dark attractions": perilous places (mostly dangerous destinations, from both the past and present), houses of horror (places associated with death and horror, actual or represented), fields of fatality (sites commemorating death or fear, such as battlegrounds, cemeteries with graves of in/famous people, concentration camps), tours of torment (visits to attractions associated with death), and themed thanatos (collections revolving around death, atrocity, or suffering; this category includes off-site Holocaust exhibitions, museums, or memorials). It seems, therefore, that in such a formulation "dark attractions" differ in terms of their emotional appeal, which is related to the site's perceived authenticity.

Another strategy of approaching dark tourism focuses on the demand for, rather than supply of, "dark attractions" and attempts at figuring out what the visitors' chief motivations to travel to these sites are. For Chris Ryan and Rahul Kholi (2006), instead of defining a site as dark judging simply on its attributes, it is crucial to explore how it is perceived and experienced by visitors. A demand-oriented approach, therefore, conceives of dark tourism as a principally behavioral phenomenon and is preoccupied with the visitors' incentives for traveling to these places as well as with their impressions and experiences of the sites. Taking into account different possible motivations of dark tourists, A. V. Seaton (1996) identifies what he calls a "continuum of intensity," encompassing various purposes of dark travels: to witness public enactments of death (public executions), to see the sites of individual or mass deaths after they occurred (death camps, sites of genocide, sites where in/famous people died, and those of notorious murders or mayhems), to visit memorials or internment sites (e.g., graveyards, cenotaphs, crypts, war memorials), to see evidence or symbolic representations of death at unconnected sites (museums, exhibitions, reconstructions of places), and, finally, travels of reenactments of death simulation (plays, festivals, reconstructions of famous battles), the latest being the "lightest" form of dark tourism. In a slightly different mode, Graham Dann (1998) perceives visitors' motivations as closely related to the specific characteristics of "dark attractions" (thus partly manufactured) and lists among them "fear of phantoms" (referring to the process of overcoming childlike fears); search for novelty, nostalgia, and desire to celebrate crime or deviance; a more basic bloodlust; and, finally, "dicing with death." Taking on a distinct position, A. V. Seaton and J. J. Lennon (2004) point to *Schadenfreude* (pleasure in others' misfortune) as an interesting (and rather perverse) aspect of this phenomenon, while Chris Rojek suggests a sense of "survival in the face of violent disruptions of collective life routines" (1997, 61) as a possible dark tourists' stimulus. Another view is offered by Tanaya Preece and Garry Price (2005), who identify three principal motives for dark travels, including education (both cognitive and affective), interest in history (both personal and general), and fascination with the abnormal and bizarre (which embraces morbid curiosity). Excluding from his investigations what Rojek termed "sensation sites" (1997, 63) and focusing exclusively on the so-called difficult heritage, G. J. Ashworth (2002, 2004) puts on the list of possible motivations the quest for roots connected to the search for specific identity, empathy for those who were the actors of the events, a pilgrimage or search for self-identification, a more general interest (or even indulgence) in death/horror, and curiosity stemming from a unique character of the place and its notoriety.

To do justice to the whole spectrum of different perspectives on these aspects of "dark attractions" that compel people to these places, I should also mention a group of psychological approaches, which resulted in the development of a number of theories. Some of them assume, for instance, that people are attracted to the sites of or associated with death and atrocity in search of a moral framework, which could (positively) impact their everyday life (Stone 2009), or because they want to realize and understand their own mortality (Uzzell 1998). Another possible motivation is to envisage, confront, and tame the eventuality and inevitability of people's own death. This is especially needed in the context of death being currently "sequestered from public view" and everyday experience due to its "medicalization" as well as a more general "professionalization" of the process of dying (Stone and Sharpley 2008). Other scholars argue that people visit these places for therapeutic reasons (Davies 1996), for compassion, or due to their narcissism (West 2004). Importantly, and quite problematically, the aforementioned consumer-oriented approaches assume that all dark tourists must have at least minimal interest in death. These perspectives, however, do not exhaust the heterogeneity of stimuli to visit and experience dark sites.

There have also been attempts to combine the supply and demand perspectives on dark tourism with the aim of sketching a more comprehensive typology of "dark attractions" and dark motivations by adopting a more experiential understanding of this phenomenon. A (rather confusing) matrix of dark tourism's demand and supply is offered by Richard Sharpley (2005), who claims that there exist a "continuum of purpose" of supply of dark tourism, ranging from accidental to intended attractions and that this should be combined with the intensity of demand, varying from the lightest to the darkest. What stems from this combination are the four "shades" of dark tourism, that is, pale tourism (sites unintended to be tourist attractions, which draw attention of people with minimal interest in death), gray tourism demand (which points to tourists fascinated with death, who visit unintended dark sites), gray tourism supply (referring to sites intended as tourist attractions appealing to visitors with a limited interest in death), and black tourism (where a deep interest in death is satisfied with purposefully constructed and exploited sites).

To recapitulate, despite many (futile) efforts, it is not possible to sketch a precise, widely shared definition of dark tourism, which would refer to a well-defined set of sites or patterns of traveling. This should come as no surprise taking into consideration the artificiality of the classificatory schemes and their rather reductive, if not simplistic, approach to reality, which I outlined in the introduction to this book. Whereas the supply-oriented classification focuses on certain attributes of places and perceives all tourists visiting them as dark (regardless of their motivations), the demand-oriented perspective centers on the visitors' characteristics (and claims that all of them must have some interest in death). In a different manner, an integrated supply-demand approach surveys possible links between dark sites' attributes and the experiences that are sought after by visitors. It is also argued that the consumer-oriented research on dark tourism is still underdeveloped (Seaton and Lennon 2004); thus, the issue should be further explored. Dissatisfied with the earlier-described approaches, some scholars notice that these perspectives offer a rather superficial view of tourist experiences. For Nell Smith and W. Glen Croy (2005), for instance, it is the perception of the site as dark by visitors (and not the nature of the site itself), which in fact makes it a "dark attraction." Such an approach acknowledges the possibility that not all visitors to dark places are actually engaged in any form of dark experience and that other forms of experiencing the sites are also important, if not prevailing (e.g., education, spiritual experience, identity building).

There are critical voices underlining the fact that the thorough examination of visitors' possible motives should be made in the context of heritage tourism, especially because—as mentioned earlier—the conceptual location of the so-called difficult or dissonant heritage sites within the broader concept of dark tourism is unclear, if not entirely problematic (Biran et al. 2011, 825). Henceforth, in the context of genocide tourism, a distinction is often made between the visitors who have some kind of connection with the commemorated/represented events (survivors, their families as well as families of the victims; those who share the heritage of those exterminated) and those without a specific connection. Whereas the motivation of the first type of travelers is a sort of pilgrimage (religious or understood in terms of remembrance), the second type of tourists visit these sites for educational reasons or because they perceive such travels as a moral/social obligation (Beech 2000; similar position is taken by Poria et al. 2003 and Poria et al. 2006). Analogously, in reference to difficult heritage tourism, Dallen Timothy and Stephen Boyd (2006) conceive of visits to dark places in terms of obligation of memory rather than of purely tourist activity.[10] In sum, researchers tend to differentiate between those with and those without a personal connection to the site, that is, between those who travel because they feel a specific moral obligation to do so and those who travel for widely understood leisure. In terms of visitors' experiences of these places, while the former's are seen as deep and revealing, the latter's are often considered superficial and fabricated.[11]

Taking into consideration both supply- and demand-oriented research, it seems that a certain general pattern of thinking in entirely dualistic terms can be discerned within this scholarship. As Michael Bowman and Phaedra Pezzullo aptly notice,

> Tourist research conducted in relation to the "dark tourism" trope seems inevitably trapped in questions of authenticity versus commodification, which falsely present the matter as one of either/or, suggesting that such places must be serious or frivolous, educational or entertaining, authentic or inauthentic, and historically accurate and edifying or devoted to nostalgia and tourist kitsch. (2010, 195)

This dichotomy also refers to tourists' experiences that are conceptualized as authentic (in case when the sightseers have some sort of connection to the visited site) or artificially fabricated (when they travel out of *mere* curiosity). Nevertheless, these dualistic framings of both "dark attractions" and experiences of "dark visitors," which surface in most of the approaches to dark sites, are problematic if we take into account a number of sites, which cannot be clearly classified as belonging to any of these (artificially established) categories.

Such "disciplining" strategies rely on a positivist orientation, aiming at developing well-justified and transparent classifications that would hierarchically order the types of the sites on the one hand and the visitors' motivations on the other. These inclinations are grounded in a thoroughly negativist logic resting on a set of binary oppositions—"dark attractions" are seen as either genuine or artificial, accidentally or purposely created, while experiences of visitors are considered either authentic or fabricated; the visitors themselves are perceived as either having or not having a personal connection with the site visited. As explained in the introduction to this book, this confrontational system of thinking embodied in the logic of either/or is derivative of the Western metaphysics that always juxtaposes one against its other, expelling the other to the margins and equipping it with a pejorative loading (in this particular instance, stemming also from the connotations the term "dark" traditionally produces in Western culture). Visits to sites considered "dark" are necessarily perceived in negative terms, while tourists' experiences emerging from them are often constructed as unnaturally stimulated and hence fictitious. Noteworthy is the fact that most of the aforementioned classifications of tourists' motives for traveling to "dark attractions" take into account intellectual cognitive or, alternatively, emotional aspects of these visits, bracketing off the issue of immediate bodily experience that actually takes place on site while tourists physically encounter the place. Meanwhile, as the phenomenological investigations have to some extent revealed, tourists must also be seen as people who experience sites and events at an immediately enfleshed, sensuous level.[12] This refers to the material dimension of any experience/event and applies both to the materiality of the landscape/place and to that of the body. Consequently, the tourist experience must also be conceptualized in terms of bodily investment in the place (Crouch and Lübbren 2003) or a generative sensible encounter engaging a whole spectrum of micro-perceptions, both material and intellectual. Visitors seek to personally absorb certain (im)material qualities and assemble with the site in an affective manner. As Birgit Trauer notices (2006), they are interested in feeling ambiance and atmosphere, in looking for intimate, intense, and complex experience. In a similar vein, Horst Opaschowski puts emphasis on the fact that nowadays many tourists search for emotional stimuli and experiencing feelings rather than for traditional sightseeing (2001). Such an experience necessarily has a bodily dimension and involves the process of "sensing" the place. Taking these aspects into consideration, certain current academic reflections on the nature of dark tourism follow, at least to some extent, deliberations on changing patterns of tourist experience, which now increasingly relies on "feeling" the site rather than simply gazing at it. Consequently, some scholars conceive of dark traveling in terms of a hunger for the real, or a quest for experiencing authentic feelings (Knudsen and Waade 2002) or a "way of relating to and witnessing the past and its victims" that "encode the past differently through their specific more or less developed site designs" (Knudsen 2011, 56).

If this bodily, sensuous, and sensible dimension of tourist activity is to be seriously taken into account, a novel theoretical approach to memorial places referring to trauma seems to be necessary. I consider it vital to look at these sites adopting a more affirmative standpoint grounded in the approach that I outlined in chapter 1. A perspective relying on a synaesthetic perception and redefining the concept of aesthetic experience towards a multidimensional material-semiotic event engaging intellectual-affective apparatus of cognition lets us approach dark tourism in a different manner, divorcing it—at least to a certain extent—from its typically negative valance. It also allows us to perceive the experiences of dark travelers in a positive, productive fashion, yet one that still pays critical attention to the political aspects of operation of "dark attractions." Such a framework lets us more comprehensively grasp the modes in which contemporary memorial institutions and sites function, taking into consideration the complex assemblage of affective-emotional procedures involved in the process of their interactions with visitors as well as recognizing the dynamic nature of the knowledge production on which these sites rely. Taking on a new materialist lens, in the section that follows, I will specifically look at three distinct museums—from different cultural and geographical locations—devoted to the memorialization of the Holocaust, critically examining their material-semiotic nature and exposing the ways in which they convey context-informed messages. These meanings, however, could not be transmitted if it were not for the material organization of the sites. Neither is it possible to grasp the ways in which they operate without taking into consideration the affective dimension of experience generated in the bodily-intellectual encounter with the materiality of these dark sites.

NEW MUSEUMS AND QUESTIONS OF "AUTHENTICITY"

Recently, noticeable has been a substantial shift in patterns of organization of history museums and exhibitions as well as of memorials, which—as Rosmarie Beier-de Haan (2006) notices—currently tend to arrange their displays in terms of memory rather than history and are oriented towards performative techniques aiming at eliciting specific mental, emotive, and bodily responses of visitors. The past two decades have witnessed the emergence of what Kylie Message (2006) calls "new museums," including "memorial museums," defined by Paul Williams as sites "dedicated to historic events commemorating mass suffering of some kind" (2007, 8). A slightly different term—"memory museum"—is also used by Susan Sontag when she refers to the Holocaust or Jewish museums erected in Washington, DC, Berlin, and Jerusalem in 1993, 2001, and 2005, respectively. As she writes, "Memory museum in its current proliferation is a product of a way of thinking about, and mourning, the destruction of European Jewry in the 1930s and 1940s" (Sontag 2003, 77). However, Sontag's original conceptualization can well be extended to encompass a great number of other museums, guided with the same logic and commemorating atrocities worldwide. Since both of these definitions are based on the nature of specific "content" of those places (i.e., one referring to collective traumas and horror), the category of memorial museum (or memory museum) encompasses a broad range of sites. To this genre there belong both original genocide sites transformed into museums and institutions erected in areas unrelated to the original trauma and built with a purpose to make visitors acquainted with past traumatic events. To do justice to the specificity of different places embraced under the single category of memorial museum, Patrizia Violi (2012) introduces a distinction between what she calls "ex novo created memorial museums" and "trauma site museums" (or simply "trauma sites"). Whereas the former term refers to purposely constructed (mostly educational and memorial) institutions located away from the original crime scenes, the latter stands for "memorials built on sites of historical traumas, transforming places originally designated for imprisonment and extermination into museums" (2012, 38). Violi also makes clear that this analytical and formal distinction is just provisional as there are cases when these two categories overlap, when, for instance, a new museum is built on the actual trauma site (2012, 39).

Notwithstanding its limitations, Violi's classification allows for shifting attention from the museum's content to its formal features and focuses on "the diverse semiotic natures of these two kinds of memorial" (2012, 39). This distinction, as she argues, testifies to the specificity of visitors' experience, which for her is obviously different in trauma sites since the perception of the memorial as an original location of a massacre (because of its "indexical semiotic character" related to a "real spatial contiguity with the trauma itself") substantially influences their understanding of the place (2012, 39–40). This is, for Violi, due to a complex process of transforming original traces into signifying items through both interpretation (which involves recognition of a trace and making visitors aware of the "indexical nature of the place") and enunciation (which relies on the transformation of the original space and traces into a narrative, equipped with specific meanings) (2012, 39). She also underlines the re-presentational (versus representational) character of trauma sites, noting that they do not represent anything, exposing instead some precise material traces of original traumatic events. This persistency of material elements translates into a perceived supposed authenticity of the place, although—Violi admits—representational sites can also induce very realistic effects (2012, 41). This issue seems to be central to understanding how contemporary memorial museums operate. Yet, it is also very problematic, especially when we acknowledge the fact that the experiences these sites offer to visitors are not purely narrative or representational, but also sensual, bodily, and affective. Also, as I want to emphasize, there is here no question of either/or. Rather, their operation draws on the entanglement of the textual and the material and emerges in the encounter with the material-semiotic nature of the visitors' bodies. Taking this into consideration, one can assume that the authenticity and intensity of visitors' experiences do not necessarily have anything to do with the memorial's location or it being the actual (genuine) crime scene. Instead, it is related to the level of intellectual-bodily inter-/intra-action that one allows for as well as to the archives of narrative-affective memories that visitors bring to the memorial site.

In a somewhat similar vein, drawing on Walter Benjamin's distinction between traces and auratic objects, Jøgen Bærenholdt and Michael Haldrup (2004) explain that while the former rely on a close relationship between the representation and what is represented, the latter instill a distance between the two. This is related, as Britta Knudsen notices, to the important difference between genuineness and authenticity of the place, where, in her words, "genuineness relates to the object's character of being a genuine trace (hair, shoes, or suitcases that belonged to prisoners) . . . while authenticity concerns the bodily-phenomenological experience of the place, which can involve various types of stage-setting at and of the sites" (2006, 11). Whereas "genuineness poses the question of truth of the trace . . . authenticity always concerns the reception of an event" (2006, 11). Yet, Knudsen concludes, "Stage-set traces can also make for extremely authentic experiences, just as genuine traces need not have an experiential value" (2006, 11). This depends, on the one hand, on the various strategies that memorial sites employ to affect visitors at their cognitive and bodily levels (i.e., on their material-semiotic operations) and, on the other hand, on the level of the visitors' involvement in the material-semiotic encounter with the site. Inspired by Tom Selwyn's (1996) distinction between "cool" and "hot" authenticity of visitors' experiences, Knudsen distinguishes "cool strategies," which involve a search for knowledge and create an "analytic-reflexive distance," and "hot strategies," which refer to the bodily dimension and inscribe visitors affectively, "fundamentally creating fellowships" (2006, 11). The latter techniques and, consequently, their effects are not connected to genuineness of the site in any straightforward way. The intensity of the affective encounter may be triggered by a specific material arrangement of the site that combines with its symbolic, discursive layer. Importantly, we cannot thoroughly approach these sites and grasp the ways in which they generate effects and knowledges without taking into account the dynamic entanglements of their narrative and affective dimensions that form vibrant machine-like assemblages with visitors. What I want to point out is that we should not lock these experiences in the dilemma of authenticity versus inauthenticity. This would be very much in line with a positivist way of thinking in terms of mutually exclusive oppositions or binary pairs. Any experience, whether accidently or artificially stimulated, is always in a sense authentic because it is always about feeling or undergoing something, a dynamic metamorphosis that sometimes happens on the imperceptible level, a movement of becoming that generates change. It might stem from being exposed to something, affecting and being affected. Something is experienced (in an authentic way), even without immediately making sense of these intense transformations. This is, I argue, an important point of departure for analysis of memorial museums erected away from the actual site of trauma, which I offer here. In what follows, therefore, I will briefly look at three memorial museums: the USHMM in Washington, DC, Yad Vashem—The World Holocaust Remembrance Center in Jerusalem, and Jewish Museum in Berlin (JMB), paying special attention to their material organizations and how they creatively enter into generative dialogue, or complex intra-actions, with (different) narratives that they convey. By analyzing the entanglements of the semiotic and the material, I want to point out the fact that a new materialist approach to these memorial spaces enables a deeper understanding of not only *what* messages they sent to their audiences but also *how* their representational dimensions come into being through their embeddedness in their material facets synaesthetically affecting, and being affected by, visitors' bodies.

Importing Trauma: The Holocaust Memory in the United States

Taking into consideration the fact that the Shoah had never really been perceived as a part of American history, it is quite interesting that the first narrative Holocaust museum was constructed on American soil. The official decision to build a national Holocaust memorial museum in the United States was announced by President Jimmy Carter in May 1978 to commemorate the thirtieth anniversary of the establishment of the Israeli state, to express US support for it, and—importantly—in order to alleviate tensions between the administration and the Jewish community in the United States concerning the sale of F-15 fighters to Saudi Arabia. This military transaction significantly fueled the construction of the USHMM. Erected in 1993, the institution has performed an important role in popularizing the knowledge about these traumatic events among American audience, which it specifically targeted.[13] Undoubtedly, the museum functions within a particular political and cultural context—through its construction, the trauma of the Holocaust has been in a sense "imported" to the United States, ideologized, and incorporated into a more general discourse on American values. Differently from many European memorials devoted to the remembrance of the Holocaust victims, often located in situ and positioning themselves as extensions of the traumatic past, the institutions built in the United States must necessarily consider the remoteness of these events not only in time but also in space. As Edward J. Young notices, memorials in America are "removed from the 'topography of terror'" (1993, 283) and "inevitably call attention to the great distance between themselves and the destruction" (1993, 284). This spatial gap is cleverly instrumentalized for the purpose of promoting American ideals.

As many authors point out (e.g., Flanzbaum 1999, Mintz 2001, Novick 2001), in order to effectively operate in these specific geopolitical and sociocultural circumstances, the Holocaust had to get Americanized and, henceforth, to make a part of US historical policy. Such a strategy sits at the origin of the USHMM, which aims at shaping "American story of the Holocaust that speaks of American values and resonates with the national experience of all Americans," as Michael Verenbaum, a later-to-be director of the USHMM, notices (quoted in Hall 1987). This aspect of the exhibition was also raised in the report of the President's Commission on the Holocaust, with Eli Wiesel as its head. Issued on September 27, 1979, the document suggested that the institution take shape of a "living memorial" with a memorial museum, an educational center, and a "Committee on Conscience." It also underlined the need to place a significant emphasis on

> the American aspect of the Holocaust—the absence of an American response (exclusion of refugees, denial of the Holocaust, etc.), the American liberation of the camps, the reception of survivors after 1945, the lives rebuilt in this country and their contribution to American society and civilization, the development of a new sensitivity to the Holocaust, and the growing respect for multi-ethnic, multi-dimensional aspects of American culture. (Wiesel 1979)

The process of the Americanization of the Shoah has also been effectuated through selection of Washington, DC,[14] and—specifically—the area adjacent to the National Mall as the location for the museum, side by side with most renowned US heritage institutions and memorial sites. This decision was also justified by President Jimmy Carter in his address during the Days of Remembrance ceremonies at the Capitol Rotunda on April 24, 1979:

> Although the Holocaust took place in Europe, the event is of fundamental significance to Americans for three reasons. First, it was American troops who liberated many of the death camps, and who helped to expose the horrible truth of what had been done there. Also, the United States became a homeland for

> many of those who were able to survive. Secondly, however, we must share the responsibility for not being willing to acknowledge forty years ago that this horrible event was occurring. Finally, because we are humane people, concerned with the human rights of all peoples, we feel compelled to study the systematic destruction of the Jews so that we may seek to learn how to prevent such enormities from occurring in the future. (Press release, quoted in Young 1993, 336)

Selection of this location clearly suggested an incorporation of the Holocaust into the narrative on American history and implied a national preoccupation with this event (Shosh Rotem 2013, 12). Obviously, it also determined the final character and arrangement of the museum, interlacing the Shoah with the more specific discourses on American values. The "added value" of such a strategy of representation was to offer an image of America as a new promised land, or a new haven, for those persecuted by totalitarian systems, which—rather unsurprisingly—was in line with the dominant US self-image.

The final architectural project of the future building and its exhibits was delivered by James Ingo Freed, who had been asked to work on it in 1986. This was preceded by a turbulent discussion of the concept of the museum and the messages it should convey. As Stephanie Shosh Rotem explains, "The concepts he [James Ingo Freed] chose, the way he subjected the building's architecture to its contents—and the way he subjected the contents of the museum to its architecture—established the ideological standards that have since become the guidelines for all subsequent architects of Holocaust museums" (2013, 99). The contrast between the building's exterior and its interior is striking. This embodies the architect's idea to conform to the Fine Arts Commission's regulation on the architectural design of the principal district of the city built in a neoclassical style, yet, simultaneously, to achieve a shocking effect in visitors on their entry into the building. Paradoxically, neoclassicism was also praised in Nazi Germany; therefore, the decision to erect thusly conceived building to serve as a home to the Holocaust museum was both a compromise and a critique of this style, especially taking into consideration the architectural tendencies of postmodernism flourishing at that time.

Whereas exterior joins the architecture of the principal district in urban and aesthetic terms, the interior brutally removes the visitors from the friendly space of the US capital. The contrast between the building's exterior and interior stimulates a very concrete perception of the events—as both integrated into the narrative on American history and ideals and, at the same time, removed from the strictly American context. Such a spatial arrangement prepares visitors for their historical journey into the Holocaust. This is also facilitated through the construction of a fake neoclassical facade, which opens to the sky and forms a portico with three rectangular arches. Four cubed openings are cut off above, creating a symmetrical wall. Behind it, the true opening gate is hidden. A more cameral entrance faces the green space of the National Mall on the other side of the building. It consists of the hexagonal limestone-clad block of the memorial hall and a flat wall made of bricks.[15] Bridging the building with the rest of the principal district and the US capital's coherent architecture, the details of the exterior of the museum still refer to the Holocaust motifs (such as the symbolism of the number 6, a "watch-tower," and ghetto-like bridges), offering a smooth transition from the contemporary American context to the historical events that took place in the 1930s and 1940s in Europe.

The interior of the building creates a distance from the architecturally familiar space of the National Mall. The events of the Holocaust, also in terms of the spatial arrangements of the exhibition, are represented as remote, removed, and radically contrasting with the most fundamental American values. As Michael Berenbaum, the project director, argues, "In America . . . we recast the story of the Holocaust to teach fundamental American values . . . pluralism, democracy, restraint on government to enter into freedom of religion" (quoted in Crysler and Kusno 1997, 52). The juxtaposition of the Nazi regime and the Western democratic system is achieved through a specific arrangement of the museal space as well as through the design of a premeditated route that visitors are encouraged, or rather forced, to follow. The interior of the museum is strikingly unfamiliar and chaotic—it is completely different from the area left outside the walls of the building.

The space of the Hall of Witness is architecturally hectic, asymmetrical, and loaded with such elements as staircases, doors, and windows, scattered around without creating any coherent whole. The familiar limestone landscape of Washington, DC, is replaced with a modern factory-like space offering dark brick walls, occasionally strapped with steel. The décor evokes the impression of complete disorientation, havoc, and confusion. The materials and structures seem to induce fragmentation and scarring—the floor is made of marble with natural cracks, and the skylighted roof is skewed and fragmented with metal trusses. Originally, the architect of the building had planned to include a gigantic fracture in the granite wall that would stand for a breach in civilization, yet he later resigned as persuaded by Richard Serra, with whom he collaborated on the final arrangement of the Hall. Nevertheless, all of these elements elicit the feeling of irreparable brokenness and unmendable wounding. Such a design translates into the impression of impending horror that haunts visitors throughout their stay at the museum. On entry, the visitors have neither a precise sense of direction nor any intuitive idea where they should proceed. At that time they do not yet realize that in fact there is just one path they can take. However, the prescribed route includes some affectively intense spaces and exhibits that the visitors may leave out—to this category there belong, for instance, the interior of a genuine cattle car used for transportation of the Jews to concentration camps as well as open showcases containing piles of shoes of people transported to and exterminated in the Nazi death factories. These parts of the museum, directly affecting visitors' senses, invite their powerful somatic, bodily participation, turning their journey into an intense and dreadful experience. Such is the logic of the whole museum, yet most of its spaces impact visitors in more subtle ways. Nevertheless, the bodily, sensual participation is constantly and systematically enforced; thus, visitors are discouraged from adopting a critical distance from the narrative that the museum relays. Throughout, the institution operates via physical organization of the site as well as through material-affective interactions with the bodies of the visitors. The story offered within the display, on the one hand, equips particular material objects with specific meanings and senses. Yet, on the other hand, the overall message is also sustained with the artifacts and spaces. The persuasive materiality enables further understandings, triggering feelings of deep involvement and participation in, as well as the connection to the represented events. The symbolic and the material dimensions of the museal experience clearly co-constitute each other, strengthening the compound impact into which these entanglements translate. The affective and the emotional work together to evoke an intense experience emerging in the encounter of the visitors' bodies and the space of the building with exhibited artifacts and conveyed narratives, even though the effects such entanglements produce can never be completely predicted in advance. Although always singular and situated, these dynamic perceptual processes, enriched with individual experiences, knowledges, and emotions brought with visitors, are at the same time carefully designed with an aim to evoke specific responses as well as their concrete interpretations. This, however, cannot remain under full control of the museum's creators, no matter how hard they try to direct, manage, and supervise the affective-intellectual responses of museumgoers.

The prescribed journey starts with a trip on the purposely overcrowded elevators to the highest floor, where the story begins. There is an oral testimony of an American soldier taking part in the liberation of concentration camps in Europe being broadcast during this short ride; thus, from the very start, the museal narrative is situated in an explicitly American context. On their entry, the first thing visitors notice in a shadowy corridor is a lone enlarged photograph representing American troops surrounding charred human remains at the Ohrdruf concentration camp, the first one liberated by the US army. As Shosh Rotem notices, the picture is taken and displayed in such a way that spectators seem to complete the circle of the soldiers, strongly identifying with their position and adopting their stance (2013, 104). The objective of such a strategy is obvious—to create a kind of connection between the audience and the represented events as experienced by American soldiers during the war. It also clearly signals the fact that the story is being told from an

American point of view, boosting the role of the United States in the processes of liberation and praising their heroic deeds. This testifies to the fact that the museum and its displays target specifically American audience and position US soldiers as munificent liberators of the persecuted ethnic groups.

With an aim of inferring a greater level of empathy towards the victims of the Nazi regime, each visitor is offered an ID admission card that tells the story of one Holocaust sufferer, witness, or survivor. To elicit a longer-lasting meaning of the journey through the exhibit as well as to build a more intense affective liaison, visitors are encouraged to get acquainted with these personal stories at different stages of their trip in order to more fully realize the fate of the people whose chronicles they read and to put themselves in their positions. Visitors are guided through subsequent stages of Nazism rising to power, the persecution of Jews and other minorities, the aggressive expansion of Hitler's power, the massive extermination, and—eventually—the fall of the totalitarian regime. In these changing historical circumstances, they follow the lives of people who were part of these traumatic events as witnesses, sufferers, victims, and survivors. In a similar manner, an immediate and personal form of visitors' engagement is also triggered by inclusion of autobiographical storytelling of the survivors in the display (especially at the end of the museal journey), which is a technique that allows for transforming visitors into "secondary witnesses" (Baer 2002, 87) and, consequently, encourages an emotional bonding. This process is accompanied with the display of enlarged photographs documenting the life and death under the Nazi regime, in the ghettos, and in the extermination camps, establishing emotional links between those visiting and those whose tragic fates are depicted.

This poignant investment happens within a concrete narrative context, advancing well-defined responses and intended reactions as possibilities for a self-reflexive critical engagement with the exhibition are to a large extent limited. The meanings the museum conveys are carefully designed and premeditated—there is not too much space for a more individual negotiation of the narrative as well as for a singular interaction with the artifacts that sustain the projected meanings. Nevertheless, at least on the immediately bodily level, the induced experience is always different and constantly differing, contingent on the individual's archives of sensual memory, from which it partly emerges. The virtuality of past memories actualizes itself in an encounter, producing enfleshed reactions and (in)corporeal knowledges. Yet this singular production of bodily experience gets entangled with more general signifying discourses and available representational structures that serve as facilitators in canalizing and making sense of personal responses produced in the encounter with, or through the vulnerable exposure to, the museum's display. The arresting atmosphere of the interior of the cattle car—its smell, humidity, confined space with no window that would enable looking out and watching what is happening outside—is partly created through the awareness of what purposes it possibly served. These semiotic meanings, generated through the encounter with the museum's narrative, come into being within the material confrontation with the physicality of the artifact, as well as with the traces of the historical uses that it bears. Similarly, the persuasive, disturbing smell of the large piles of shoes belonging to the people exterminated in the death camps helps visitors realize that the atrocities of the Holocaust affected real people with real bodies and that the scale of the horror was virtually unfathomable. The nature of these realizations, or of these bodily-intellectual collisions, is necessarily material-semiotic. Such is also the character of the knowledge with which the guests leave the exhibition. Certainly, every visitor will bring a different experience to the museum and will leave with a different kind of memorable traces of it.

On exit, visitors again encounter the landscape of the American capital, with the Washington Monument and Jefferson Memorial as the most immediately visible features. The effect was also planned—after the dark and disturbing journey into the Holocaust (somewhat removed from the American context), the familiar and bright scenery is seen afresh as referring to democratic values, freedom, and tolerance, and as such it is strongly contrasted with the nightmare offered by the museum's interior and its content. The landscape of the National Mall is vast and generous as compared to the narrow, oppressive, and claustrophobic spaces of the exhibition. In such a way, the narrative on American values, offered side by side with the story of the Holocaust, is reinforced through the spatial organization of the whole area and works within the discourse on the American nationhood with its core principles and beliefs. In such a way, the dark story of the Shoah is in this case not only imported to the United States but also recast to reinforce the narrative on American values. The physical arrangement of the whole site, together with its location in the direct proximity to the space whose task is to praise American heritage and the nation's achievements, work to convey very particular messages that emerge from the materiality of the site and its surroundings as well as, simultaneously, equip these material artifacts and their organization with symbolic meanings.

As I want to make clear in my analysis, in the case of the USHMM certain political aspects of the operation of this narrative museum cannot be fully grasped without a reference to the affective dimensions of the experience it offers. This is especially meaningful in the context of educative functions performed by memorial institutions, as these aspects substantially reinforce the ideological message conveyed by the site. As Mark Johnson argues, "There is meaning that comes through bodily experience and [the] figurative process of ordering, all of which are ignored by dominant objectivist treatments of language, meaning, understanding and reasoning" (1987, 17).

Accordingly, the architectural arrangement and the décor of the site—that is, its material becoming—play a seminal role in how it is experienced, felt, and, consequently, remembered by visitors. It translates into knowledges that—although singular—are still immersed in an ideological context and rely on premeditated meanings and impressions. Thus, the materiality of the place, as Nicole Boivin (2008) underlines, does not solely serve as a medium for encoding, expressing, and transmitting social values. It is not a set of passive objects serving as sites for cultural inscription. Quite the contrary—it remains an active agent, entering into transformational assemblages with representational schemes and narrative structures, producing important effects. The matter of the site triggers understanding and generates feelings through the physical features, which offer themselves to visitors as opportunities for intense bodily and sensual engagements and invite active responses. These encounters are generative of knowledges. The architecture should therefore be understood as an active material-semiotic (Haraway 1988, 588) assemblage, which facilitates, or enables, the flow of meaning. The latter would not be possible without the former. Therefore, I insist, we should think of such museums not just in terms of the well-defined tasks they perform, but also as artistic objects (or *works* of art) that—in a way similar to art—produce sensations not necessarily graspable in purely figurative terms. Importantly, memorial museum is not just an educational institution or a site of remembrance. It is also an aesthetic product with certain material qualities, which usually serve to support socially mediated meanings. This assemblage performs work, leaving memorable material-semiotic traces on the bodies that encounter it, yet—at the same time—itself undergoing constant material-semiotic transformations as an effect of these intensive collisions.

Summing up, as Greig Crysler and Abidin Kusno (1997) claim, the USHMM intends the Holocaust to be remembered in very American terms. The narrative it offers and reinforces with the material aspects of the place speaks of democracy as counteractive to genocide and antithetical to atrocious occurrences that it depicts. Contemporary American values are removed in time and space from the presented events but are immediately encountered in symbolic form right before the entrance as well as right on leaving the museum. Although highlighting American pluralist ideals, the museum at the same time approaches cultural difference—embodied by Jewish as well as other religious, racial, ethnic, and political victims of the Holocaust—as a thing of the past. These differences are presented as a source of oppression or as something to be annihilated by the Nazi nation state. Yet, by constructing the museum's narrative from the point of view of the American liberators and portraying the American nation as a rescuer of those who survived the Holocaust, the differences among the visitors are evacuated, as they are all invited to identify with the American values of freedom and democracy as adversative to the Nazi regime. In Crysler and Kusno's words, "The spectator's identification . . . demands an attitude of indifference towards the particularities of his or her ethnic/social/sexual/gendered/classed body" (1997, 52). In a sense then, USHMM instrumentalizes the predominantly non-American experience of the Holocaust in the construction of a homogenous national identity and its projection of an idealized citizenry of the present. This is achieved by various material-semiotic means. Hence, an analysis focusing exclusively on how this site is shaped by social discourses would simply have not been sufficient to wholly grasp its complex operations.

Past in the Present Tense: The Israeli Memory of the Holocaust

In Israeli politics and culture, since the establishment of the state, the events of the Shoah have remained a crucial issue and a subliminal always-present theme. As James E. Young explains, "History continues to assert itself as a locus of Jewish identity, memory as a primary form of Jewish faith" (1993, 210). It does not mean, however, that the strategies of remembrance have not changed over time. Daniel Gutwein distinguishes three periods as far as Israeli memory of the Holocaust is concerned: "The divided memory period, the nationalized memory period, and the privatized memory period" (2009, 36). Typical for the first stage, preceded by the disclosure of the atrocities of World War II to the wide public and associated with the discourses on the establishment of the Israeli state, was the interplay between the private and the public dimensions of memory. This intermingling was connected, on the one hand, to the need to mourn the fate of the victims and, on the other hand, to the necessity of setting up the values of the newly emerged political organism, so that the memory of the Holocaust would simultaneously belong to both individuals and the nation. Since pilgrimages to the tombs of the lost relatives were not possible, as it was difficult to establish where the latter had been buried, the long Jewish tradition of mourning could not be fully put in practice. In response to this, the state determined a national "Day of Remembrance" on which Holocaust memorials could be visited by those who lost their families during the Shoah, which initiated public practices of commemorating the trauma of the war and the extermination of Jewish population connected thereto. Interestingly, this period was also characterized by the implementation of the forestation plans meant to serve as forms of monuments, a symbolic act standing for a metaphor of the nation's return from a protracted exile. Newly planted forests worked as symbols of regeneration as well as referred to the atrocities of the Holocaust so often concealed by the sinister thicket of immense Eastern European woods. Even though controversial—since planted on the former Palestinian habitation territories—the forests served as living memorials to those who perished, being integrated at the same time within the Israeli strategies of settlement and turning the inhospitable land into a more habitable environment. Importantly, the immediate after-war period gave birth to more tangible projects of institutionalized memorials, museums, and practices of remembrance, among them the notorious Yad Vashem site of memory, erected on the hills of Jerusalem.

The first stage of Israeli memory of the Holocaust identified by Gutwein (2009) finished with the Eichmann Trial, so crucial for the transformation of Jewish attitudes towards the traumatic events. From passive victims, the Jewish nation has, in the public imaginary, gradually evolved into active accusers, executing penalty on their persecutors, on behalf of those whose lives had been lost. This was happening in the circumstances of the Yom Kippur war, which further contributed to the emergence of the symbolic figure of a heroic Jew, actively involved in the struggle to defend the country and zealously fighting for its independence. Such an association, especially in the context of the unfolding conflict, made empathizing with the Holocaust victims easier for contemporary Jews (Zerubavel 1994, 86). This was also the moment when the narrative on the Holocaust remembrance started to embrace discourses on resurrection of the nation, which was accompanied with the erection of a number of memorials commemorating heroic deeds by Jewish people (like the Warsaw Ghetto Uprising). Unsurprisingly, in that period, the Holocaust memory started to incorporate a more nationalistic rhetoric, heavily influenced by the Zionist movement. The trauma of the Jewish people started to be instrumentalized in the project of Jewish settlement and used for shaping the nationalist ideology connected therewith, especially considering difficult relations Israel had with its neighbors at that time. Incorporation of the Holocaust narratives into the everyday politics resulted in a somewhat paradoxical situation. As Young underlines, “By linking the state’s raison d’être to the Holocaust, the early founders also located the Shoah at the center of national identity: Israel would be a nation condemned to defining itself in opposition to the very event that made it necessary” (1993, 212). In the times of blooming of Zionist ideology, the trauma of the Holocaust has been further politicized and employed for advancement of the most up-to-date interests. The interlacing of the Holocaust memory and the current political projects is still discernible in the organization of many memorial institutions.

The third period of Israeli memory of the Holocaust, Gutwein asserts (2009), started in the 1980s and resulted from political and cultural changes happening in Israel at that time. This produced a number of diversified accounts connected to the Shoah and dismantled one official narrative that had crystallized earlier. This period is depicted by Gutwein by the term “privatization,” as the memory of the Holocaust turned it into “a personal experience that is concerned with the fate of Jews as individuals: victims, displaced persons (DPs), survivors, and the 'second generation'" (2009, 37). These processes, again, translated into a radical transformation of the Holocaust discourses pervading Israeli politics, society, and culture at that time. All these metamorphoses of the prevailing ways in which the national trauma has been remembered and rehearsed had a tremendous impact on the shape and functioning of the memorial institutions located there as well as on the ways they tended to affect visitors. A predominant view was also to assert an Israeli primary right to be an international authority on the Holocaust. In this context worth noticing is the fact that the decision to completely reorganize the architecture and the display of the Yad Vashem memorial complex in Jerusalem was triggered by the opening of the USHMM and its impressive exhibition in 1993. This was connected to the fear that it could replace the Israeli institutions as far as their role in spreading knowledge of the Shoah is concerned. Before I focus on a more detailed analysis of the most important Holocaust memorial in Israel, let me first briefly discuss the circumstances in which the institution was originally established.

The decision to erect a national memorial of the Holocaust was taken relatively early after the establishment of the state of Israel. In legal terms, the resolution setting up such an institution was passed by the Knesset on August 19, 1953, yet the conceptual plans for its development had already been envisioned earlier. As Young claims, "Conceived in the throes of the state's birth and building, Yad Vashem would be regarded from the outset as an integral part of Israel's civic infrastructure" (1993, 243). Today the national law still regulates the funding and functioning of Yad Vashem, and the institution is positioned as the primary national (and international) authority on the issues of the Holocaust research and education. It operates under governmental supervision and is financed from the state's budget. As such, it offers an official narrative on the events of the Shoah from a Jewish perspective, inscribing it within more general discourses on national values and incorporating the Holocaust onto political agendas. Crucial was, in this context, the location of the memorial institution, which shapes its reception by visitors and strengthens the connection between the utmost national trauma and the project of building and sustaining the Israeli state. When it was eventually decided that Yad Vashem would be located in Jerusalem, the main architect of the project Mordechai Shenhavi suggested erecting the memorial complex next to Mt. Herzl, the official military cemetery and the burial site of the nation's leaders, including Theodor Herzl—a primary ideologue of Zionism and propagator of Jewish settlement on the territories of the historical "promised land." This suggestion was enthusiastically accepted and, consequently, in July 1954, the land was formally allocated to Yad Vashem—the area was named Mt. Remembrance (*Har Ha'zikaron*). Significantly, a walking path connects the two sites, weaving together the two narratives so important in contemporary Israeli politics.

Similar to the USHMM, both the physical location of Yad Vashem and its material organization shape the messages the institution conveys in a quite substantial way, offering a bridge between the difficult past of the Jewish nation and the long-awaited projects for the future. This has become even more visible after the extensive reconstruction of the memorial complex completed in 2005,[16] which—as mentioned earlier—was triggered by the opening of the museum in Washington, DC. From its inception Yad Vashem was meant to function as primarily a memorial institution. Its museal and educational functions were initially considered secondary to the emotional message that the site was intended to convey—sentimental connection came first, only after the knowledge on the traumatic past was to be added to visitors' experience. Even though today's exhibition—which is four times as big as the original one—attempts to offer visitors a most complete narrative on the Holocaust depicted from a Jewish point of view, it still does it in a very affective fashion, triggering sensitive bodily involvement and empathetic response. The way the new museum is situated and how it relates to the surrounding landscape and the nearby institutions translates into the complex interlacing of its official account with more political discourses on the contemporary Israeli state and the challenges it faces. This is achieved through affective-emotional means as well as through the material guiding of the visitors along a preplanned path, from which in no place could they divert. Such a strategy produces very concrete meanings that could not be so persuasive if it were not for the physical organization of the memorial site and the *mattering* materiality of its contents.

The "new" Yad Vashem museum was officially inaugurated on March 15, 2005, yet its reconstruction had begun already in 1993. The site comprises the International School for Holocaust Studies, the International Institute for Holocaust Research, the Yad Vashem Archives and Library, the Visitors' Center and the museum complex containing an historical museum, a Hall of Names, art museum, and display halls for temporary exhibitions. The memorial complex also hosts the Children's Memorial, the Alley of the Righteous, the Warsaw Ghetto Plaza, Remembrance Hall, the Sunken Courtyard, Synagogue, the Valley of the Communities, and the Monument to the Deportees. The whole site is immense and offers a complexity of memorial, educational, and emotional experiences. Moshe Safdie, the author of the design of *Yad Layeled* (1987), was chosen to deliver the final project of the whole renovated site—as Stephanie Shosh Rotem underlines, "The main argument for selecting Safdie's proposal was his general plan of the campus. The layout that he suggested wove together the various monuments and memorial spaces scattered on the hillside to form a continuous walk that created a coherent narrative of commemoration" (2013, 61). Even though the architect himself used to claim that his purpose was to avoid a highly ideological message, the meticulous knitting together of the Holocaust and the more contemporary politics of Israel is very present in the museal journey. This is especially strengthened by the geographical location of the memorial site as well as its responsive attitude towards the surrounding space.

A premeditated narrative route—dictated by a material-symbolic organization of the site—translates into a deep emotional and sensorial experience produced in a dynamic assemblage of visitors' bodies, their private contexts and knowledges, political and cultural discourses, and the meaningful physical arrangement of the memorial space. Crossing the delicate and fragile wooden bridge spreading between the temple-like Visitors' Center and the museum building seems to fulfill the role of metaphorically cutting off visitors from their everyday life and giving them an impression of going on a long journey into a distant past, now existing exclusively within the realm of memory. The museum building is made of concrete, which puts it aside all other architecture of Jerusalem (and which demanded special permission), as Safdie's intention was to take visitors to an alien and secluded place as well as to create a feeling of anxiety and strangeness connected to the displacement experienced by Jewish people. That is why he resigned from using the familiar limestone and decided instead to erect a severe concrete block. The entrance is not inviting—it seems as an opening of an abyss; the exit cannot be seen from this perspective. As a result, visitors have an impression of penetrating a space without a way of return.

The museum is shaped as a prism—the permanent exhibition is hosted by galleries placed on both sides of the centrally located corridor running along the building. The prism itself is built underground, with both ends hanging above the edge of the cliff. Joan Ockman offers a convincing description of the building's architecture, which I quote here at full length:

> The diagonal flanks of the cast-concrete structure are post-tensioned with steel reinforcement to support the compressive load of the hill, while the glazed vertex of the building's triangular section protrudes through the earth, allowing light to filter down to the circulation spine. From outside, the architect's act of violence in slitting open the ground is felt viscerally, expressing itself as an archeological scar symbolically healed by the landscape itself. Inside, along the nearly six-hundred-foot length of the tunnel, the already compressed triangular geometry is likewise visceral, constricting to its narrowest diameter at one of the darkest points in the curatorial narrative—the extermination of more than 1.1 million Jews at Auschwitz-Birkenau—before eventually widening to a generous equilateral conclusion. In tandem with this modulation in the building's longitudinal section, the floor and roof planes also ramp five degrees downward and then back up, producing a perspectival distortion that destabilizes the

> visitor's sense of equilibrium and creates a haptic sense of down and up, dark and light, contraction and expansion, weight and suspension. (2006, 22)

The purposeful arrangement of the length and height of the museum rooms and corridors is used in the building on many occasions. For instance, when visitors enter the space of the historical exhibition, the ceiling lowers; the room seems to be oppressive as if it was weighted down by the horrific events. Then, visitors pass under a concrete bridge, with deep pits excavated on their both sides—the arrangement of exhibits gives an impression of unfriendliness and hostility; the space is inhospitable; one needs to be careful surrounded by the uninviting environment. The story unfolds with different levels of intensity, which results from the building's architecture, the spatial deployment of artifacts, and the material design of the exhibit. Thus, as mentioned earlier, the museum offers not exclusively narrative but also thoroughly sensorial experience—visitors are in the midst of material artifacts, digital exhibits, recorded testimonies, and photographs; they are surrounded by sights, sounds, voices, and lights, which trigger specific emotional-affective responses. As Avner Shalev, the chief curator of the museum, explains, "The museum did not aim to project a history lesson, nor would it provide a substitute for history textbooks. The exhibition was intended to let visitors go through a process that generates a sense of empathy and identification with the narrative" (2006, 11). The aim of the team of designers and curators was, in Dorit Harel's words, to achieve "that subtle and informed balance between the abundance of items in the storerooms of Yad Vashem, and the relating of the historical narrative as a museological experience" (2010, 19). Nevertheless, the exhibition seems to be overpacked with artifacts, which gives an idea of how difficult it was to deal with the orgy of available evidence to the Nazi's horrendous crime.

On entering the museum, visitors can see the bright balcony at the end of the journey through the dark building, yet they cannot reach this site without embarking on a long, predominantly chronologically narrated route that guides them from one hall to another. The navigation through the galleries is prescribed—practically no part of the exhibition can be skipped; there are no shortcuts or abridgements. The circulation is closed. As Harel explains, by cutting the central corridor of the prism with six indentations filled with historical objects symbolizing meaningful changes in the course of the events, the architectural prism was transformed "into an ideological timeline of longitude—the axis of historical memory. There is no axis that visitors can walk along uninterrupted, for their progress is halted by each rupture. They must follow the path of historical memory in the dictated museological route, advancing from one gallery to the next" (2010, 25). Somewhat paradoxically, the arrangement of light that enters through the glass ceiling of the prism highlights the route from the entry to the wide window at the end of the building, yet—because of the trenches in the floor—visitors are clearly prevented from following it. Even though they feel like getting to the balcony at the end of the spine first, this remains impossible—the only way to follow is to visit all the galleries and engage in a historical narrative that tells the difficult story of the Jewish nation right before and during the war. This creates a weird feeling of corporeal confusion—the body seems to hurry to get to the final point of the long spine, as if it was magnetically attracted to it, but it is physically barred from the desired destination. Instead, visitors have to proceed along the narrative story that systematically unfolds from one gallery to another. Eventually, reaching the glassed terrace emerges as a culmination of the journey—it offers a bright redemptive view of the hills of Jerusalem, creating a sense that the return to this exceptional area was a logical conclusion of the atrocities the nation had had to suffer. Certainly, such an impression is achieved not exclusively through architectural means, yet the construction of the building (as well as prescription of the visiting route) contributes extensively to fulfilling this objective.

The commencement of the journey is equally moving as its termination. The story that the exhibition recounts begins by briefly presenting vibrant Jewish communities in prewar Europe that visitors encounter right on entry, on the left side—a short filmic montage by Michal Rovner is projected on the triangular wall of the building. Having watched the installation, visitors are forced to turn their back at it, putting the vanished world behind them, and start their exhausting route through the exhibition. They zigzag through the spine, from one gallery to another. The displays located there offer personalized accounts of the story—viewers encounter the testimonies and memories of witnesses and survivors, which are offered to them via screens located at the eye level of visitors enabling an almost direct contact. The exhibition is organized around ninety individual records and includes genuine objects originally belonging to those whose stories are told. Employing such a strategy, the museum strives to intensify the emotional experience and trigger empathy, experienced in a sensorial memorial space. Moreover, unlike many other Holocaust museums, Yad Vashem is unique in that it displays principally authentic artifacts rather than copies or reconstructions. This might strengthen the intensity of responses of the visitors, who are confronted with the original material objects from the distant and horrifying past.

When advancing from one section of the exhibition to another, visitors are offered glimpses of what awaits them. There are some openings through which they are able to discern what they would find in the following galleries—yet they cannot see clearly; they can only anticipate. Such a strategy refers to the situation of the Jewish people during the war—they could imagine, or suppose, what would happen to them; however, they could not be completely sure, as the information provided was scarce and fragmentary. With an aim of inferring a greater level of identification, in one of the opening galleries, visitors encounter a typical room in the home of a respected German Jewish family. They can realize how regular lives these people had led before they were persecuted, enslaved, and exterminated. The direct proximity of physical objects and a familiar space of a study let the visitors build an empathetic, affective connection with those whose stories the museum tells. This stimulates more passionate feelings as well as a sense of affinity and withness.

The overall message that the museum conveys in material-semiotic terms is openly political. Interestingly, the closing galleries are not those presenting the "final solution" and the Nazi death camps, offering instead a rather nationalistic memorandum in a form of recording from 1930 of a children's choir from Mukacevo (then in Czechoslovakia) singing *Hatikva*, a composition that was to become the Israeli anthem. With the melody still in their ears, the visitors reach the sunlit balcony overlooking the Jerusalem Hills. In such a way, the museal route rehearses the narrative of "from ashes to resurrection," glorifying the final fate of the nation as belonging to where it eventually settled down. From darkness, symbolically located underground, visitors eventually emerge to the light, which is embodied in the spacious balcony located higher, outside the hill, and offering generous views. Obviously, with this highly ideological ending, the material-discursive composition of the museum writes an openly Zionist narrative.

As mentioned earlier, these political meanings are relayed in intricate manners, through complex material-semiotic means. The building's architecture, as combined with sensorial narrative exhibits, conveys a persuasive message. As Joan Ockman underlines, in Yad Vashem, architecture "aspires beyond its sheer functional obligation to produce an emphatic identification or unmediated apprehension of something ineffable, something that cannot be represented—an aesthetic experience" (2006, 24). The museum operates both through its spatial, aesthetic qualities and through its representational, narrative layer. These two dimensions are entangled and co-constitute each other in order to evoke a particular material-semiotic experience, yet with always-singular qualities. The architecture establishes a "place of displacement" (Ockman 2006, 24), interlacing the narrative on the Holocaust with a more contemporary political context of the state of Israel. It does not function solely as a background, or vehicle, for a narrative content—it is itself an active and potent agent that substantially shapes visitors' experiences, entering into creative assemblage-like synaesthetic encounters with their sensual bodies as well as with representational knowledges that they possess. All involved bodies bear memorable traces of these intensive material-semiotic encounters.

Shameful Memories: Remembering the Shoah in the German Context

Similar to the case of Israel, the Holocaust memory in Germany is locked within the dilemma between remembering and forgetting, although it is so for a different reason. Troubled with the record of World War II and the difficult times of division afterward, German society has long struggled with the issue of how to remember the victims of the Nazi regime. The horrendous crimes the Third Reich was charged with have always been resisting incorporation into the dominant public discourses—they have tended to leave the society speechless. As heirs to the legacy of their parents and grandparents, contemporary Germans are still divided on the question how, or in fact whether, to include both the trauma of the Holocaust victims and that of the bystanders and perpetrators into the official public narratives of remembrance. Thus, memorialization of these painful events in Germany, as James E. Young argues, "remains a tortured, self-reflective, even paralyzing preoccupation" (1992, 269). How should a nation remember the victims of crime it has perpetrated? How should it commemorate its own dreadful barbarity? How should the void left after expulsion and extermination of the German Jewish community be represented? Since the shock of the unspeakable done to victims haunts and disquiets perpetrators' descendants and is embedded in memory as a constant reproach, the Holocaust remembrance in the contemporary German context embodies intractable questions rather than answering them.

Worth noticing is also the fact that the effort of memorializing these terrifying deeds has to be necessarily undertaken by those who have never been themselves part of these events. Even though a similar situation is dealt with also elsewhere, in Germany the nature of this memory is radically different, as the artists often face the dilemma of evoking the shameful activities perpetrated by and on behalf of the same nation to which they now belong. Whereas in other contexts the discourses on victimhood and resistance are primarily evoked as commemorative themes, in this case the mnemonic strategies need to be of different character, referring to the convoluted nature of Germans' participation in World War II. The aesthetics of commemorative art is, in such an instance, unavoidably postmemorial (more on this in chapter 3).

Whereas the practices of remembering the shameful, difficult past seem to be one challenge, the problem with the fascist loading of the massive architectural forms in Germany is another one. As Young reminds, "German memory-artists are heirs to a double-edged postwar legacy: a deep distrust of monumental forms in light of their systematic exploitation by the Nazis and a profound desire to distinguish their generation from that of the killers through memory" (2000, 96). Hence the emergence of a countermonumental format—it seems that the best strategy to celebrate the fall of totalitarian regimes is by celebrating the fall of their monuments (Young 2000, 96). Isn't destruction the most adequate manner to commemorate destruction?—some German memory-artists seem to ask. Isn't a void, or vanishing, self-abnegating and self-effacing memorial site the most suitable vehicle to honor the memory of an exterminated community? How to evoke nonexistence, immateriality, or nothingness? How to memorialize absence? Any monumental form seems to be completely inappropriate if it comes to evoking something so brutally removed from the texture of society that is now to commemorate it.

The indeterminate and perplexed nature of the German memory of World War II has produced specific strategies of remembrance. The earlier-signaled shift towards "countermonumental" aesthetics (Young 1992, 1993, 2000), or invention of ambiguous memorial formats, counts as an important characteristic of this memorial genre, which often seems to reflect on the character of memory itself rather than offering a narrativized discourse on the specific events. Since remembrance and self-indictment seem to be completely at odds, countermonuments tend to avoid the certainty inscribed in monumental forms. Is it possible for a nation to openly mourn its own victims and dedicate space to them in the national memorial landscape? How to incorporate shame and the guilt of an unimaginable crime into a collective memory of a nation? How to express or embody the dreadful past in a work of art, especially considering the fact that squeezing aesthetic pleasure from memorial art commemorating crime and mass murder seems to be an ethically controversial issue? Because of the rather convoluted nature of the German memory of the Shoah, the aesthetics of countermonuments resist redemptory closure so typical for most memorial formats worldwide. Rather than offering already-interpreted accounts and narratives, they tend to ask questions and open public debates. As such, they remain in contrast to the conventional memorial institutions (including museums and monuments) that seem to be entirely incapable of fulfilling the needs of a tortured, angst-ridden nature of memory of the Holocaust in Germany. "Brazen, painfully self-conscious memorial spaces conceived to challenge the very premises of their being" (Young 1993, 27) serve as a means to both express and experience the difficult relations to the shameful past and to trigger critical reflection on the work of memory as well as how it shapes and is shaped by more contemporary contexts and circumstances.

The history of the JMB reflects in a way the troubled character of the German memory of the fate of Berlin's Jewry. In fact, the contemporary exhibition has roots in a tiny collection of artworks and coins gathered by Albert Wolf and donated to the Jewish congregation in Berlin after his death in 1907. Other artifacts and more contemporary works by Jewish artists were added to this. Officially, the Jewish Museum, housed in a building next to the synagogue at 31 Orienburger Strasse in Berlin, opened in 1933, which coincided with the rise of the Nazi regime and the installation of Adolf Hitler as Third Reich's chancellor. The institution functioned in an increasingly unfriendly environment and under constant pressure, yet it testified to the deep entanglement of Jewish and German culture. As Young recounts,

> With the advent of Nuremberg laws defining "the Jews" as essentially "un-German," the Nazis suddenly forbade all but Jews to visit the museum, and all but Jewish artists to exhibit there. With this sleight of legislative hand, the Nazis thus transformed the institutional "fact" of an inextricably linked German-Jewish culture into a segregated ghetto of art and culture by Jews for Jews. (2000, 157)

Neither the synagogue nor the museum survived the *Kristallnacht* from November 9 to 10, 1938. They disappeared from the landscape of the city, as did the Jewish community from Berlin. After the war there had been plans to reopen the Jewish exhibition, yet it turned out to be a long and difficult process. Eventually, in 1975 the Berlin Senate voted for establishment of a Jewish section within the Berlin Museum, pointing to the deep interweaving of the two cultures and communities. It was not at that time clear whether the Jewish Department would sit inside or outside the Berlin Museum. Only in 1988 did the Senate approved the financial measures for the Jewish Department that would be administratively hosted by the Berlin Museum but would have its own building—the idea was to both extend the original museum and give the Jewish exhibition its own place. This was to manifest the interconnectedness of the two institutions and the two cultures they represented. They were to be considered inseparable.

The competition for the design of the JMB was announced in November 1988. A conceptual paper was developed and offered by the Berlin Museum and the Jewish Department to the invited architects. In planners' minds, as Young explains, "the Jewish wing would be both autonomous and integrative, the difficulty being to link a museum of civic history with the altogether uncivil treatment of that city's Jews" (2000, 161). This was an immense challenge for the competitors. In response, in April 1989, a total of 165 design projects were submitted and evaluated according to such criteria as general concept of the museum, urban development type of building, and its relationship to other buildings. An execution plan, construction, materials to be used, feasibility, and economic efficiency of the project were also taken into consideration. Even though Daniel Libeskind's proposal contradicted many of the original requirements established for the winning design, and although it was even considered unbuildable (because of the tilted walls he originally planned),[17] in June 1989 his proposition was elected and commissioned as the future concept of the JMB. Considered as a masterpiece of process art, offering much more than usual museums typically offer, it presented a spatial debate on a philosophical and ethical theme, a building as an intellectual-material becoming whose qualities emerge in an encounter with the visitors' bodies. The architectural convincingness of his proposal lay in the way he dealt with the capturing of both the autonomy and integration of the Jewish Museum in the history of the city of Berlin. This was achieved by connecting the new building to the old *Kolliegenhaus* by way of an underground tunnel—the visitors enter the JMB via the building of the Berlin Museum; then they proceed through the subterranean corridor to eventually find themselves in a new building hosting the Jewish exhibition. Thus, the two structures—as the two histories—are both interwoven and separate at the same time.

The whole site has been approached as an "embodiment of absence" (Libeskind 2000, 28), "a critique of the historiographical apparatus" (Stead 2000), and an "antiredemptive" memorial (Young 2000, 154) offering participation in "a traumatic affect" and "distinctly material experience of trauma" (Heckner 2008, 63–65). Praised as a piece of deconstructivist architecture, Libeskind's building seems to both be a part of the surrounding landscape of Berlin and stand aside of it. The architect made an effort to trace the addresses of the famous Berliners of Jewish origin and draw lines connecting them, situating the museum's building on top of an old map of the city—"I felt that certain people and particular certain writers, scientists, composers, artists and poets formed the link between Jewish tradition and German culture" (Libeskind 1991, 8). What emerged from this web of imaginary lines was a system of squared triangles that formed together a shape of a compressed and distorted Star of David—an emblem of Jewish culture as well as a symbol of persecution of Jews during the war. The building is partly inscribed in the lines connecting the addresses, embodying the materiality of Berlin's cultural, social, and ethnic geography. This topography, however, is not completely revealed to those visiting the site, yet it attests to the importance of the building's context and its immediate surroundings. The invisible, ghostly presence of the vanished community incorporated into the architecture of the museum turns it into a memorial to the perished culture, once so important to the texture of the city. The building is haunted by the absence of these people, which translates into it being a Holocaust museum rather than a Jewish Museum. The trauma of the Shoah is ever present throughout the journey due to the deeply felt material experience of a void.

As seen from the preceding text, the building is shaped like a jagged lightning bolt, with sharp edges, corners, and angles that make it inhospitable to any traditional display. From the outside, it is built from the concrete coated with zinc planks with no window frames. The diagonal slits in the facades, forming scar-like signs, create an impression of distortion and deformation. Windows slash through the zinc panels, offering a dramatic display of light onto the walls of the museum's interior. Their trajectories are not accidental—as it is the case with a general placement of the building, they refer to the imaginary topography of the city emerged from the lines connecting the homes of its Jewish citizens. The whole building, therefore, offers a map of Jewish history within Berlin. From the inside of the building the windows offer glimpses of disfigured fragments of city's landscape, which looks unfamiliar and alien through these irregular fissures.

Both the shape and the construction of the museum stand aside the typical architecture of the city. Yet the use of the zinc is not accidental. As Shosh Rotem points out, this is a material traditionally used to cover roofs of the buildings in the capital of Germany. Libeskind, however, decided to choose a traditional type of zinc, which "will take some years to become part of the city" (Libeskind and Binet, quoted in Shosh Rotem 2013, 151), as it will take time to absorb the brutal reality of the memory of the Shoah in the German context. Wrapped in reflective zinc cladding, the facade would age, change color, and grow into the architectural material texture of the city. Its material becoming is intermingled with the processual transformation of the tangled Holocaust memory. The surface of the structure is equally evocative—while the seams between the panels run perfectly vertical and parallel to one another, the horizontal seams are skewed. This results in an illusion that the walls are not perpendicular to the ground, eliciting an effect of disjunction.

Libeskind called his project "Between the Lines" since, as he explains, "it is a project about two lines of thinking, organization, and relationship" (1991, 3). He elaborates further:

> One is a straight line, but broken into many fragments; the other is a torturous line, but continuing indefinitely. These two lines develop architecturally and programmatically through a limited but definite dialogue. They also fall apart, become disengaged, and are seen as separated. In this way, they expose a void that runs through this museum and through architecture, a discontinuous void. (Libeskind 1991, 3)

At the intersections of the two lines there are six empty towers erected to form an empty spine of the whole construction. The central void cuts the building at many points so that the emptiness that it embodies is always felt by the proceeding visitors—their route is systematically interrupted. This translates into a narrative of a fragmented story of German Jewry, which is experienced viscerally as an always-haunting absence. Such a feeling is present throughout the whole exhibition, as an element constantly alluded to. Consequently, even though only a part of the permanent exhibition is devoted to the depiction of the Shoah, this trauma is present all the time during the journey through the museum, as embodied by voided spaces. In line with deconstructivists' claims, Libeskind decenters the traditional thinking about architecture—he leaves the center voided and mostly inaccessible to the visitors. No longer does the center exist—rather, it embodies nonexistence that ghostly haunts all other spaces that it cuts through, brutally wounding them and thus eerily reminding about its ephemeral existence. Importantly, by introducing the void as a chief element of the building's architecture, Libeskind successfully materializes absence. The materiality of the void, its running through the whole building and cutting it violently into irregular pieces, is an index of ever-present nothingness, standing for the Jewish people's drama experienced during World War II. The museum's architecture elicits questions: How to represent the nonexistent? How to give voice or speak for the perished culture? Even though these questions remain unanswered, the materiality of the space triggers reflection on the perplexed nature of the Holocaust memory. Consequently, what is most evident and palpable about the building is the empty spine that runs through it rather than its walls. The latter are important insofar as they materialize the central void as the most real element of the building. Even though the zigzagging structure is not sensed as such by the museumgoers when they are already inside the space, it translates into the weird feeling of meandering within narrow, shadowy corridors, with unusual shapes, and diagonal windows that all translate into an unfamiliar bodily experience generating powerful affects and dreadful intensities.

Unlike in the USHMM and Yad Vashem, on entry into the dark and unfriendly basement of the JMB, the visitors have to choose out of three possible routes intersecting there. The hall is rather confusing, offering a feeling of entrapment beneath the ground, and there are no indications of which way they should first follow. The names of the possible paths are inscribed on the wall: Axis of Holocaust, Axis of Emigration, and Axis of Continuity. As the architect explains: "The road leading to the Holocaust tower . . . has no entrance except from the underground level; the road leading to the garden; and the road leading to the main circulation stair and the void. The entire plane of the museum is tilted toward the void of the superstructure. The building is as complex as the history of Berlin" (Libeskind 1995, 34). The first two routes are dead ends—if visitors choose to follow them, they will have to eventually come back into the basement and embark on another one.

The Axis of Holocaust takes the visitors to the void located right outside the building—it gradually turns narrower and darker and eventually ends before the heavy metal door leading to the empty, stony, and alien space lit only by a single ray of light entering through a slit at the top of the room. There is no other way out of the tower—it gives the visitors a moment of reflection but also a feeling of petrifying dread and horror. They can hear the remote noises coming from the outside while being totally isolated from them. The external space of a familiar landscape of Berlin is beyond their reach, as they are locked in the dark tower, with no window to look out. There is a life outside, but there is an appalling abyss inside the space. Solitude and alienation are experienced viscerally. The Axis of Emigration, another cul-de-sac, takes visitors to the Garden of Exile, a tricky space of contemplation designed by the architect as a complementary element of the museum, composed of forty-nine pillars on a tilted floor (more on this installation in chapter 4). As in the case of the first route, here again visitors have to turn back and return to the entrance hall. The Axis of Continuity meanders through the museum building, starting with a narrow staircase that takes visitors to the highest floor where the chronological voyage through many centuries of Jewish tradition in Germany begins. The route is premeditated, but because it snakes through the confusing spaces of the zigzagging building, it always reminds the visitors about the ghostly architecture of the unusual construction, regularly interrupted by the central void penetrating the museum. Contrary to its name, the route seems to alter any sense of continuity, suggesting instead architectural, spatial, and narrative gaps in the presentation—the void interrupts the displays and alerts viewers to what awaits them. One might even have an impression that the displayed items and information, although arranged in an interactive, thought-provoking fashion, remain secondary to the exhibition space itself. Occasionally, they even seem inappropriate, somewhat artificially arranged in the overpersuasive space of Libeskind's building. As Young argues,

> Instead of merely housing the collection . . . the building seeks to estrange it from viewer's preconceptions. Such walls and oblique angles . . . defamiliarize the all-too-familiar ritual objects and historical chronologies, and cause museumgoers to see into these relations between the Jewish and German departments as if for the first time. (2000, 175)

By planning the three routes, the architect made the trauma of the Shoah always implicitly present during the journey through the museum, even in the galleries and halls devoted to the pre-Holocaust history of Jewish community in Germany. The premonition of an impending drama and a feeling that something horrible would eventually happen to the depicted people is felt at every stage of the visit, which is due to the evocative materiality of the building. Worth noticing is the fact that the Holocaust was not planned as a central theme of the museum but rather as one of the elements that were to be subtly incorporated into the overall narrative. The reminiscent physicality of the structure, however, turned the Jewish trauma of the war into the dominant motif of the whole exhibition, viscerally experienced by visitors at every stage of their journey. Libeskind turned the museum's material space—with its lighting, cold concrete floors, narrowing and tilted walls—into the most significant artifact of the museum. It is more important how the museum feels rather than how it looks like. What counts is the experience and not the practicality of the interiors. Experienced affectively, and absorbed in material-semiotic manners, the building's shattering materiality elicits destruction and the abyss that it left in the texture of European society. It impacts visitors on their intimately bodily level, materially inscribing them with wraithlike sensations, opening rooms for singular production of affective-emotional knowledges.

Contingent on always-unstable assemblages, the effects of the encounters with the architecture of the museum bear potentials for disturbing, subverting, or transcending the well-established institutionalized frameworks for cultural remembrance, opening them to more singular negotiations as well as exposing numerous vulnerabilities and susceptibilities of mnemonic processes. The museum is, in its designer's words, "on the verge of *becoming*" (Libeskind 1991, 54; original emphasis), opening its experience to always new interpretations, combinations, sensual intensities, metamorphous flows, and differing potentialities, and offering a multiplicity of personalized memorial encounters. This is especially salient in the context of remembering the trauma of the Holocaust in Germany, taking into consideration the discourses and political prescriptions that have translated into the countermonumental memorial aesthetics.

THE *MATTERING* OF MATTER: CONCLUDING REMARKS

Although the complex relation between public memory of the Shoah, politics, and representation in different national, gendered, or generational contexts has recently been widely explored (e.g., Reading 2002, Kantsteiner 2006, Rothberg 2009, Hirsch and Spitzer 2011, Hirsch 2012), it is still necessary to look at *how* public memory of trauma is shaped, packaged, and spread. A new materialist perspective enables drawing attention to the *process* of memory itself and lets us recognize the complex roles of mediation and transmission in Holocaust commemoration. Writing about art practices referring to the events of the Shoah, Dora Appel asserts that they rather tend towards the nonnarrative, the polyvalent, the enigmatic, and the ambiguous, paying attention to the processes of cultivation of absences, gaps, omissions, and silences (2002, 4). This is also the case of many memorial museums—in a way similar to art, they affect visitors on the immediately embodied level, imperceptibly inscribing them with memorable traces and persuasive knowledges. The latter are contingent on the rich and diversified archives—symbolic, affective, emotional, and so on—that the visitors bring on their memorial journeys. Therefore, the most important space of memory is the space between the memorial and the viewer, between the viewer and his or her memory: the place of the memorial in the viewer's mind, heart, body, and conscience. What counts is the compound collision that entangles the variety of bodies in a generative, experiential encounter. These interactions, however, are immensely shaped by cultural contexts and political discourses in which they occur.

The logic of the Holocaust memory only seemingly operates in a cross-cultural fashion. How these traumatic events have become a part of national discourses and historical policies in different cultural, political, and geographical locations is therefore worth analyzing. Necessary is a strategy that "always places the Holocaust in relations to the circumstances of its representation in the present" and "recognizes the altered ideological contexts of the present, the fragmented and conflicted nature of experience and subjectivity, and the difficulty of retrieving knowledge from the past" (Appel 2002, 7). The subjective character of meaning (or content) precludes the possibility that any interpretation of history, any emotional narrative, or any affective relation to the past and its contemporary rehearsals can be universal for all members of a particular group (national, racial, ethnic, etc.). It is not possible to assume any interpretations and representations as normative, as experiences stem from material-semiotic entanglements that are always in motion, shaped by the immediate circumstances of their emergence. Yet, as Andreas Huyssen notices, "no matter how fractured by media, by geography and by subject position representations of the Holocaust are, ultimately it all comes down to this core: unimaginable, unspeakable, and unrepresentable horror" (1995, 259). As exposed in the analysis of the three museums discussed earlier, this difficult nature of the Shoah is never presented in universal terms, yet always depends on the material-semiotic contexts in which and by which these representations are produced. The story of the Holocaust is told in different manners and used for different purposes in the United States, Israel, and Germany (as well as in any other context). In order to highlight these differences, diversified strategies are persuasively used with an aim of conveying specific messages. This is achieved with narrative-affective means.

As Jeffrey Alexander reminds us, material and sensuous objects, such as art or architecture, allow us to experience intimate feelings that are otherwise inaccessible (2008, 785). The contact with these objects takes place primarily at the intimately sensuous, or affective, level. Affectivity, as explained in chapter 1, refers quite simply to a body's capability to affect and be affected. It stands for a faculty, immanent to all matter, to enter into temporary, intense, dynamic, and creative interactions or encounters with others (other bodies, objects, images, sounds, etc.). Importantly, affects are those qualities that define artistic creation. Art produces and generates intensity, which directly impresses the nervous system and intensifies perception. This translates into a system of dynamic and mutually impacting forces and not exclusively a set of images functioning under a regime of signification. Sensation, or affect, is in such context understood as "the capacity of both matter and life to exchange with each other, to enter into becomings that transform each" (Grosz 2008, 7). Material—stone, concrete, bricks, canvas, color, and so on—is a support for art, that is, sensation. For Deleuze and Guattari, "It is difficult to say where in fact the material ends and sensation begins," yet "sensation is not the same thing as material" (1997, 166); "It is affect that is metallic, crystalline, stony, and so on; and the sensation is not colored but . . . coloring" (1997, 167). Therefore, both the architecture and the design of the site, experienced in primarily bodily material terms, actively participate in the processes of producing impressions, experiences, and knowledges that visitors absorb while taking a journey through the museum. The texture, weight, density, shape, temperature, color, and so on of the materials used in the construction of the place are primarily experienced bodily at the surface of the skin and only then are they subjected to conscious representational analysis. The material and the symbolic co-constitute each other, enabling production of experiences and knowledges. Logically, the eye and the language would be nothing without the former sensuous bodily memory of how materials *feel*. Yet what needs to be highlighted is that the apparent chronology of cognition can only be understood in ontological terms (as detailed in the previous chapter) rather than as an ordered sequence of events.

Taking the preceding discussion into consideration, noticeable is the fact that many contemporary museums have modified the nature of their material architectural design. Whereas the importance placed on the display of artifact diminishes, the impact of the museum's materiality and architectural structures intensifies. No longer a blank space, or a neutral packaging for the narrative, architecture has to be seen as at least an equal partner (or a rival) to the contents the museum exhibits. As Shosh Rotem notices,

> The museum architecture is one of the most effective means by which to transmit messages and values to visitors, and Holocaust museums are generally characterized by unique and innovative design that are sometimes stronger in effect than the museum exhibits themselves, and become the focus of the visit. (2013, 15)

It is so because in some particular cases, architecture, or a specific spatial arrangement, is able to transmit more than narrative configurations based on language and meaning. As Daniel Libeskind claims, there is also a "substance beyond the visible" (2001, 25). This kind of knowledge is transferred through affective means. That is why such sites should be located at the intersection of the social and the material. As active agents, they increase our perception through visual, acoustic, olfactory, and haptic complexity. This, in museums, is achieved with various methods and techniques, including the display and particular interpretation of selected artifacts, as well as a purposely designed architectural landscape that offers specific experiences to visitors, understood in intellectual-affective terms. This corresponds well with the recent approach to memory, that is, one acknowledging not only its narrative but also its bodily nature (more on this in chapter 3).

Offering a strong emotional and corporeal involvement through specific material elements seems therefore to be a recurrent tendency in contemporary memorial museums. Importantly, a memorial museum is itself an interesting construction. Whereas, as explained earlier, memorials are typically seen as places inviting passive contemplation, museums are primarily tasked with achieving educative objectives, aimed at providing an interpretation and historical contextualization of their contents. As Paul Williams writes, in the case of memorial museum the "coalescing of the two suggests that there is an increasing desire to add both a moral framework to the narration of past events and more in-depth contextual explanations to commemorative acts" (2007, 8). This is performed by offering a complex, multidimensional material-semiotic experience, affecting visitors both emotionally (through symbolic meanings) and physically (by inducing sensory-perceptual responses).

This generative character of new museums, positioned often as "dark tourist attractions," enables approaching them in a more affirmative manner, disavowing the negative framework within which they are typically located. Relying on evocation of sensations, they operate in a way similar to art and are purposely arranged in artistic terms. It does not mean, however, that the experiences produced at the dark sites should be seen as purely affective and as such asocial. Neither are affect and representation delinked from each other. Quite the contrary, as my analyses show, they are intertwined in complex ways and often harnessed for political purposes. Also for this reason, memorials should be seen as irreducible in their complexity to a set of straightforward meanings or content, thus partly resistant to the structural analysis made possible by discourse research. As vibrant in their operations, they rather require us to think through and account for the dynamic and unexpected potential of affect with all its possible effects. A synaesthetic new materialist account of the complex modes of functioning of contemporary memorials and the ways visitors engage in, and are absorbed by, their material-semiotic operations provides us with a manner of approaching them through a more affirmative lens. Philosophically, affect is always positive; it is about production, generation, movement, transformation. As Deleuze and Guattari notice, pure intensities "are all positive in relationship to the zero intensity" (1983, 19). And they further explain that

> affect, even if it tortures or kills . . . manifests something new and different, a solar force . . . a pleasure that can rightly be called autoerotic, or rather automatic: the nuptial celebration of a new alliance, a new birth, a radiant ecstasy . . . an intense feeling of transition, states of pure, naked intensity stripped of all shape and form. (1983, 18)

As a bodily response connected to an experienced (aesthetic) intensity, affect is about a constant production, a permanent becoming with the other, or becoming-other. In such an instance, to engage with the memorial site no longer implicates just immediate intentional recognition of what it refers to. Rather, it is also a living body which simultaneously produces, radiates, and receives sensory impulses, thus immanently and sensuously transforms with and in the world. This sheds an altogether different light on the conception and reception of memorial "dark attractions." While referring to atrocity and stimulating rather disturbing emotions and sad reflections, many of them simultaneously offer positive aesthetic bodily experiences, which are about production, emergence of the new, floating, progressing, rising, flying, breathing. Affirmation of these encounters, however, is by no means mindless and uncritical.

In memorial institutions the production of knowledge is stimulated by the material-affective qualities of the space. Even though there cannot be a direct social control over individuals' perceptions and values, through the hyper-abundance of the dominant and culturally available (and known) signs, as well as through the material that they are supported with, social guidance is exerted, pushing even the critical or resistant viewer towards certain interpretations and reactions. Since "material aspects of the environment not only encode cultural messages but also support these messages independently of an individual's ability to 'read the signs' " (Beckstead et al. 2011, 199), it is necessary to explore how these materialities provoke "socially mediated responses, guiding the individual physically, cognitively, and affectively through the landscape" (Beckstead et al. 2011, 203). As Ingrid Josephs (2000) posits, it is through applying concepts to feelings that we are able to "stabilize" the flow of affective experience and to construct meaning out of our lived and felt sensations. However, as elaborated in chapter 1, emotional terms are not neutral, and using them can also escalate or block the feeling. This labeling, for Joseph, allows for reconstructing it (in a personal way) through culturally provided dominant semiotic means (2000, 824). This is why the contemporary mnemonic practices of incorporating trauma into the dominant discourses, also through triggering and controlling the material-semiotic flow of perception, deserve sharpened critical attention.

NOTES

1. See, for instance, works by James E. Young (1993) and Marita Sturken (1997).
2. In his analysis of "Black Spots," Chris Rojek includes the crash site in Cholame in which James Dean was killed in 1955; the annual communal gatherings in memory of Elvis Presley at Graceland, Tennessee; the regular celebrations of John F. Kennedy's assassination in Dealey Plaza in Dallas, Texas, to which he further adds

other examples, such as the forecourt of the Dakota building in New York City, where John Lennon was murdered, and Kurt Cobain's suicide site in Seattle, as well as such events as the large number of tourists arriving to the shores of Zeebrugge where in 1987 the ferry *Herald of Free Enterprise* capsized or to the site of Pan Am 103 crash in 1988 (see Rojek 1993, 1997). Importantly, "Black Spots" is a term that for Rojek carries a dual meaning. First, it refers to a marker of a death site (e.g., monuments and cemeteries, which Rojek describes as "nostalgic" sites); second, it applies to disaster sites and those connected with notable deaths (e.g., concentration camps, killing fields, and numerous places where famous people were assassinated or tragically died) (Rojek 1993, 137–45). Later on, Rojek differentiates between disaster sites and black spots, where the latter he conceptualizes in terms of sensation (1997, 63). In his words, "these are places in which violent death has occurred, or where abduction, chase or siege is occurring, or has recently occurred, and to which sightseers travel both physically and through reverie" (1997, 63). These sites, as Rojek remarks, "permit much higher levels of voyeuristic participation than travelling to cemeteries or monuments" (1997, 63).

3. Thomas Blom defines the "morbid tourism" "on the one hand, as the form of tourism that focuses on sudden death and which quickly attracts large numbers of people and, on the other, as an attraction-focused artificial morbidity-related tourism" (2000, 32).

4. Other distinctions mentioned by Philip Stone refer, first, to the motivations of sightseers flocking to these places with a purpose to, for example, witness, learn, or dice with death (i.e., to the nature of the demand for such sites), and, second, to reasons for production of these places, which include political motivations, remembrance, education, entertainment, or economic gain (i.e., the issue of supply of dark sites) (2006). See also Richard Sharpley (2009, 13).

5. Such a conceptualization, situating this phenomenon in the context of postmodernity, is in line with both Chris Rojek's idea of "Black Spots" (1993, 1997) and Blom's notion of "morbid tourism" (2000), which identify both the emergence of "dark attractions" and, consequently, increased interest in traveling to these sites, as recent trends associated with the condition of postmodernity. Rojek's sensation sights (1997) are problematized in terms of postmodern spectacles, whose popularity relies on the audiovisual media and global communication technologies, where "the process of gazing at the events involves either on-the-spot observation or TV viewing" (1997, 63). Notably, attention is being paid here to commercial aspects of "dark attractions" (Rojek 1993, 85). In a similar vein, for Thomas Blom "morbid tourism" is a form of postmodern tourism, which "has significant elements of what can be labelled deviant, dubious, macabre and even frightening and is often linked with death and destruction" (2000, 29). For this kind of attractions, as Blom notices, the media play a crucial role as they "create an image or symbol, which produces associations in the individual" (2000, 30). Among the proponents of the idea that dark tourism is an essentially postmodern activity, there is also Paul Williams (2004) with his studies concerning the killing fields in Cambodia and Sharon Slayton (2006) focusing on the Hiroshima disaster.

6. I explored these questions in more detail elsewhere (cf. Golańska 2015).

7. The set of key tenets of modernity, identified by Foley and Lennon and questioned within the phenomenon of dark tourism, includes "progress, rationality, science, technology, industrialization and liberal democracy" (2010, 21).

8. This tendency is obviously connected to the (not necessarily fortunate) marriage of tourism studies with marketing and management studies (this, however, is an issue that goes beyond the scope of this book).

9. Philip Stone's typology of "Seven Dark Suppliers" includes dark fun factories ("those visitor sites, attractions, and tours which predominantly have an entertainment focus and commercial ethic, and which present real or fictional death and macabre events"), dark exhibitions ("those exhibitions and sites which essentially blend the product design to reflect education and potential learning opportunities"; they "are manifested within an eclectic product range and are often located away from the actual site of death or macabre event"), dark dungeons ("[former] prisons and courthouses"), dark resting places (cemeteries and grave markers), dark shrines ("sites that essentially 'trade' on the act of remembrance and respect for the recently deceased," constructed "very close to the site of death and within a very short time period of the death occurring," they tend to "dominate the media agenda for relatively short periods of time" and are temporal in nature), dark conflict sites (sites that "revolve around war and battlefields and their commodification as potential tourism products"; they "essentially have an educational and commemorative focus, are history-centric and are originally non-purposeful in the dark tourism context"), and finally dark camps of genocide ("those sites and places which have genocide, atrocity and catastrophe as the main thanatological theme"; they are "produced to provide the ultimate emotional experience," and their design revolves around "education and commemoration"; importantly, they "are located at the actual site of the death-event" and "have a high degree of political ideology attached to them") (see Stone 2006).

10. A comparable approach is offered by Debbie Lisle (2004) in the study of Ground Zero visitors and, in the context of Holocaust tourism, by Grizelda Pollock (2003), who writes about diversified kinds of experiences associated with the site and involving different sorts of visitors (tourists vs. pilgrims). When tackling the issue of Holocaust tourism, Pollock draws an important distinction between pilgrims and tourists who visit memory sites. As she explains, pilgrims are those who go to the place that they or their relatives once knew and are somewhat connected to it. For them the place is a memorial, a site to mourn and to deal with the past. Conversely, for tourists, the same place is merely a "sight" or an attraction, "a packaged, planned, itinerized experience, preshaped by the new cannons of the museum educators and heritage industry" (Pollock 2003, 177).

11. Interestingly, all the supply-oriented and some of the demand-oriented classifications of "dark attractions" implicitly acknowledge that dark tourism is (at least to some extent) related to leisure (if not pleasure), which is discernible in putting in the same line experiences and infrastructures offered by entertainment parks or fun factories on the one side of the spectrum and genocide camps or sites of mass catastrophes on the other. Visitations to both "lighter" and "darker" "dark attractions" are also usually seen as tourist activities, regardless of their motivations.

12. See, for instance, works by Jøgen Ole Bærenholdt et al. (2004), David Crouch (2005), David Crouch and Nina Lübbren (2003), or Tim Edensor (2001).

13. Before, the discourses on the Holocaust had only been present among members of Jewish-American communities, and its remembrance had been limited to synagogues and Jewish culture centers. The situation significantly changed with

the decision to create a federally financed national museum to commemorate the Shoah.

14. Alternatively, the New York City was also considered as a future home to the national memorial museum. Yet this location would rather connote a Jewish character of the institution, as the city is considered a site of the biggest Jewish community in the United States.

15. For a detailed and attentive overview of the USHMM's architecture, see Stephanie Shosh Rotem (2013, 93–106).

16. The first exhibition at Yad Vashem memorial complex was opened to the public in 1958. In April 1961 Ohel Yizkor was initiated, and a year after the project of planting of the Avenue of the Righteous was launched. The synagogue opened in 1965, the historical museum in 1973, and the art museum in 1981. In 1987 Children's Memorial (*Yad Layeled*) was added to the memorial complex. The construction of this memorial site spanned the entire history of the state of Israel, paralleling its self-construction.

17. The original design of the building envisioned sloping, tilted walls. Libeskind decided to set the walls upright after the fall of the Berlin wall and the unification of Germany. In his opinion the project "no longer influenced by that kind of schizophrenic which dominated the two nature character of the city. The museum had to represent something else—and face a reunified and wall-less city" (Libeskind 1992, 47).

Chapter 3

Memory and Trauma: The Unspeakable

ENTANGLED MEMORIES: AN INTRODUCTION

When referring to her intimate traumatic experience of the Shoah, Charlotte Delbo writes about the complex and multidimensional nature of mnemonic processes, pointing to the different ways the horrific event could be remembered, (re)felt, and recounted:

> When I talk to you about Auschwitz, it is not from deep memory my words issue. They come from external memory, if I may put it that way, from intellectual memory, the memory connected with thinking processes. Deep memory preserves sensations, physical imprints. It is the memory of the senses. For it isn't words that are swollen with emotional charge. Otherwise, someone who has been tortured by thirst for weeks on end could never again say "I'm thirsty. How about a cup of tea." This word has also split in two. Thirst has turned back into a word for commonplace use. But if I dream of the thirst I suffered in Birkenau I once again see the person I was, haggard, halfway crazed, near to collapse; I physically feel that real thirst and it is an atrocious nightmare. If, however, you'd like me to talk to you about it. . . .
>
> This is why I say today that while knowing perfectly well that it corresponds to the facts, I no longer know if it is real. (2001 [1990], 3–4)

As it can be inferred from this meaningful passage, the bodily, sensuous, or "deep" (as Delbo prefers) memory seems to operate in different registers than the narrative ("intellectual") memory, yet the two remain deeply interconnected. The goal of this chapter is to shed light on the entangled nature of memory, focusing on its different aspects and taking into consideration its bodily-intellectual structure with an aim of working out a monistic and encompassing perspective on the way mnemonic processes function. New materialist philosophical framework will be instrumental for developing my argumentation. Taking into account different yet intensely entwined modes of memorizing and remembering, and considering the fact that they are deeply anchored in the corporeal, sensory experience, the chapter's objective is to overcome the dichotomy of the bodily and the intellectual as far as the ways in which memory operates are concerned. By focusing on trauma as an analytical category, my objective here is to point out that the fierce debate on whether traumatic experiences could be represented or not is falsely constructed as a binary. Even though often eluding representational processing (and as such fairly incomprehensible), the traumatic experience is still there and haunts the subject on an everyday basis. Consequently, I also aim to override traditional oppositions between the past, the present, and the future (that I partly tackled in the previous chapter), emphasizing their co-constitutive and relational nature. In this context, I also turn to the issue of atemporal connectivities associated with traumatic occurrences.

I begin the chapter with mapping recent scholarship on trauma. At first, I focus on the dominant paradigms in trauma studies. This is followed by an extensive discussion of more recent theoretical perspectives (grounded in contemporary cultural studies) developed by Bessel Van der Kolk (in cooperation with his associates) and Cathy Caruth. They both conceive of trauma as a form of bodily memory, which resides beyond representational realm of thinking. In this context, I also refer to the concept of postmemory (developed by Marianne Hirsch), signaling the transgenerational transmission of trauma. Although deeply intimate, bodily, and affective, this process remains immersed in more general representational practices available to wide publics. Such a peculiar operating of postmemory indicates its material-semiotic nature, which corresponds well with the new materialist optic that the book adopts. From there I turn my analysis to art related to traumatic experiences (particularly Holocaust) as a unique category of artistic production, that is, one relying on distinctive artistic (affective) means. This serves as an important inspiration for developing a novel conceptualization of the politics of experience as derived from the affective-emotional encounter with a *work of art* (understood in new materialist terms). In order to illustrate these processes in a more tangible way, I offer analyses of selected contemporary material memorial artifacts immersed in the complex meaning-making practices. I also reflect on the ways they affectively and intellectually relate to and interact with the bodies of spectators/visitors. This implies an understanding of memorial art in terms of intermediality of connections produced within different interactions, which seems to correspond with the multimedia nature of memories in a more general sense.

APPROACHES TO TRAUMA: AN OVERVIEW

Recently, trauma—in its different manifestations—has become emblematic for cultural sensibility, while trauma theory has been turned into a prominent analytical tool in contemporary cultural and literary criticism. This resulted in a thorough (re)examination of the existing theories of and approaches to the concept of trauma as well as in the development of new theoretical perspectives and their novel applications. Obviously, the increased interest in such issues as trauma or, more generally, memory, especially as related to the Holocaust studies, has to be understood in a broader historical, political, and cultural context. One thing is undoubtedly the turn of the millennia, which—rather unsurprisingly—evokes decadent reflections on the past and triggers discussions on how it is implicated in the present as well as in the future. Another thing is the passing away of the Holocaust survivors and witnesses, and so the disappearance of those who can provide personal testimonies of these events and validate them historically. This situation stimulates thinking on how their first-hand knowledge of what happened could be preserved and passed on to new generations. Yet another thing is the increasing politicization of memory, and especially of traumatic events, as they are often instrumentalized and turned into tools in current political conflicts in which they repeatedly serve as a means for advancing specific national(ist) projects (which I discussed in the previous chapter). This list of factors contributing to the growing interest in trauma studies is certainly not exhaustive, yet it already sheds light on why this research area has recently emerged as an important field for interdisciplinary criticism as well as a meaningful subject of multidisciplinary investigations.

Already from its inception at the turn of the nineteenth and twentieth centuries, scholars and practitioners located within the field of trauma studies have not spoken in one voice. Broadly, two lines of historically theorizing (and, subsequently, treating) trauma could be identified. In her complete and impressive study Ruth Leys, taking on a genealogical perspective, scrutinizes the record of psychotherapeutic approaches to trauma and concludes that there have been competing and conflicting tendencies on how it has been conceptualized and cured. She also points out that the field of trauma studies today continues to lack cohesion and struggles with much the same conundrums and challenges (2000, 6–7). Yet it also poses new problems and offers novel understandings and theorizations. Noticeably, in recent years, a lot of attention within trauma studies has been devoted to the research on the body and *corporeal* memory (rather than the mind and *narrative* memory associated therewith), while "traumatic memory" has started to be explained in neurobiological terms (Van der Kolk and Van der Hart 1995). This shift of perspectives has stimulated the development of a number of fresh approaches to trauma, focusing more explicitly on the embodied forms of knowing and how these modes differ from more conventional (or representational) ways of generating knowledge or memorizing and remembering events.

Yet, in order to provide a general overview of this research field, it is necessary to first briefly come back to the genealogies of trauma. As Leys aptly notices, "From the moment of its invention in the late nineteenth century the concept of trauma has been fundamentally unstable, balancing uneasily—indeed veering uncontrollably—between two ideas, theories or paradigms" (2000, 298). What she calls a *mimetic* approach can be aligned with Freudian psychoanalytical developments and focuses on processes of the unconscious identification and psychic regression that result in certain compulsive behaviors, and prompts the traumatized subjects to (re)enact the traumatic event. Trauma overwhelms the victim in such a profound way that it precludes any possibility of "specular distance necessary for cognitive knowledge of what had happened" (Leys 2000, 9). And, as such, the traumatic scene remains dissociated and unavailable for representational processing. This is prevailingly why the victim has no recollection of the original traumatogenic event, as the extremity of this experience "shatters or disables the victim's cognitive and perceptual capacities so that the experience never becomes part of the ordinary memory system" (Leys 2000, 298). Yet the victim can be stimulated to reenact it through, for instance, hypnosis (Leys 2000, 298).[1] The *antimimetic* perspective, by contrast, mostly ignores the work of the unconscious in positioning an experience as traumatic and argues instead for a "strict dichotomy between the autonomous subject and the external event" where the latter is seen as befalling "a fully constituted if passive subject" (Leys 2007, 9). The traumatized person is essentially aloof from the traumatic experience and in a sense "remains a spectator of the traumatic scene," which means that the very scene can be "seen," recognized, and represented to both oneself and others (Leys 2000, 299). For the proponents of the antimimetic approach, the issue of recollecting the event does not constitute a problem (although in practice it can pose substantial difficulties), as trauma—considered external to the subject who experiences it—remains a part of the individual's memory and thus can be recovered from it (the torturous nature of the recovery process notwithstanding). This approach, as Leys explains, has remained in concord with positivist and scientistic interpretations of trauma, so widely accepted today (Leys 2000, 10). The tension, or oscillation, between the two competing paradigms of conceptualizing trauma is, as Leys seems to suggest, still discernible within the field of trauma studies even though new theories are being formulated and new approaches are being adopted.

In the 1990s a novel strand within the theories of trauma emerged. These new theorizations drew heavily on deconstructive linguistics on the one hand

and on neurobiological research on the other hand. Inspired by philosophies of language and applying analytical tools worked out within the field of literary studies, they have been extremely influential for contemporary cultural criticism focusing on trauma, especially in the context of post-Holocaust memory. Consequently, they have gained significant respect among scholars working on issues connected with testimonies of witnesses, post-Holocaust art, and diverse strategies of remembrance. Since some of these formulations are particularly salient for the argumentation that this book offers, a cursory overview of the recently developed theorizations of trauma would provide a necessary background for my investigations. Importantly, I also find these approaches particularly interesting in the context of the new materialist perspective that this book fosters, as they put emphasis on the hitherto-neglected bodily, or extralinguistic, aspects of processes of remembering, pointing simultaneously to the substantial limitations of representational thinking.

In 1992 Shoshana Felman and Dori Laub published their remarkable work entitled *Testimony*, which since its release has started to be considered a milestone in contemporary trauma studies. Surprisingly for the critics, in their analysis, the two authors brought together a deconstructive literary criticism and the recordings of testimonies of Holocaust survivors. The deconstructive strategy implemented in this work served as a tool to identify the means by which the traumatic past can be revealed indirectly, that is, through silences, gaps, omissions, and erasures. Noticeably, such literary devices had usually been seen as irrelevant, or of marginal importance at most, for the meaning of the texts. These repressed elements of both survivors' testimonies and literary works emerged in the study as ways of dealing with the traumatic past, contributing to a more persuasive (and affective) account thereof. Thusly construed, the work examined a complex relation between history and witnessing. The abundance of different points of view discernible in survivors' accounts pointed to, according to the authors, "the crisis of witnessing" and revealed significant shortcomings of the mechanism of representation in this regard. This resulted in what has come to be known as, in Michael Rothberg's words, a new "traumatic realism" (2000). As Allen Meek notices, the work by Felman and Laub contributed to the "validation of testimony as cultural form"; at the same time "trauma had been isolated and elevated as a cultural category," yet it has also been in a sense removed from a wider cultural and political context (2014, 21–22). This, undoubtedly, has been a meaningful move, offering substantial contribution to the broader field of trauma studies. Moreover, it should also be perceived as an important addendum to the field of literary studies. As a result, trauma theory—in its diverse formulations and shapes—constitutes an indispensable aspect of cultural criticism nowadays.

An interesting, and extremely influential (although not received uncritically), contribution to the contemporary trauma studies was made by a literary critic, Cathy Caruth (1995a, 1996), whose oeuvre draws heavily on the work of an American physician Bessel Van der Kolk and his associates. Bearing in mind this important inspiration, before I turn directly to Caruth's argumentation (salient in the field of contemporary memory studies, in general, and Holocaust studies, in particular), I need to offer a brief comment on Van der Kolk's findings, located at the intersection of neurobiology and psychiatry. Central for this author is the claim that external trauma leaves a *literal imprint* on the memory of the victim. This trace, however, resides in the traumatic memory system (i.e., it does not function as a part of narrative memory) and defies any possibility of representation, hence also of expression. For Van der Kolk traumatic memory is of a "non-declarative" type; it involves bodily responses that lie outside verbal-semantic-linguistic representation (Van der Kolk and Van der Hart 1995, 160). Such conceptualization points to the crisis, or limit, of purely representational processing, which is a claim that has gained significant respect within the contemporary humanities.

Not surprisingly, similar formulations can be found in the works of Cathy Caruth, situated within the paradigms of postmodernist, poststructuralist, and performative theories of culture. As Leys notices, Caruth's approach (although critiqued) has received a significant approbation among humanists as well as psychiatrists and physicians (2000, 266). In her argumentation Caruth combines the work on literary deconstructive criticism on trauma (more precisely, performative theories of language) with neurobiological findings and empirical neuroscience.[2] Her main claim is that massive trauma lies beyond linguistic cognition and, therefore, beyond conventionally understood knowledge. This is mostly because of the fact that in the case of traumatic experience ordinary mechanisms of consciousness and memory are temporarily sustained or destroyed. What occurs instead is a material and undistorted (or *literal*, as Caruth prefers) registration of the event that cannot be known or processed in cognitive terms but repeatedly returns in the form of nightmares. A nightmare is exactly what Caruth (1996) calls an "unclaimed experience"—a literal and nonrepresentational memory of the trauma. Consequently, in her influential book entitled *Trauma: Explorations in Memory* (1995a), while introducing essays by Claude Lanzmann and Dori Laub, Caruth argued for substantial difficulty in, or even impossibility of, adequately representing any traumatic experience. In that sense, not only does a traumatic event pose a limit case for psychiatry but also it remains impervious to historical or literary analysis (1995b, 4). Therefore, it should be seen as an authentic yet cognitively inaccessible experience—the traumatic event "is not assimilated or experienced fully at the time, but only belatedly, in its repeated possession of the one who experiences it. To be traumatized is precisely to be possessed by the image or event" (1995b, 4–5). For Caruth traumatic events are nonsymbolic and in that sense they should be considered *immediate* and *material* historical embodiments of the traumatic past, as they return in the form of petrifying flashbacks.[3] The *literal* nature of such memory signifies that in trauma, in Caruth's words, "the outside has gone inside without any mediation" (1996, 59). The act of witnessing the past is therefore paradoxical since it resists representation and, consequently, also memory. It means that the conventional notion of memory (as necessarily narrative and, therefore, fundamentally representational) cannot be applied to approach such cases. Instead, both Caruth and Van der Kolk conceive of traumatic memory as consisting of direct, indexical traces left by an empirical identity. Since the original traumatic event eludes conscious memory, for Caruth, it must keep on returning in a form of literal repetition, or truthful experience of a traumatic event.[4] The flashback is here defined as "an interruption . . . that . . . cannot be thought simply as a representation" and associated with the "interruption of a representational mode" that Caruth relates to Paul de Man's work on deconstruction of language (1996, 115, note 6). Therefore, although the traumatized person cannot narrate or symbolically represent the traumatic event, he or she still reexperiences or performs it. Logically, trauma, for Caruth, "is not fully perceived as it occurs," and henceforth, any recollection of the traumatic past "can be grasped only in the very inaccessibility of its occurrence" (1995b, 8). If Caruth's approach were to be situated in the context of the two traditional lines of theorizing trauma referenced earlier, it could be argued (following Leys) that it, at least partly, contributes to the collapse of this distinction. As Leys writes, "Caruth posits an absolute opposition between external trauma and victim in ways that have been associated historically with the repudiation of mimesis." Yet, on the other hand, "by imaging that trauma stands outside representation altogether, she also embraces a version . . . of the mimetic theory" (Leys 2000, 17).[5]

Obviously, locating trauma beyond the representational realm poses challenges for the conceptualization of the notion of memory, especially as far as mnemonic storage of traumatic experiences is concerned. Let me then come back to the issue of traumatic memory and its positioning vis-à-vis a more common concept of narrative memory in order to both clarify differences between the two and, somewhat paradoxically, point to their profound entwinement. This will be instrumental in developing later a new materialist view on both memory and knowledge, indicating their material-semiotic as well as virtual-actual nature.

TRAUMATIC MEMORY, OR A HAUNTING PAST

The question of the presence of traumatic experience within, or its translation into, the representational realm has been widely discussed by trauma studies scholars focusing on whether a traumatic event can or cannot be represented (i.e., also remembered and expressed) in linguistic terms. Towards the end of the twentieth century, and partly thanks to the emergence of such works as those by Felman and Laub (1992), Van der Kolk and Van der Hart (1995), or Caruth (1995a, 1995b, 1996) mentioned earlier, the issue of (un)representability of trauma acquired currency among cultural critics and has become a major concern for memory studies scholars, especially in the context of (post) Holocaust studies. Within this field of multidisciplinary research, the Shoah is often considered a watershed event of the modern times, a uniquely terrible and unspeakable experience. Considering the inexpressible nature of traumatic occurrences, most up-to-date research on trauma, as discussed in the preceding part of this chapter, has indicated that we should think of memory also in corporeal terms and that trauma could be considered an assemblage of embodied experiences, often eluding the processes of signification. For if trauma escapes representational framing, how (if at all) could this experience be memorized, remembered, and—eventually—transmitted to others? What kind of theory of memory is needed if we want to incorporate traumatic events into it, especially if we consider the latter as unutterable and situated beyond the cognitive realm? Such a perspective necessarily demands a nonrepresentational, or more-than-representational, approach to memory and calls for a considerable expansion, or pluralizing, of the traditional understandings of memorizing processes.

As referenced in Bessel Van der Kolk and Onno Van der Hart's work, Pierre Janet—a French psychiatrist working at the beginning of the twentieth century to whose theorizations their research is indebted—introduced distinctions between three modes of memory. These include habit memory, narrative memory, and traumatic memory (1995, 158–82). Accordingly, habit memory automatically integrates new information without paying conscious attention to what is actually happening. Narrative memory is about making sense out of experience through imposing existing recognizable mental constructs and meaningful structures on it. Traumatic memory, different from the previous two, consists of events and experiences that resist integration within the accessible cognitive schemes—they can either be vividly remembered or resist memorizing altogether (Van der Kolk and Van der Hart 1995, 160). These "memories" (although the use of the term "memory" here is only for the purpose of convenience, as typically understood memory is fundamentally representational) are stored differently and cannot be easily retrieved—they become "dissociated from conscious awareness and voluntary control" (Van der Kolk and Van der Hart 1995, 160) and, therefore, remain suspended in an unintegratable mode. Trauma, as a failed experience, is impossible to remember in voluntary ways; it cannot be narrated. Narration would demand certain distance towards the event as it is effectuated after it has happened. In the case of trauma, however, the person remains within the event that resists mediation and reimposes itself directly as present, that is, it is always happening "here and now." Such a division between the different modes of storing information clearly sets the traumatic experiences aside all others, granting them a specific status and situating them away from the representational, or symbolic, manners of remembering. Virtualized and lingering beyond the cognitive schemes, the traumatic memory can actualize itself unexpectedly (in a form of, for instance, specific bodily symptoms), absorbing the subject who is temporarily (and often passively) possessed by the traumatic event, hanging in between what is conventionally called the past and the present. In fact, it is both—a sudden actualization of the virtuality of the always-present past. Here and now.

Adopting a stance similar to Janet's, when writing about her experience and memories of Auschwitz, Charlotte Delbo (quoted at the beginning of this chapter) points to the meaningful difference between what she calls "common memory" (*mémoire ordinaire*) and "deep memory" (*mémoire profonde*) (cf. Delbo 1965, 1970, 1971). For her, common memory manages to situate the traumatic event chronologically in the past, which might testify to the survivor's redemption from the horror of the Holocaust. Conversely, deep memory never adopts such a distance. In that sense, the event still operates as present and haunts the survivor on an everyday basis. This distinction corresponds with another one made by Delbo, that is, a difference between external memory (articulated, for instance, in the act of narration, again through establishing a distance between the event and its narrative representation) and sense memory (a physical memory, symptomatic for Auschwitz, that defies narration, yet whose ongoing presence constantly makes itself experienced and felt). Sense memory, for Delbo (2001), registers a physical imprint of the event. As such, it operates always in the present, although it is not continuously experienced.

The nature of these two modes of remembering remains dynamic and entangled as they never operate in complete isolation from each other. They might account for varying degrees of working through the traumatic past, that is, for gaining a critical distance towards it that would testify to the process of coming to terms with trauma. Nonetheless, as Delbo's case reveals, the survivors of trauma are often subjects to distinctive yet overlapping modes of remembering that could manifest themselves in different situations and contexts. Any attempt at singling out one mode of "memory" from the other must therefore remain solely provisional.

Such views as Janet's or Delbo's are not isolated; however, the distinctive work of these two authors constitutes a meaningful inspiration for more contemporary theoretical formulations. Akin claims about unrepresentability of traumatic experiences have been expressed by Shoshana Felman mentioned earlier, who writes about this matter in the important context of what she refers to as "the crisis of witnessing," that is, an epistemo-ontological puzzle (which is a crisis manifested at the level of language itself). These critical developments have translated into trauma theory being mostly concerned with the contradictory, or in a sense inconsistent, condition of traumatic memory as well as with the challenges that these understandings pose for such concepts as truth, representation, a historical account of events, or a testimony (Felman and Laub 1992, Felman 2002). Trauma, as in a way a liminal condition, explodes the traditional distinction between fiction and fact, generating what Felman and Laub called "a crisis of truth" (1992). Its literal reality refutes metaphysical recognition and resists linguistic framing; therefore, trauma cannot entirely enter the realm of what is called a narrative memory. Eluding processes of signification, trauma remains in a limbo, as never actually recognized and known, a virtuality on the verge of actualization, yet never completely actualized. Adopting an analogous logic, Judith Herman asserts that traumatic memories "are encoded in the form of vivid sensations and images" rather than being captured in "verbal narrative and context" (1997, 38). For Joshua Hirsch, similarly, there is a fundamental gap between the witnessed or experienced event and its mindful comprehension. Trauma cannot be situated within a coherent narrative and its recollection remains "intact and unassimilated" (2004, 15). It lingers between a mode of memory that is communicable through bodily symptoms or sensations and translates into a constant reenactment of the traumatic event and a mode of memory that is profoundly mediated and indirect, partly interpreted through symbolic schemes.

What I want to make clear in this chapter is that acknowledging the entangled nature of the manners of memorizing demands an extended understanding of the processes of "seeing," which are not solely grounded in a traditionally conceptualized procedure of registering the event and—through the mediation of the subject (and linguistic concepts)—representing it to oneself. Rather, it is about seeing with the whole body, *a synaesthetic perception*, a material process that engages bodily senses and sensibilities, an immediate registering that eludes purely representational structuring (as discussed in chapter 1). In such a case we do not deal exclusively with the process of "slowing down" of the input of experiences (images) that need to be recognized and ordered into logical sequences with an aim of being intellectually captured and comprehended. As exposed in the earlier-referenced works of many scholars, trauma does not follow this logic; rather, it dislocates this way of thinking, exposing its inconsistencies and serious limitations. As Ernst Van Alphen argues, the experiences of Holocaust victims have radically disrupted the link between the traditionally conceived seeing and comprehension; in survivors' testimonies, "the visual functions more like the unmodified return of what happened, instead of as a mode of access to or penetration into what happened" (2002, 207).

When discussing an account of an act of witnessing devoid of any emotional or ethical dimension, yet functioning as a visual recording, Van Alphen introduces a distinction between images understood as imprints and images functioning as representations. Whereas the former are neither worked through nor emotionally experienced, the latter have been representationally processed and automatically comprehended, that is, turned into knowledge (2002, 206). Accordingly, the nature of witnessing the events of Shoah (as well as of other traumatic occurrences) is, for Van Alphen, more like a visual imprint left on the memory that defies representational processing—"The image is there; it refuses to budge," he writes (2002, 207). Importantly, these imprints are never *purely* visual. Their nature is at least partly material, as they leave impressions on the traumatized subject. After all, the etymology of the verb "to impress" comes from Latin *imprimere*, meaning "to press into" or "to stamp," which already signals a certain physicality of this process. Thusly conceived, trauma leaves material-semiotic imprints on both the body and the mind of a subject; traumatic experience, therefore, should be conceptualized and approached in affective-emotional terms.

As mentioned earlier, theoretical perspectives situating trauma beyond a purely representational realm have gained significant respect among scholars located within the fields of memory studies, cultural studies, and Holocaust studies. Apart from that, they could also serve as an interesting inspiration for philosophers of knowledge or epistemologists, and especially those interested in new materialism. Worth noticing is the fact that in the context of such conceptualizations of trauma not only do we have to recognize the crisis of representation but also we need to tackle a more general issue of the crisis of traditionally defined knowledge. For if knowledge—in its most prevalent formulation—emerges from representational practices, something that cannot be captured by words or images (or that does not function within the linguistic structures and schemes) cannot be comprehended and (re)cognized (recognition, in the end, is about canalizing an experience into the already-existent cognitive schemes; it is therefore about "knowing" by subordinating "the new" to "the already known"). Yet, as evidenced in the works of many scholars, these memories or "knowledges," although representationally "unknown," still exist as well as haunt and inform the present (and future) on an everyday basis. A question should be posed: How, in such instance, shall we do justice to these forms of knowing? In order to be capable to think about these memories *as* knowledges, it is necessary to both transcend the historical metaphysical dualism between the mind and the body and concede that bodies are equipped with certain cognitive faculties and function as active entities generating knowledges, even though these knowledges do not necessarily or easily (if at all) translate into recognizable schemes.

In this context, it could be informative to briefly come back to the etymological origins of the notion of trauma, which initially stood for a physical wound (from *trau-* [extended form of *tere-*], meaning "to rub" or "to turn"). Trauma, in its most literal sense, is a wound inflicted on the body. And, as Roberta Culberstone writes, "no experience is more one's own than harm to one's own skin, but none is more locked within that skin, played out within it in actions other than words, in patterns of consciousness below the everyday and the constructions of language" (1995, 170). Such a formulation explicitly signals the enfleshed, physical nature of traumatic memory. Only in the late nineteenth century was the current understanding of the term "trauma" forged. Since then it has started to be associated with a psychic wound/injury or an experience causing abnormal stress. Yet the "physicality" of the traumatic event (and its embodied consequences or its corporal dimension) still informs even the most up-to-date definition of this concept.

As it can be concluded from the earlier theorizations, in the case of trauma, the notion of conventional memory as constituted in the process of transforming experience into a representation should be overridden. At the same time, however, the distinction between narrative (representational) and traumatic (uncontainable in language) modes of memorizing must remain solely analytical and profoundly unstable, as it is impossible to clearly divide between the different manners in which memory operates. The various forms of remembering—symbolic (semiotic, representational, or emotional) and enfleshed (material, sensory, or affective)—are entangled and coexist simultaneously nourishing and informing each other. Consequently, if we adhere to this provisional distinction, it may be argued that whereas the narrative memory can be consciously referenced and represented in figurative terms, the traumatic one can be activated only through mobilization of affects. As Jill Bennett underlines, unlike the former, the latter mode of memory cannot be linguistically canalized in any uncomplicated ways, yet it can be still revived and felt (2005, 22–26).

Certainly, both conceptualization of trauma in terms of a material-semiotic experience and theorization of traumatic memories as partly residing beyond the representational realm have had salient implications for thinking about eventual transhistorical, transgenerational, or transgeographical transmission of the knowledge of the disturbing past/present to others. It also poses important challenges for critically approaching artistic production related to trauma. The issue of (un)representability of traumatic experiences is therefore vividly present in current debates within the fields of cultural, art, and literary studies, in general, and in the research on memorial art, in particular.

TRANSMISSION OF TRAUMA

If trauma defies purely representational signification, how can these difficult experiences be passed to others? How (if at all) those who came after can know (and learn from) the traumas of the past? How is trauma transmitted across generations? Can it be intimately "remembered" by those who did not live through it nor witness it? Can the legacy of a distant past be "inherited" as a bodily knowledge and shape the lives of those who did not experience it? If trauma cannot be expressed in language, could the accounts of the difficult past ever be reliable? As discussed in the previous section, the issue of realism in the representation of traumatic events has been a salient topic in trauma studies (Van Alphen 1997, Rothberg 2000). The field has recently been rather dominated by an anti-representational paradigm—it has been maintained that no representation is capable of fully transmitting the "truth" of the trauma. Although this position has lately been challenged (e.g., Guerin and Hallas 2007), and although Caruth's work on trauma as precluding representation (1995a, 1995b, 1996) inspired substantial critical considerations (e.g., Kaufman 1998, Hungerford 2001, LaCapra 2001, Wolfreys 2002), the view about traumatic experiences being unspeakable still pervades the field. It therefore seems that the problem of representation/unrepresentability of trauma is constructed as a binary, or as a question of "either/or." The construction of a debate between the proponents of mimetic and antimimetic approaches to trauma and its treatment is similar. Grounded in a new materialist framework, both my theoretical argumentation and analyses of case studies serving as its illustration should be perceived as a refusal to participate in such dualism. Instead, my perspective aims at approaching this problem in a more conciliatory fashion, adopting an affirmative, diffractive strategy that allows for combining several—sometimes very different or seemingly conflicting—theorizations together or reading them through one another. Such an approach offers a productive reformulation of the binarized way of thinking, focusing on a complex, entangled nature of mnemonic processes. Moreover, in the context of memorial art, and especially in the case of artistic production related to trauma, such a perspective may possibly lend itself to remembering (and commemorating) histories that resist purely figural representation.

The concept of postmemory tackling the issue of an intergenerational transmission of traumatic experiences is instrumental for my analysis. Coined by Marianne Hirsch in the context of the post-Holocaust memory, it—in her words—"describes the relationship that the generation after those who witnessed cultural or collective trauma bears to the experiences of those who came before, experiences that they 'remember' only by means of the stories, images, and behaviors among which they grew up" (2008, 106). She also emphasizes that "these experiences were transmitted to them so deeply and affectively as to *seem* to constitute memories in their own right" (2008, 106; original emphasis). In that sense, Hirsch explains, postmemory is not connected to the past by "recall." Rather, it is so through "imaginative investment, projection, and creation"—"to grow up with such overwhelming inherited memories, to be dominated by narratives that preceded one's birth or one's consciousness, is to risk having one's own stories and experiences displaced, even evacuated, by those of a previous generation" (2008, 107), Hirsch adds. Although originally employed in the post-Holocaust context, the term may be applied in the analyses of other violent events, dramatic upheavals, and traumatic occurrences, indicating the intense yet atemporal connections between remote situations and distant people. Importantly, as Hirsch claims, the notion of "postmemory" can serve as a point of reference for "connective approaches," as a "form of affiliation across lines of difference" (2012, 21). As such, it can well serve as an important figuration and a starting point for developing a new materialist politics of connectivity (or *sym*pathy, as I will explain later in this book), especially taking into consideration the material-semiotic, or bodily-intellectual, nature of processes of remembering. The "transversal" (Dolphijn and van der Tuin 2010, 2012) philosophy of new materialism offers a useful framework for such ethico-politics.

The link with the past in the case of postmemory is very intense, passionate, and affective; it constantly shapes the present and thus blurs the division between what belongs to the past and what is happening here and now. The inherited trauma of the parents (or, broadly, of the previous generations) manifests itself on an everyday basis. As Hirsch elaborates:

> Children of those directly affected by collective trauma inherit a horrific, unknown, and unknowable past that their parents were not meant to survive. Second-generation fiction, art, memoir, and testimony are shaped by the attempt to represent the long-term effects of living in close proximity to the pain, depression, and dissociation of persons who have witnessed and survived massive historical trauma. They are shaped by the child's confusion and responsibility, by a desire to repair, and by the consciousness that her own existence may well be a form of compensation for unspeakable loss. Loss of family, home, of a sense of belonging and safety in the world "bleed" from one generation to the next. (2012, 34)

On the one hand, the condition of postmemory might be due to a long-lasting exposure to the trauma of close relatives or friends, or a result of living in the shadow of the drama that has never been verbalized and recounted. On the other hand, however, postmemory is triggered by widely available narrativized accounts of the past, the plethora of images and stories populating culture and feeding the public imaginary. Related to both the intimate and the public at the same time, the concept of postmemory testifies to the virtual character of the past and its constant implication in the present. And vice versa—it reveals that the present is always about the past; it continuously molds and reshapes it, nourishing it and being nourished by it; the distinction between the two in the case of postmemory is entirely blurred.

Noticeably, when theorizing the transgenerational nature of postmemory, Hirsch suggests that trauma can be shared, at least to a certain extent, and that although deeply personal and intimate, it might, in a powerful way, affect the lives of those, who were not directly involved in the traumatic events. In fact, similar formulation can be found in Caruth's work (1995a, 1995b, 1996) referenced earlier.[6] She is also convinced that trauma experienced by one person can be passed on to others through the direct encounter between the traumatized subject who (re)enacts the difficult experience from the past and a vulnerable witness of this process, who subsequently becomes contaminated by the trauma of the other spreading contagiously from one individual to another. Moreover, Caruth's model assumes that transmission of trauma can also occur across space and time, and affect later generations whose representatives take over the traumatic memories of others, including of those who died long ago (1996, 71). This signals the possibility of "remembering" someone else's experiences, which would testify to the collapse of the history into the personalized memory. It also indicates certain politics of reflexive connectivity based on the consideration of how trauma—characterized by temporal unlocatability—"may lead . . . to the encounter with another, through the very possibility and surprise of listening to another's wound" (Caruth 1996, 8). This, for Caruth, applies to both individuals and groups (1996, 71). Similar mechanisms of remembering and reviving the traumas that are not one's own in an affective way have been identified by Hirsch in her theory of intergenerational transmission of difficult experiences.

For the purpose of developing the concept of postmemory, Hirsch draws on her own experiences as well as on the works of the artists with a similar background. The starting point for her investigations is provided by the specificity of lives of Holocaust survivors' children (like herself). In her analysis she wonders whether these people can have memories of their parents' suffering or whether in such instance we can deal with some sort of "transactive, transferential processes—cognitive and affective—through which the past is internalized without fully being understood" and how these processes and acts of transfer "enable memories to be shared across individuals and generations" (Hirsch 2012, 31). When elaborating on postmemory as a form of remembering, Hirsch refers to Eva Hoffman's accounts of her intimate experiences concerning the familial trauma. Let me quote this passage at full length:

> Certainly, we do not have literal "memories" of others' experiences, and certainly, one person's lived memories cannot be transformed into another's.

> Postmemory is not identical to memory: it is "post"; but, at the same time . . . it approximates memory in its affective force and its psychic effects. Eva Hoffman describes what was passed down to her as a fairy tale: "The memories—not memories but emanations—of wartime experiences kept erupting in flashes of imagery; in abrupt but broken refrains." These "not memories," communicated in "flashes of imagery," and these "broken refrains," transmitted through "the language of the body," are precisely the stuff of the postmemory of trauma, and of its return. (2012, 31)

Memory, however, must be seen as different from, almost opposed to, history, especially in what Hirsch describes as the "presence of embodied and affective experience in the process of transmission" (2012, 33). Memory, in that understanding, "signals an affective link to the past—a sense, precisely, of a material 'living connection'—and it is powerfully mediated by technologies like literature, photography, and testimony" (2012, 33). The familial, affective (i.e., material) postmemory is therefore also culturally interceded and negotiated. In her famous analysis of Art Spiegelman's *The First Maus* (1972), Hirsch pays attention to the important role of widely circulated photographs that drift from the public realm into private imaginary archives. This testifies to the fact that often the Holocaust victims' or survivors' children can only imagine their parents' experiences as filtered through the well-known images and representations, which means that—in Hirsch's words—"even the most intimate familial transmission of the past is, it seems, mediated by public images and narratives" (Hirsch 2012, 30; see also Hirsch 1992–1993). The material imprints produced by the fact of living for years in the shadow of traumatic experiences of a close relative could therefore make sense only in the cultural context of collective or even institutionalized instances of memory that are accessible to those who come after, and facilitate mediation of the otherwise incomprehensible or unthinkable (in representational terms) bodily affects and sensations. In the weird mixture of the bodily and the symbolic, or of the private and the public, the widely accessible images and stories connected to the collective traumatic past become part of and get integrated within an "inner storehouse" (Hoffman 2004, 193). In fact, as Hirsch declares, postmemory "is distinguished from memory by generational distance and from history by deep personal connection" (1997, 22); it falls somewhere in between the two as a memory removed from its source and a personal interpretation of history at the same time. These (non)memories are also situated at the overlap of the private and the cultural, familial, and affiliative and are contingent on both the material, direct connections and the social or cultural factors. These two aspects co-constitute and shape each other—the acts of interpretation, or reading, of the affective bodily memories expose the cultural, often-politicized codes of meaning that are profoundly marked by social differences, generating varied, situated, experiences. Such "events" are simultaneously personal and political, individual and collective, discursive and affective, symbolically interpreted and bodily felt. These diverse dimensions, importantly, can never be separated or singled out from each other; they remain entwined.

Taking into consideration the entangled nature of (post)memory, oscillating between the material and the symbolic, for Hirsch, it cannot be seen in terms of an identity position. Rather, it signals "a *generational* structure of transmission embedded in multiple forms of mediation" as family life is always situated within a broader context, even in its most intimate moments, and as such it is partly shaped by shared fantasies and projections as well as mediated by a collective archive of narratives, images, and stories. It is, therefore, not solely a "biological" transmission but rather one that is culturally structured and socially translated (2012, 35; original emphasis). It does not mean, however, that the trauma from the past can be fully understood or known by those who come after. This idea of missing, or of never being able to comprehend, is present in Ellen Fine's concept of "absent memory" (1998, 187). In her words, the second-generation Holocaust survivors "continue to 'remember' an event not lived through" (1998, 187). Yet an inherent paradox is present as far as the nature of such mnemonic processes is concerned—the sensation experienced as a memory is not in fact a memory. For Fine, "this nonmemory or lack of memory comes from the feeling of exclusion both from the experience and from knowledge about the experience" (1998, 187). Importantly however, in such cases what might be called "the sensation of memory" is present and vividly felt. The knowledge of the event, nevertheless, remains incomplete and imaginary, never fully graspable and comprehensible. It is there; it is not there.

TRAUMA AND THE ARTS

As clarified earlier, within the field of trauma studies traumatic events are prevailingly considered to be uncontainable within existing representational systems, words, images, thoughts, or fantasies; they breach the limits of representation as they are without any historical precedent.[7] Their extremity and horror fall outside of the existing meaning-making structures and cannot be expressed with available words and representations. Neither can we make sense of them by referring to the accessible concepts or terms. Their affects, however, can be registered and—to a certain extent—sensed. What happened has, in the case of trauma, no representation. Henceforth, no communicable knowledge of the event can exist. If there is no knowledge, however, how can others "know" anything about the traumatic past? This is one of the reasons why the problem of trauma's alleged unrepresentability has raised major concerns. For if trauma cannot be adequately represented, there is a risk that it would remain solely an experience of very particular groups (or individuals) and be politicized. Or, as pointed out by other critics, assuming unrepresentability of the traumatic past, we are deemed to make a choice "between inadequate telling and the relegating of trauma to a mystified silence" (Kaplan and Wang 2004, 12). Still others raise the fact that if not captured linguistically, the image of the past will disappear forever and will never be retrieved (Benjamin 1999, 391). For instance, as Hirsch recounts, she turned to the study of memory and—more specifically—of the traumatic past "out of the conviction that . . . it offered a means to uncover and to restore experiences and life stories that might otherwise remain absent from the historical archive" (2012, 15). Furthermore, she continues, the work on memory, understood in terms of a counter-history, "offered a means to account for the power structures animating forgetting, oblivion, and erasure" (2012, 15–16). Moreover, the fact of adopting a feminist lens in these investigations opened an important and previously unacknowledged space for "the consideration of affect, embodiment, privacy, and intimacy as concerns of history" while shifting attention to the "minute events of daily life," tackling "the particular vulnerabilities of lives caught up in historical catastrophe," and acknowledging "differential effects trauma can have on different historical subjects" (2012, 16). Such arguments place emphasis on certain necessity to spread the "knowledge" of traumatic events across individuals, communities, and generations so that they could serve as important sources of reference for more contemporary politics.

The increased interest in trauma theory expressed by scholars working within the fields of literary studies and film studies has led to the eruption of a new set of debates focusing on whether and how trauma could be represented and what the risks of translating it into the realm of language are. These discussions have been conducted in the context of growing proliferation of representations of the traumatic past (and especially of the Shoah) in popular culture, encompassing all sorts of different media—from literary texts and big-budget cinematic productions targeting mass audiences to museums and memorials accessible to wide publics. Considering the difficulties concerning the introduction of trauma into representational realms, are these images not overly inadequate or even obscene? Is it ethical to present these stories, exposing the vulnerable conditions of those who can no longer speak for themselves? What are the risks of such procedures? For Caruth (1996), for instance, the problem lies in an attempt to represent the inherent alterity of trauma. This effort might also result in retraumatization of those who had originally experienced it. Other risks of potential trauma's capturing within the representational structures of language, especially as an expression of, or a vehicle for, personal experience, are those of its possible appropriation or reduction. Trauma becomes obviously mediated and deformed—it is no longer the initial experience but rather a mere imitation (or simulation) of the original event with its affects and emotions.

Concerns about a "secondary traumatization" of those who witness or interact with the imagery of trauma are worth mentioning in this context. Dominck LaCapra (1998) argues that engagement with a work of art related to trauma may enable an experience of a "muted" dose of trauma. Geoffrey Hartman (2000), in a similar vein, writes about spectators of the traumatic imagery as vicariously experiencing a milder version of the original shock that the primary witnesses lived through. Paying attention to traumatic art and considering ethical dilemmas that artists face, Grizelda Pollock writes about a work of art as an "aesthetic event" or "the occasion for an encounter," yet one which "must risk being *traumatising* by releasing affect not immediately containable" (2010, 847; original emphasis). She also critically reflects on whether there are ways of reconnecting with atrocious past events in non-traumatizing ways and opts for politics of connectivity grounded in aesthetic wit(h)nessing (the former concept emerges from the works of Bracha Ettinger; I will come back to it in the last chapter of this book).

Considering the aforementioned problems and challenges, it is necessary to develop different ways of thinking about trauma and its possible shareability, as well as to work out a framework that would do away with a realist aesthetics and focus instead on the ways in which knowledge on trauma can be transmitted interpersonally (or trangenerationally) without remaining vulnerable to appropriation or instrumentalization. Artistic production can be of help here, especially if we approach art in new materialist terms (as I outlined in chapter 1). Such an understanding deals primarily with the processes of art rather than with its "aboutness." In that case the affective responses triggered by a work of art do not necessarily have much to do with an emotional identification but rather emerge from a material-semiotic engagement with a sensation registered in the artwork or sensation that it produces. It is a touching event although not one that would necessarily be communicative in a sense of transmitting personal experience of the other. This can only be understood if we pay attention to the processual nature of a work of art, that is, to the affects that emerge out of the (*synaesthetic*) encounter with it as well as to the intellectual production that this encounter triggers. This is quite different from approaching art through representation (which constitutes our predominant form of knowing). If we stubbornly stick to the traditional definition of art referring to it in representational ways, we will remain blind to the possibility of a different conceptualization of the politics of experience. The latter, in a new materialist spirit, might be derived from the manner in which art registers and embodies affects and how they are encountered in material-semiotic ways. Focusing on affects and sensations (with which the field of art has been engaged for a long period of time, by moving spectators and turning them into the viewers of their own feelings) lets us approach art related to trauma in a different way. No longer is art considered solely a vehicle for an interpersonal transmission of traumatic experience. Instead, what is more important in such an account is how art bears imprints of trauma and how the affective responses engendered by works of art emerge from a direct, material engagement with sensation registered in the work. It poses new challenges for the art—instead of imaging within the realms of the already-known, art needs a creative invention if it is to transmit knowledge about events that overwhelm our capacities to "know." As Michael Rothberg argues, there is a "need for new forms of representation capable of registering the traumatic shock" (2000, 58). It calls for new forms and new ways of imaging to trigger affective, passionate, and knowledgeable modes of engagement. It seems then that only art is capable of negotiating and taming the crisis of knowing, so often indicated in the case of unintelligible traumatic events causing the preconceived cognitive systems to balk.

In the remainder of this chapter I will have a brief look at three permanent artistic installations/permanent commissions that seem to tackle an issue of a corporeal nature of traumatic experiences. Drawing on the assumption that this sort of memory is profoundly material (as related to the body and materialized in it), they also tend to transmit the knowledge about dramatic occurrences via sensual, material, and bodily engagement of viewers, entering in complex interactions with them that potentially leave unforgettable material-semiotic traces. Certainly, as in the case of postmemory, these memorable imprints necessarily function in a sociocultural semiotic context, both widely shared and intimately individual. The three cases analyzed here also seem to trigger reflection on the character of remembering processes, a profound material-semiotic entanglement of past, present, and future. These cases exemplify how contemporary public memorial art embodies trauma and deliberates its compound, multidimensional nature. They also offer a critical insight into ways in which traumatic past actualizes itself in singular, transformational, and dynamic artistic situations.

2146 Stones against Racism (Jochen Gerz, 1993)

Adopting unconventional aesthetics, the memorial work by Jochen Gerz, created clandestinely in cooperation with art students from the Hochschule für Bildende Kunst Saar (Saar College of Visual Art) in Saarbrücken, announces its presence by words rather than traditional visual forms. Plaques reading "Place of the Invisible Memorial" (*Platz des unsichtbaren Mahnmals*) are installed throughout the space, informing passersby that there is something more to this site than what immediately meets the visitor's eye. Reflecting on the nature of mnemonic processes, the memorial seems to exemplify the tension between the representable and the unrepresentable, in a way referring to the character of traumatic memory itself.

The invisible memorial *2146 Stones against Racism* is situated in front of Schloss Saarbrücken, the castle that in the past served as home for the Gestapo and located in the square where on *Kristallnacht* in 1938 the Nazis brought and humiliated the local Jewish population. From the same square in October 1940 the town's remaining Jewish community was deported to Southern France and then further to camps all over Europe. To commemorate the fiftieth anniversary of the horrendous events, as well as to do justice to the material memory of the site, between April 1990 and May 1993, a group of students led by Jochen Gerz (then a visiting professor in one of the Saarbrücken's colleges) made an uncommissioned intervention in public space. This project was initially completely unnoticed by anyone but those involved in this three-year secret, and in fact illegal, activity. Consequently, what commenced in a private context of a classroom soon turned into a guerrilla-style successful memorial project aimed at drawing meaningful connections between past, present, and future.

One group of Gerz's students removed a number of cobblestones from the square, usually at night or at opportune moments, and replaced them with temporary substitutes with metal nails inside so that they could be later easily found with a metal detector. Another group of students were at that time busy researching the names and locations of all Jewish cemeteries existing in Germany before World War II. These sites were later abandoned, vandalized, or shattered. The research was undertaken with a substantial help of Jewish communities in Germany and, eventually, a long list of 2,146 sites was drawn up. Following this, the names of the cemeteries were engraved on the removed cobblestones. They were also inscribed with the date Gerz and his team had rediscovered information of the erstwhile existence of the cemeteries (see Hapkemeyer 1999). Later on, the original—yet already engraved—stones were gradually, in batches of ten to twenty, resituated in place in front of the Saarbrücken Palace, the seat of the state parliament. All the 2,146 stones were, however, placed with the inscribed side facing the ground and therefore the inscriptions made by the artist(s) were completely invisible, so that the monument remained permanently hidden and impossible to be noticed by those without knowledge about its existence. Even though in the course of the project's realization the measure was made public, and the memorial was eventually approved by the state parliament and retrospectively commissioned, there is still nothing to be seen in Saarbrücken's square. The only information about it is in fact the site's official name, which—as a result of approval of the memorial—was renamed as *Platz des unsichtbaren*

Mahnmals. Although every single trace of research performed for the fulfillment of this artistic project, the joint collaboration of the artist and students, and the process of creating the memorial over a total period of three years is concealed, the site attracts visitors inviting them to engage in individual memory exercise. As Andrea Pinotti writes, the project is "an invisible work, a monument structurally kept out of sight in a structural sense of nonumentality" (Pinotti 2015, 79). Actually, the name of the site is the only technique used for making the invisible installation visible. Employing aesthetic strategies based on displaying nothingness, yet simultaneously leaving material traces on the stones-witnesses of the events of the Shoah, *2146 Stones against Racism* constitutes an antithesis of more traditional memorials. Untypically, it is a memorial site to be walked over, reflected on, and negotiated individually by every single passerby. As Mark Callaghan notices, "The conditions found in The Place of the Invisible Monument create this opportunity for personal imaginative authorship of one's own memory-work that, like Gerz's version, remains internal, concealed" (2010).

This invisible, in fact subterranean, memorial seems to embody the compound nature of processes of remembering the traumatic past. It alludes to the complex entanglement of the material and the semiotic, or the unrepresentable and the representable. The memorial character of the site is in fact inscribed into its deep and hidden materiality, which cannot be accessed through visual means. It remains subcutaneous, enfleshed, and etched in the materiality of the site, yet—in fact—its physical traces or material wounds could not be easily narrated in visual manners. Such aesthetic strategy is likely to question the very possibility of building memorials to the atrocious events as well as testifies to the impossibility of expressing traumatic experiences, to making sense of them, and passing knowledge about them to others via representational means. At the same time, these traces in the memorial got reintegrated back into the fabric of everyday life of the city, invisibly documenting its history and bearing testimony to the merciless destruction of a great part of the legacy of German Jewish culture. Therefore, the engraved cobblestones constitute a vanishing monument to vanished people, signaling an irreparable loss, a disappearance of a whole ethnic community. It seems that this great loss left an incurable wound in the texture of the city—it is there, yet it is no longer there at the same time.

Certainly, the knowledge of the material existence of the invisible memorial is activated by linguistic structures, that is, through the name of the place. When visually encountered by the visitors, it triggers the process of memory work. The scarred materiality of the square's cobblestones gets transformed into meanings, conveying a sense of the irrevocable ephemerality of constant material-semiotic becoming, of metamorphous passing and transformation that never leaves the affecting/affected bodies unaltered. Even though the stones were purposely engraved with carefully selected information, in fact their materiality "remembers" the events to which the memorial refers regardless of these inscriptions. These traces, however, remain invisible to observers, as much as those effectuated by Gerz's team. By adding the representational, yet invisible, layer to the site, the artist seems to refer to the imperceptible marks left on the surfaces of the bodies and testifying to their complex histories. They seem to encourage reflection on how to think these tangled memories in times of postmemory, where contemporary relations to such traumatic events exist solely in the ways their histories and details have been passed to generations that came after those who witnessed them. This process makes them necessarily mediated and infused with widely circulating codes and meaning-generating structures, which never do justice to their complex character. It seems to suggest that trauma has not, and could never have, any narrative structure and is deemed to remain partly hidden, engraved deeply in the texture of the affected bodily materiality, a trace that shapes the body, yet never fully actualizes on a representational level.

It appears that by granting agency to the visitors with regard to memorialization, Gerz puts the common meanings at risk, opening them to more singular becomings and negotiations. In that sense, the memorial does not function as a vehicle for preservation of memory but rather fuels its inventive recreation. Gerz attempts to find a means for speaking against authority of imposition of a collective meaning or a single code of remembrance. He favors instead a format of an artifact as intercessor stimulating a debate on the memory work. Such a strategy appears as especially successful as far as inexpressibly horrendous events are concerned. It envisions articulating more personal meanings and individual reflections on both the traumatic past and the processes of incorporating memory of them into the tissue of contemporary social and cultural life. Yet, in this particular case, what is to be remembered—death, destruction, vanishing, absence—cannot be directly recognized, even though these are completely (im)material phenomena.

Concealed underground and embodying a trajectory of disappearance as well as vagueness of memory, this "buried monument" (Malcolm 2004, 130) seems to "commemorate absence" and its own "passing in oblivion" (Kear 2009, 193). Through nonpresence of the representational layer, it re-evokes the materiality of the objects as well as the materiality of loss. It gets discreetly smuggled into here and now. In fact, all that is seen there is that nothing is to be seen. Yet the memorial assumes a direct, bodily contact with the visually nonexistent—it is to be experienced viscerally but also materially as visitors have to walk on it while knowing what lays hidden in the ground. Hence, although the memorial remains physically invisible, the recording of its existence is there and can be "felt." Its representational dimension is reduced to a form of modest narration, which activates a material-semiotic process of memory work. The artist employs invisibility in service of seeking new aesthetic forms of interactions relying on the materiality of the quasi-immaterial, or the quasi-incorporeal.

Realized through "the artistic choice of physical disappearance of the visual image from the viewers' field of perception" (Aceti 2009, 31), Gerz's work exemplifies a nonrepresentational, self-thematizing memorial that self-reflexively debates the difficulties inherent in public commemoration. Such self-abnegating formats, in Henry Pickford's words, "do not provide a convenient closure of universal reconciliation, [but] do provide another kind of closure, that of historical causality and agency" (Pickford 2013, n.p.), pointing to the transience of the ever-incomplete task of remembrance, especially as far as traumatic past is concerned. *2146 Stones against Racism* embodies the dynamic entanglement of the visibility and invisibility, or the discursive and the bodily, so emblematic—as explained earlier in this chapter—for processes of remembering embedded in both the narrative and the corporeal memory. Combining the intimate (the material) and the monumental (the semiotic), it is a memorial about memory itself, a landscape of experience, or an attempt to create a fragile immediacy while eliciting historical consciousness.

The Memorial to the Murdered Jews of Europe (Peter Eisenman, 2005)

Erected in 2005 in direct proximity to the Brandenburg Gate, Peter Eisenman's *Memorial to the Murdered Jews of Europe* comprises a grid of approximately 2,700 rectangular-sectioned gray stony pillars. The material organization of the vastly spreading site is arresting. Occupying an immense urban territory, the memorial can be approached from all sides. Neither does it possess one point of entrance nor one premeditated route to follow. It has no specific point to be reached by visitors, no central focus, no culmination of the architectural space. The site emerges as boundless and inexhaustible. Remaining in accord with countermonumental aesthetics, Eisenman's memorial—already in its conceptual phase—evoked mixed reactions. It was described as open to interpretation (Carrier 2005), an "inextricable maze" (Rauterberg 2005),[8] or a narrative without continuity (Till 2005). Offering opportunities of civic engagement of visitors with themselves rather that history (Dekel 2013), the site tends to refrain from, in Irit Dekel's words, "imposing memorial etiquette" (2009, 82). Instead, it implodes "existing systems of memorialization" (Dekel 2009, 173). The massive scale of the centrally located memorial site triggered, on the one hand, ferocious criticism—the site was perceived as embodying "monumentalization of shame" (Walser 1998, 15), as too vast and too central. Yet, on the other hand, it was also read in positive manners—Aleida Assmann expressed hope that due to its centrality and extensiveness, the memorial would serve as "a kind of replacement cemetery for the cemeteries that do not exist" (Assmann and Frevert 1999, 69–72). Certainly, the memorial site functions within an important context of the troubled German memory of the Shoah (as it was described in chapter 2), but its most intense operations rely on its persuasive materiality as well as its impressive breadth. Interestingly, the memorial's wavy format seems to suggest the unfinished nature of procedures of memory work. It also implies singularity of processes of commemoration as the pillars are separate from each other; nevertheless, they form a consistent block. Such a design may also be read as referring to the same trauma, yet experienced individually by each person involved (cf. Young 2000, 210).[9]

The compound material-semiotic character of the site translates into visitors' complex memorial experience generated within the affective-intellectual encounter with the memorial space. Interestingly, the nature of this assemblage evokes the composite construction of mnemonic processes. This was very well captured in Giorgio Agamben's review of the site (2005). In his short analysis, Agamben distinguished between the "memorable" (*Erinnerbares*) and the "unforgettable" (*Unvergessliches*). Whereas the former refers to the representable and the recognizable (i.e., to what can be conveyed by texts, photographs, numbers, maps, and documents), the latter is a dimension of memory that could not be so contained, that which is unspeakable and illegible. Contrary to most traditional memorials and monuments functioning through provision of representations (images and texts), Eisenman's oeuvre offers a "book of stone" whose illegible pages "can neither be inscribed or read" (Agamben 2005). Agamben's discussion identifies two—nevertheless entangled—modes of memory: one grounded in representational structures and straightforward narratives and one located beyond the representational realm. Such a distinction clearly refers to the investigations presented earlier in this chapter testifying to the complexity of mnemonic processes, especially as it concerns the memory of traumatic events. The strikingly irresistible material organization of the site embodies the horror of the perished, yet also testifies to the torturous process of incorporating the perplexed memory of the Shoah into the texture of contemporary German society and culture.

Both the overwhelming structure and imposing appearance of the site result from a sagaciously planned designing process. As Mark Godfrey explains, the arresting form of the memorial field was determined through the circumspect procedure of inventing two distinct wavy topographies, each undulating differently. He further clarifies that "each topography was then divided into an identical grid of rectangular sections, with narrow pathways between them. One topography was placed above the other. . . . The columns simply joined the rectangular sections in the top grid to these in the bottom grid. The columns vary in height and tilt because the two topographies were not parallel sheets, but differently irregular" (2007, 244). There is a striking contrast between the rational, carefully conducted process of designing the memorial and the surprisingly violent effects that it generates. Even though the space seems to be outstandingly regular, resulting from the customary geometrical distribution of the pillars and the uniformity of the navigational choices left to visitors, the actual walk through the memorial generates distorted experiences and unexpected physical impressions. The pillars differ in height, and while most of them rise up perpendicular to the ground, some suddenly lurch and lean at different angles while the ground tilts and undulates. As Godfrey notices, when facing east or west, the corridor's soil seems to be constant and the space homogenously oppressive; when facing south or north, there is more of a sense of disturbance and intrusion because the ground undulates (2007, 241). Hence, the space is only seemingly repetitive and monotonous. In fact, its rational or geometrically predictable design produces distorting and thwarting effects.

The forceful operations of the memorial do not rely solely on the material persuasiveness of its appearance. They are contingent on, and result from, the continuous spatial movement of the visitor's body through the field. Only in motion do the qualities of the site emerge with their full articulacy. This is when the seemingly systematic site actualizes as physically discomforting and inhospitable. The walk within the outwardly structured architectural space is likely to make the visitor conscious of the ostensibly random nature of the navigation as well as it reveals a superficial standardization of the directional choices offered to the visitor. Every encountered crossroad invites the visitor to move forward or backward, and turn to the right or to the left. Even though the choice seems to be always identical, in fact it recurs as always new and forces the visitor to decide where to proceed. One might expect that the arresting regularity of the grid makes steering through the stony field uncomplicated and predictable, but after taking the first navigational choices, the visitor may easily become confused and disoriented. This feeling gets amplified by the lack of a more general perspective and turns the walk through the memorial into an unsettling adventure.

The irregular, uneven undulations of the soil are experienced by the visitor physically, turning explorations of the space into an activity surprisingly more demanding than originally expected. Depending on visitor's decision, the route through the memorial may involve different undulations, varied in terms of regularity. Sensed bodily, the encounter with such a wavy ground is likely to be disquieting and troubling—the seemingly systematic terrain evokes feelings of physical fickleness, instability, and hesitation. There is a sensation of permanent vacillation and uncertainty. The volatile interaction with the hyperrationally planned memorial field seems to generate anxious material effects.

The disconcerting spatial experience of the memorial field is complicated with its acoustic and olfactory qualities that synaesthetically combine with its visual immensity. A physical encounter of the visitor and the site generates dulled sounds that resonate with the stony landscape, vibrantly (re)entering all participating entities. A culturally mediated feeling of a dramatic solitude that the overwhelming material organization of the memorial is likely to evoke is therefore magnified with the equally material sonic sensations, jointly produced and received by the assemblage of bodies, and leaving almost imperceptible, yet memorable, traces on the materialities of entities involved in the process. Severe stony smell—born in the performance of molecules emerging in contact with the sensorial apparatus of the visitor—contributes to the feeling of isolation and, simultaneously, is shaped by its cultural meaning. The materiality and the idea coexist within sensation.

As evidenced, the memorial space operates through constant, always new intra-actions of the material and the semiotic generated in a creative encounter of different bodies. If we focus exclusively on one dimension of the memorial experience produced there, never will we be able to grasp its compound complexity. The massive materiality of the site is itself physically overwhelming, yet only in the assemblage with culturally mediated meanings does it enable and trigger the enduring process of memory work.

The site gradually removes the visitor from the surrounding urban landscape, which is achieved by means of oppressive and irresistible physicality of the place. When entering the memorial field, visitors' bodies rise high above the massive stellae, but when they continue walking, the blocks become higher to the point that the visitors may feel completely seized by the stony landscape. They become immersed in the memorial field without having a possibility to see anything that surrounds the site. This transition appears to be surprisingly immediate, which is achieved by an architectural organization of the wavy space, that is, by lowering the level of the ground and simultaneously heightening the pillars. The shift is likely to be sensed bodily, as the removal of the visitor's body from the urban territory seems to be strikingly unanticipated. Hence, the spatial organization of the memorial works as a material-semiotic agent, which—in a vibrant encounter with the visitors—forms a field of emergence for meanings and signifying structures. These interpretations are produced and sustained materially, yet also the nature of their materiality itself emerges out of these interpretations.

The whole experience—triggered by the overwhelming physicality of the site, and produced in a dynamic series of visual, acoustic, olfactory, and haptic micro-assemblages constantly feeding and informing each other—has a singular and unrepeatable character. The meanings generated in this multiplicity of encounters emerge in an amalgam of visuo-tactile assemblages in which the materiality of the space and the cultural meanings ascribed to its physical qualities jointly produce entangled sensations and emotions. The body of the visitor dashes with the materiality of the field to perform together in order to produce an enduring memorial event. Various effects generated in an encounter of the terrain with visitors' bodies produce and sustain disconcerting memorial character of the site. The experiences of the viewers, however, are by no means homogenous or similar to each other. Rather, these individual performances are totally open to the precariousness and variations of memory work, assuming a never-finished character of mnemonic processes. The memorial experience produced therein exceeds the spatiotemporal boundaries of the site of remembrance, leaving resilient impressions on the bodies involved in the event.

Gravity (Richard Serra, 1993)

Commissioned by and installed in the Hall of Witness in the USHMM Washington, DC, Richard Serra's *Gravity* (1993) seems to embody the weight of the Holocaust drama and refer to the nature of traumatic memory. It is a twelve-by-twelve-foot steel plate, weighting nearly 30 tons, that tilts slightly into the base of a steep staircase. The massive slab appears as if it has just accidentally fallen from the top level, yet its placement was carefully selected. Visitors seem to follow the movement of the steel slab. Located at the bottom of the stairs—as a site-specific processual work of art—it enters into creative assemblage with its architectural environment.

The idea is to exacerbate the sense of descent (which magnifies the impression of the block's massive weight), as visitors go down the stairs and encounter the sculpture for the first time—from the top of the Hall of Witness' staircase. In the context of the Holocaust museum, it might elude a feeling of materializing a procedure of descending into the unknown darkness. When seen for the first time, *Gravity* appears as flat and two dimensional, and, initially, it is difficult to say what position the piece occupies. It cuts across the stairs, forces a rift in visitors' flow, and interrupts the most natural route they would probably take. At the same time, it looks relatively small compared to the mammoth dark granite wall against which it is situated. The form divides the space in which it is located, bisecting the steps that take visitors from the open space of the atrium to the museum's lower-level galleries. Visitors are forced to move around the sculpture—there is a decision to be taken whether they would pass it on the right or on the left side. This creates an impression of people being sorted out by the ruthless steel structure which—in the context of a space that resembles the train station—might bring to mind the process of classification of people as far as their fate is concerned (cf. Grunewald 1992).

Gravity's shape and positioning is more complex than it appears at first glance. From above, the block seems to stand upright. Then, when approached, the sculpture tilts downward to the right. After a couple of further steps down, visitors again perceive the slab as standing perpendicular to the floor—this is when they look at it along the axis of its diagonal direction. This is because, as Mark Godfrey carefully details,

> the corner of the stairs is angled away from the corner of the walls beyond it, and Gravity is (unexpectedly) aligned along the intersecting axis of the wall's corner, while cutting into the staircase off its corner.
>
> A few steps down, the viewer reaches the sculpture's edge. Now Gravity seems to tilt to the left. . . . The edge is marked by horizontal scrapes showing where the slab was cut. (2007, 231)

The truly dramatic character of *Gravity* is fully revealed only when it is experienced from a very short distance. When visitors lean down, they discern that in fact the steel block pitches into the floor. This can be noticed only at the ground level—visitors suddenly realize that the sculpture sinks into the ground while its bottom edge floats slightly above the surface. It elicits a feeling that the sculpture is actually in movement and that observers are not able to determine its full shape. Some part of it seems to be already immersed in the ground, unavailable for visitors' view. Tilted and partly sunken, *Gravity* is likely to allude to the physical entropy and evoke a sensation of falling apart, or loosing itself. As such, it elicits a feeling of visceral unease, or even fear. It makes visitors question the stability of the ground on which they are moving. The materiality of both the slab and the environment wherein it is located seems to be vulnerable and fragile, ready to unexpectedly collapse. As Harriet F. Senie explains, "Existing in the same space as the body, sculpture implies a way of being in the world" and—as she continues—*Gravity*, "either seeming on the verge of collapse or apparently sinking (unevenly) into the ground, conveys a threatened existence" (2001, 208).

Neither does *Gravity* conform to nor overwhelm its surroundings. Rather, it seems to activate the space and trigger visitors' movement. Serra's work, in Michael Kimmelman's words (1993), "underscores the theme of rupture and disjunction" so fundamental to Ingo Freed's architecture of the building. Even though it may correspond with the Hall of Witness' rectangular elements of the décor, at the same time—as tilted and partly sunken—it creates an impression of standing aside of it. It is positioned at an angle, even shaky, and seems to be about to fall down or disappear in the ground. Yet it also heightens the effects of the other elements used in the arrangement of the space, exposing diagonal skylight or weird angles, making them more appropriate although equally disquieting. There is a perpetual tension between the superficial regularity of the shapes and forms used in the architecture of the

Hall of Witness and the gentle yet paralyzing distortions of these elements. As Godfrey concludes, "Together, *Gravity* and The Hall of Witness fix viewers in a warp" (2007, 231).

Even though the artist did not intend the sculpture to have any references to the Holocaust on the representational level, on account of its being situated within the space of the USHMM, it necessarily functions within a specific code of remembrance. It concerns the convoluted shape of the block as well as its polychrome, occasionally rusty brown, surface. Scars and scratches made by eroding agents as well as digital print of numbers in one of the sculpture's corners are clearly discernible. Undoubtedly, they draw visitors' attention, especially that they can be read in relation to the tattooed numbers on the arms of concentration camps' prisoners and bearing evidence to their painful experiences marked on their bodies. In fact, these imprints are not products of the artist, but they are factory stamps left on the steel blast. These have always been typical for Serra's works as—by leaving them untouched—he wanted to expose the materiality of the sculpture as well as the materiality of the process through which it has come into being. Even though these marks have typically been ignored by critics and viewers as far as other Serra's works are concerned, in the case of *Gravity*, they get equipped with additional cultural meanings, which is due to the context, in which the sculpture is installed. These profound and meaningful scars left on the surface of the structure provide a partial history of the work's construction and material processing. They evidence a substantial amount of suffering that each piece of steel has had to endure in order to appear in its contemporary form. The marks therefore seem to invite a more intimate, sensible engagement with the materiality of the volume—torturously formed by heat and chill, fire and water, the pieces of steel bear signs of the stresses that they went through. Due to physical and chemical processes and forces, the structure becomes what it is now. The material procedure seems to be the most important part of the emergence of the work of art. Its materiality suffers and endures complex, intense, physical and chemical practices in the process of becoming a work of art. "In confronting the site I wish to create a field force so that the space is discerned physically rather than optically," says Serra about his work (quoted in Godfrey 2007, 232). The purely representational dimension is here practically without importance; what counts instead are the material metamorphoses that produce new qualities. The body of the sculpture bears memories of the procedures and processing it has endured; the permanent marks and scars testify to its material suffering and irreversible transformations. Such a construction of the work of art seems to correspond with the nature of the traumatic memory described earlier in this chapter. It is about the material past wound that actualizes itself in the present, always atemporarily dwelling at the overlap of then and now, or past, present, and future.

It belongs to the ontology of the affected body and translates into its new becomings with others. As such, the sculpture invites an active personal experience of its immense and scarred volume, engaging perceptual sensitivity, sensibility, and memory of visitors. It encourages reflection on the process of transformation and change, a constant becoming-other, permanent differing, yet in the context of consequential archives of bodily-narrative memory. In a compound synaesthetic encounter that depends on and remains in motion, the work of art generates meaningful effects.

The materiality of the work of art sustains and makes possible cultural meanings created in the encounter with it and its location. Even though gravity has been a recurring theme in Serra's works (cf. McShine et al. 2007), the fact that this work of art functions within the space of USHMM translates into it being encoded with meanings produced within the meaningful structures of the Holocaust remembrance. Therefore, the title of the sculpture may be read in reference to the gravestone (especially since the word "grave" derives from "gravity") and evokes the mass burials of Holocaust victims. It also alludes to the gravity of evil perpetuated during World War II, as well as to the gravity of existence. Since it regulates movement around it, it generates additional readings connected to the sorting of the Nazi victims (Grunewald 1992) and, on account of its arresting yet ambivalent format, it was interpreted as embodying tension between the sacral and the secular (Foster 1998b, 26–27). As scarred, partly sunken, and seemingly unstable, it can also suggest a nature of mnemonic processes themselves—fragile, vanishing, and vulnerable, yet also substantial and solid. Bearing marks of physical transformations and permanent decay, *Gravity* may also signal the impossibility of memorial work's coming to closure.

Due to its abstract form, the work of art seems to unsettle the notion of Holocaust memory, asking questions about the nature of commemoration processes rather than delivering any answers. It stubbornly avoids representation and tenaciously refuses to visualize the trauma of the Shoah in figurative terms, inviting instead physical and material responses as well as thorough reflection on materiality of the (traumatic) memory. As such, it favors more complex forms of commemoration, relying on affective means and interactions.

BODILY-DISCURSIVE ENCOUNTERS: CONCLUDING REMARKS

The memorial artifacts analyzed in this chapter seem to operate through activation of bodily, lived experience, which is both semiotic and material in its nature. In these cases, the memorial event emerges as a situated practice, or a corporeal encounter mediated by sensible action and sensory engagement rather than by representations and discourse (Crouch 2002). As such, a central role of the materiality of the body as much as of the encountered space is affirmed as crucial in understanding the transmission of knowledges and triggering critical reflection on both the past and the ways it is used or rehearsed in the present. The bodily relationships with sites are therefore fluid and contingent (Obrador Pons 2003). Important however, as exemplified by my case studies, the acknowledgment of the crucial role of the body does not translate in denying the relevance of images and culturally shaped meanings. Unquestionably, they fulfill a substantial role in shaping visitors' experiences and knowledges stemming from them. Certainly, they are individually negotiated and approached, and hence produce singular readings and interpretations, yet ones always entangled with the material dimension of experience. As Ola Söderström emphasizes, the nonrepresentational—or more-than-representational—theories focus on such agents as "the body, emotions, spatial practice, interaction, performance, 'things,' technology" and to certain extent "downplay the role of mental processes, language and vision" without, however, denying the importance of representational realm (2005, 14). In the case of (post)Holocaust memory, artistic and aesthetic strategies embodied by these memorial artifacts seem to work as agential vehicles for knowledge of the difficult past, while warning against totalizing of meanings these knowledges rely on.

Acknowledging singularity of the memorial processes being experienced and enacted by each visitor in a different manner sheds an altogether different light on practices of public commemoration. Certainly, the official and widely spread codes of remembrance matter. Yet what also counts is a more bodily and sensual engagement with the memorial event, which—as in the case of trauma—may happen beyond the representational, or speakable, realm. This idiosyncrasy of experiences, as well as particularity of ways in which certain events are memorized and remembered (discursively and semiotically), evidences the singular nature of memory work. The ways of remembering seem to follow constraining cultural frameworks, but they simultaneously negotiate and redo them, opening them to inventive rearrangements and creative reconfigurations. As David Crouch and Luke Deforges notice, it is necessary to take into considerations visitors' embodied and experiential encounters with sites and places. However, I would add that the latter need to be seen as active agents in these dynamic material-semiotic assemblages, affecting and being affected at the same time. It means, for the two authors, that the analysis of embodied perception must necessarily take into account "the importance of contexts, of representations of events, activities or places, and the role of mediators in their construction" (Crouch and Deforges 2003, 11). This entanglement of the discursive and the bodily is therefore emblematic for such memorial encounters.

In approaching the memorial through a new materialist lens, and adopting the perspective of synaesthetic perception (explained in chapter 1), it is necessary to focus in more detail on the complex cooperation of different senses, merging into compound bodily-intellectual experiential and transformational events. Relying on vision's primacy is simply not enough to grasp the complex metamorphoses at work during, or within, the memorial encounters. Hence, it is of vital importance to expand the range of sensations, mediators, and material objects working together in machine-like fashion in order to produce singular events. No longer could vision (and representation!) usurp the role of the whole body and have a monopoly for generating knowledge. As John Urry claims, we need to transcend the hegemony of visuality that totalizes the work of all synaesthetically operating bodily senses (1999). We should focus more on the contingency of memorial encounters, by undoing the well-established bodily routines and opening the body to new, often turbulent and unexpected, becomings. Bearing in mind the complex affective-intellectual nature of memory, in the next chapter, I will focus more closely on material sensuous encounters with memorial sites and artifacts.

NOTES

1. Ruth Leys argues that such an approach incites considerable "doubts about the veracity of the victim's testimony: to the extent that the traumatic occurrence is considered never to have become part of the victim's memory, it is unclear how she can truthfully testify to what befell her" (2000, 299).

2. Cathy Caruth cites Shoshana Felman's proposal that trauma provokes a "crisis of truth" (1995a, 6) and proposes a paradox "that in trauma the greatest confrontation with reality may also occur as an absolute numbing to it" (1995a, 6). Because the event could not be witnessed "fully" (1995a, 7) at the time of its original occurrence, the memory of trauma is experienced belatedly, thereby requiring an act of witnessing to validate it and to make it a part of a conscious representational understanding. Caruth's articulation of the ontology of the traumatic image or imprint serves to anchor a temporal relation between the witness and the event, validating the traumatic nature of the event as it is witnessed.

3. Ruth Leys (2000) explained how an emphasis on trauma as an exact repetition or literal trace of an original event gave rise to various speculations about establishing a neurobiological basis for trauma. A theory claiming that trauma—as retained in the body, or as an imprint of experience—is qualitatively different from other forms of memory may be used as an argument that disclosure, or revelation, of a hidden traumatic cause can help achieve therapeutic results where other forms of diagnoses and treatment might fail.

4. Leys argues that the neurobiological formulation of trauma as a literal trace of an event or experience in fact contradicts the therapeutic emphasis on the role of narrative in integrating trauma into the fabric of memory. For Leys, if trauma remains

radically outside representational realm, it cannot be narrated without compromising its status as "literal truth." Leys argues that even if the experience is visualized solely as a dream or "flashback," some degree of symbolization must always be operative (see Leys 2000, 249).

5. In her study, Ruth Leys elaborates in detail on Cathy Caruth's approach (see Leys 2000, 266–97).

6. Marianne Hirsch admits that her theory has been deeply indebted to the works by Cathy Caruth. She also claims that Caruth's theorization of trauma and transmission thereof was helpful for Hirsch in the process of making sense of her own experiences connected to postmemory.

7. For the relationship of visuality to trauma, see Ulrich Baer (2002), Jill Bennett (2005), Shelley Hornstein and Florence Jocobowitz (2002), Barbie Zelizer (1998), Bernd Hüppauf (1997), and Van Alphen (2005).

8. See also Pickford (2012).

9. In his 2000 study, James E. Young describes the long and difficult process of establishing the memorial in Berlin, its legal land financial basis, and the various controversies it arouse. Young himself served as a member of a committee in charge of selecting the winning design for the Berlin memorial. He offers interesting descriptions of the competing proposals and lists arguments in favor of Peter Eisenman's design. His discussion is very instructive with regard to the convoluted nature of German memory of the Shoah as well as to the character of obstacles the idea of a national memorial to the crime inflicted by a nation on an ethnic minority might possibly face (cf. Young 2000, 184–223).

Chapter 4

Rhythms and Movements: Sensations, Becomings, Flows

CONSTANT MOVEMENT: THE BODY AS A VERB

From a new materialist point of view, a body (of any kind) is never defined in terms of what it *is*, but rather it is conceived in terms of what it *becomes* and what it *does*, or—more precisely—of what it is potentially capable of doing. Hence, a body is an assemblage of the actual and the virtual, a bundle of intensities and flows. Its ontology, therefore, is understood as constant fluidity and dynamism, or an incessant procedure of transition. This process may be seen as a ge(nea)(o)logy of becoming, an entanglement of past, present, and future, or a zone of emerging potentiality. Let me then start these elaborations with a geological story.

> Geological strata (accumulation of sedimentary rocks like sandstone or limestone) are created through a process involving (at least) two distinct operations. . . . Geologists have uncovered one such mechanism: rivers acting as veritable hydraulic computers (or at least, sorting machines). Rivers transport rocky materials from their point of origin (a previously created mountain subject to erosion or weathering) to the place in the ocean where these materials will accumulate. In this process, pebbles of variable size, weight and shape tend to react differently to the water transporting them. These different reactions to moving water are what sorts the pebbles, with the small ones reaching the ocean sooner than the large ones, for example. Once the raw materials have been sorted out into more or less homogeneous groupings deposited at the bottom of the sea (that is, once they have become sedimented), a second operation is necessary to transform these loose collections of pebbles into an entity of a higher scale: a sedimentary rock. This operation consists in cementing the sorted components together into a new entity with emergent properties of its own, that is, properties such as overall strength and permeability that cannot be ascribed

> to the sum of the individual pebbles. This second operation is carried out by certain substances dissolved in water (such as silica or hematite in the case of sandstones) which penetrate the sediment through the pores between pebbles. As this percolating solution crystallizes, it consolidates the pebble's temporary spatial relations into a more or less permanent "architectonic" structure. Thus, a double operation, a "double articulation" gets us from structures at one scale to structures at another scale. (DeLanda 1996)

What is most important in this excerpt with regard to my argumentation is not only the fact that matter is active and that it produces (in never final ways) new transformations and new metamorphoses, but rather that out of this creation (here, the second operation), as Iris van der Tuin clarifies (2014c, 264), something new ("a new entity") emerges and this new body/movement has "emergent properties of its own." This means that what results from this operation cannot be simply reduced to the characteristics of preexisting entities (pebbles, rivers, flows, minerals) or their points of origin (which again and infinitely go back to their points of origin), but rather they should be seen as a potentiality, as something that pebbles have always already been potentially able to do; their actualization is again a new potentiality for, or openness to, new becomings and new transformations. Although seemingly a final product of the procedure of sedimentation, this "new entity" is at the same time a new beginning or a new vibrant movement.

The dynamism of transformational processes analogously applies to the perceptual events in which bodies are constantly involved. Yet perception has to be understood here in line with the views of new materialism, that is, in material-semiotic terms—as a bodily-intellectual process, or assemblage of forces reconfiguring the entities involved and creating new possibilities for their further potential metamorphoses. Bearing these ideas in mind, in this chapter, relating to my earlier investigations, I focus on the process of perceptual involvement with memorial artifacts, mostly installation art. In this context I turn rhythm and movement into chapter 4's two leading concepts through which I later approach a number of works of art. Bearing in mind my deliberations and theoretical developments discussed in previous chapters of this book, I situate these analyses in relation to notions of synaesthetic perception and bodily (traumatic) memory, elaborated on in chapters 1 and 3, respectively. This is to make clear how the processes involving matter's movements and transformations described in DeLanda's passage quoted earlier are relevant for discussing the events of bodily encounters with memorial space/work/installation. As illustrated with a few examples, the interaction with such artifacts is not a purely visual experience but rather one that is informed by other senses, and eventually translates into a synaesthetic event of a material-semiotic nature. In line with my earlier deliberations, the aim of the chapter is to point to the complexity of the procedure of "seeing," understood in terms of a set of multidimensional, embodied, and sensual dynamic processes, yet also located in particular social and cultural contexts and meanings.

Drawing on analyses of the synaesthetic experiences produced in encounters with the examined memorial works of art, the chapter scrutinizes the relevance of rhythm and movement for the theorization of embodiment and affect. I argue again for a more encompassing approach to experience that assumes dissolving the opposition between the virtual and the actual (in Gilles Deleuze's understanding of the terms). Movement, accordingly, is seen as a constant duration, or becoming of time and bodies, while rhythm—a dynamic coupling of movements—is conceived of (in a new materialist way) as a creative force, an intensive nonconscious dimension of experience, a vibration, an activity inherent to all matter, an imperceptible force of "more than" (Manning 2013; more on this will follow). Importantly, in this part of the book, I also briefly elaborate on the connection between rhythm and processes of remembering and forgetting, especially on account of the fact that rhythm is also about making and unmaking routines and habits. As such, the chapter provides an important transition between the new materialist conceptualizations of perception and memory offered in prior chapters and the feminist politics of connectivity explored in chapter 5. It also presents a more intricate analyses of the selected memorial works of art (including artistic installations and architectural sites of remembrance), paying special attention to their synaesthetic, relational operations and signaling the bodily-intellectual becoming of knowledge production processes emerging out of encounters with memorial installation art.

THINKING (THROUGH THE) SENSUOUS BODIES

As clarified in chapter 1, the approach grounded in synaesthetic perception underlines both the dynamic entanglement of the material and the semiotic and the crucial role of senses in bodily becoming with/in the world. The sensual perceptions, however, are not seen as having ground in any transcendence. Rather, they are temporary instantiations, or actualizations, of the virtual, which is—in Deleuzian terms—equally real as the actual. Accordingly, experience does not rely on the subject's consciousness but is contingent on circumstantial movements and becomings, or encounters with other bodies—material, semiotic, sonic, olfactory, organic, inorganic, human, inhuman, and so on. Moreover, these sensations are also informed by past experiences, or archives of memory, as much as they point to future potentialities and are shaped by them. This involves constant becoming-other, a perpetual metamorphosis, or a process of never-ending transformation.

"Conscious perception is . . . the most primitive form of judgment," Alfred Whitehead evinces (1978, 162). In the context of new materialist philosophy, the idea of a coherent perceiving subject in control of what he or she perceives and knows appears as completely fictional. It seems to be forged solely for reasons of convenience, allowing for situating a human being at the center of cognition. Alternatively, Whitehead proposes a manner of thinking that starts with *the process* rather than with *a subject of process*, wherein the subjective form results from experience and not vice versa—the experiences are presupposed by a subject. Although working much earlier than new materialist philosophical movement actually appeared, some of his ideas seem to resonate clearly with main postulates of this relatively recent trend. Especially because Whitehead's philosophy focuses on desubjectification of experience and underlines the notion of process defined in entirely relational terms, that is, being themselves relations, processes are shaped by relations with other processes. Life, therefore, is not constructed of bits of matter but rather from processes involving dynamic material movements. In such an account, any perceptual event is completely immanent in its unfolding, oscillating between the actual (i.e., what something has become and is still becoming) and the virtual (i.e., the realm of potentiality, or a bundle of past and future possibilities), the latter manifesting itself in its effects. There is a constant movement between and permanent entangling of the actual and the virtual—the actualization is a temporary instantiation of the virtual possibilities and potentials. The subject, in such an account, does not precede the experience but is informed by and emerges from it in the process of perpetual becoming-other, or constant differing. Such logic is completely in line with the Deleuzian way of thinking and resounds his (and Bergsonian) notion of the virtual. Accordingly, the virtuality is understood here in terms of contractions of intensity, a set of differentiating tendencies and forces, a zone of potentiality. The virtual, however, engenders the actual, being at the same time its generative force. It bears in itself the past and the future that manifest and materialize themselves in the actual. Yet not all of that actually actualizes; it is rather about a multiplicity of tendencies, plentiful of competing potentialities on the verge of becoming actualized.

As Erin Manning passionately explains,[1] for Whitehead the initial phase of perception (which he calls prehension) starts with "the force of a relational attunement (causal efficacy)" (2014, 163) shaped by always singular set of conditions. Only then, in certain cases, can we talk about sensation (which, nevertheless, intertwines with prehension). Accordingly, "relation and sensation are co-composing in experience, participatory in the direct experience of a world informing" (Manning 2014, 164). What is most important for experience to emerge is actually *a relation*, or a combination of relations, and not the preexisting subject. And what matters is the directness of relation, or of a generative collision of bodies, productive of their new becomings and new potential linkages they can form. To clarify, a body is a certain dynamic constellation of relations, emergent in the events of encounters, as some parts of experience may, in Whitehead's account (1978, 53), remain beyond consciousness. Therefore, as Manning further explains (2014), it is necessary to provisionally differentiate between the body and its awareness (even though they are always co-composing): "Consciousness invades the becoming-body, tunes it, attunes to it, even as the becoming-body invades awareness" (Manning 2014, 177). There is always a co-constituting dynamic intra-action of the perceiving body and its awareness (which is more *with* than *of* the body); they are entangled in the constant process of connective becoming, which affects and is affected by its immediate environment (relational circumstances) with which it enters into direct processual encounters.

Consequently, the body emerges in relentless movement, being itself a precarious, unstable assemblage of micro-movements—it does not preexist its movement but is manufactured in it. Even its temporary stasis is full of imperceptible movements producing provisional, fleeting equilibrium. In Manning's words, "Movement courses through the me that is in formation: experience, perception, feeling—all of these are movements, and each of them contributes, in an infinity of ways, to what 'I' will become in any given occasion" (2014, 166). Forms emerge in the event as a secondary process, within the ecology of relations, and exist only as transient instantiations, as provisional actualizations of the virtual possibilities. Forms are mirage-like, as movement never really stops: "What has stopped and taken form is but a subtraction from the total field of movement—a step, a shape, a figure always already on its way to something else" (Manning 2014, 169). Neither should forms be seen as referring to any transcendental realm, nor are they the same each time they return—they remain active and changeable. Stasis is merely a perceived freezing of movement as the latter is a vibrational force and it constantly moves, producing new relating bodies, new sensations, new intensities, and new connections. In Manning's words, "Relation folds experience into it such that what emerges is always more than the sum of its parts" (2013, 2). Thus, the movement (of life) remains generative of new possibilities; it is an inventive force of virtual-actual becomings. Writes Manning,

> Every event is relational. Events create relation as much as relation creates events. We cannot know in advance what an event can do, any more that we can know what a body can do. Spinoza's question will remain unanswered: to know of what a body is capable would be to divest a body of its elasticity. The essence of a technique of relation is not its content per se but its capacity to become more-than and to create more-than. (2009, 41)

Exploring the nature of perception, Manning also notices that a key to understanding Whitehead's process philosophy is his notion of the "non-sensuous," through which the philosopher points to what exceeds sense-presentation. In a non sensuous perception we deal with "an overlapping of pastnesses into presentings that are already anticipating the immediate future—a direct perception of time out of sync" (Manning 2014, 176). It is a feeling that "pastness can become contributory to the present in-act, not as the past that was, but as a dimension of the present it will have become" (Manning 2014, 176). Sense-presentation comes afterward, as different from sensation and feeling. Feeling is a zone of potentiality and "non-sensuous perception is full of feeling. Every movement in-act is imbued with pastnesses—every step is composed of the millions of steps that preceded it, and yet every step is also uniquely itself" (Manning 2014, 176). This understanding draws on the complex entanglement of past(s), present(s), and future(s), always oscillating between the realm of actuality and the realm of virtuality. The synchronic coexistence and co-constitution of different dimensions of time contributes in a sense to the fact that memory persists and sustains an illusion of personal, yet fluid, subjectivity, even though each actual occasion remains entirely singular and unrepeatable. In each event the past is *still* and the future is *already* present (cf. Manning 2014). The becoming of the present is informed by virtualities of the past and the future alike, and weaves them together into always different and always new singular events and experiences.

In a similar vein, Elizabeth Grosz points to a complex coexistence of different realms of time, indicating that time is in fact a constant duration, a movement of transformation, recruiting from the material and the symbolic alike. It is a life itself. As she explains,

> Life, even the simplest organic cell, carries its past with its present as no material object does. This incipient memory endows life with creativity, the capacity to elaborate an innovative and unpredictable response to stimuli, to react or, rather, simply to act, to enfold matter into itself, to transform matter and life in unpredictable ways. (2008, 6)

In a Deleuzian fashion, Grosz's approach subscribes to the concept of time as perpetual becoming or duration of movement. Instead of freezing time into an ideal of the present, it suggests that time's duration is the very condition of simultaneity. As Peter Eisenman explains, "In the division of duration into past and present, the past is seen as a virtuality of the present, while the future is that which overwrites or restructures the virtual that is the past. Duration is that flow which connects the future to the past" (2001, xiii).

Thus, the becoming of time (the duration) as well as the becoming of bodies involves the atemporal entanglement of past(s), present(s), and future(s), which coexist within a body. Yet bodies are also becoming with other bodies as they are totally relational. The environment is not external to the body dwelling in it—it co-constitutes the body as much as the body is productive of and affects its surroundings. Such understanding of the body and the ways in which it encounters other bodies resonates clearly with Deleuze and Guattari's conceptions and is interesting from a feminist point of view. As Grosz underlines, "Their notion of the body as a discontinuous, nontotalizable series of processes, organs, flows, energies, corporeal substances and incorporeal events, speeds and durations, may be of great value to feminists," especially taking into consideration feminist attempts "to reconceive bodies outside the binary oppositions imposed on the body by the mind/body, nature/culture, subject/object and interior/exterior oppositions" (1994, 164). Instead, their proposition situates the notion of the body in the context of "its connections with other bodies . . . linking organs and biological processes to material objects and social practices" (Grosz 1994, 165). There is directness in these connections—bodies do not connect solely through mediations of ideological apparatuses or representations but rather via formation of machines and direct linkages by means of intensive affects and forces. This, however, happens in complex sociocultural and political contexts. The body, accordingly, is envisioned as a multiplicity of different surfaces, facets, and plateaus, always remaining in dynamic, undetermined flux. It is conceived in terms of liaisons it is capable to establish, the potential transformations it can undergo, the affects it can generate or intensify, the machine-like becomings it can endure, the knowledges it can produce, the effects it can have in and with the world, or the acts it can perform. Thus, such theorization fosters a conception of the body as entirely relational, which does not reduce it to a mere biological organization (or an organism) nor to an entity subordinated to the phantasm of its consciousness (cf. Deleuze and Guattari 1987, 74).

While defining bodies in terms of incessant becomings, or surfaces of affects, intensities, and speeds, Deleuze and Guattari offer an idea of a body that is centered neither biologically nor psychically. There is no hierarchy, no organization, and no stratification in how the body is composed. Rather, it is a singularity—there is in it "a kind of wildness, pivots of unpredictability, elements whose trajectories, connections, and future relations remain unpredictable" (Grosz 1994, 174). There is no predetermined trajectory that the body has to follow in its becomings. And there is no teleology in this process. Its metamorphosis is completely contingent on the circumstances in which the body is located, or on other encountered bodies—there is no transcendence in this transformation, no external, "ideal" framework that should be put into practice. Also, there is reciprocity of becoming—the bodies are formed by the relations in which they enter as much as these relations are shaped by the participating bodies. They connect through the forces of affects: "Sensation . . . designates a relation between a subject and the world preceding rationality and knowledge, perception and intellection, in which there is always a mutual transformation between them," Grosz clarifies (2008, 8). Thus, being themselves consequences of a practice, bodies remain proliferative and productive, yet always in new, experimental ways.

Summing up, a new materialist conception of a body—diffractively drawing on ideas and theories of different philosophers (of the body, of the immanence, or of the process) as well as its more contemporary interpreters and practitioners—conceives of it in completely dynamic terms, as an assemblage produced in encounters with other bodies, connecting with them and forming temporary linkages. Such proposition is totally different from theories of subjectivity subordinating it to the idea of consciousness and portrayed as an autonomous being in control of his or her actions and generated knowledges. It is also away from the concept of knowledge as necessarily cumulative and produced by a detached, unengaged subject of knowledge, isolated from the object on which knowledge is generated. Similarly, it gives up the idea of learning as a progressive quest for a total grasp of the studied issue effectuated by a conscious mind. Instead, it offers a concept of knowledge as a dynamic bodily-intellectual practice produced together with other bodies—these bodies are not necessarily human and not necessarily organic. Like the body, knowledge is also seen in terms of constant becoming-with, a process that does not follow any prescribed route but can potentially move in different directions. It embodies a continuous tension between remembering and forgetting, or between sustaining old habits or routines and opening to something new or unexpected. Knowledge, accordingly, is not about recognizing what is already there or subordinating the newly encountered to the already known and recognizable. Rather, it is about exposure to novel unexpected potentialities and possible metamorphoses revealed in perceptual events, which are not grounded in any predetermined structures or formations. The permanent becoming-other, which is also *becoming-with-other-bodies*, leaves memorable traces on those involved in this relational process, reconfiguring their subsequent becomings as well as their machine-like composition. Every single encounter, every collision as well as every established linkage affect the participating bodies, whose trajectories change, even if in minute or imperceptible ways. Thus, bodies should be understood as fluid entities, remaining always in motion; they are the waves of intensities and flows. Such a dynamic concept of the body implies, therefore, that we start to conceive of it as a verb. In new materialist spirit we need therefore to focus on what the body is capable of doing rather than on what it simply is.

THE RHYTHM OF *UN/LEARNING*—A PERMANENT VIBRATION

As explained earlier, in my investigations, I rely on a theorization of life as a vibrating movement, a creativity that always involves entanglements of the actual and the virtual as well as of the material and the semiotic. It is a force dealing with what happens to us, what happens with us as well as how we happen. These complex processes are contingent on the rhythm of life's becoming. Starting from Deleuze and Guattari's statement that "rhythm is the milieu's answer to chaos" (1988, 313), I argue that rhythm should be considered as an antidote for anarchy, a dynamic coupling of movements that spontaneously gives forms to chaos and lets us think and process it. It is a creative energy that constitutes an intensive imperceptible dimension of experience, a vibration inherent to all matter, regardless its composition or nature. While remaining immanent to chaos as its dynamic force, rhythm is also about constant reconfigurings and constitutes a part of all dynamic processes of becoming-other. Consequently, it oscillates between the molar and the molecular, or—in other words—between the disciplinary formations tending towards sedimentation or stasis and creative experimentations involving inventive connectivities and unpredictable linkages. Although rhythm, in its more conventional understandings, might suggest repetition of old ideas and habits at precise frequencies, it is so in unrepeatable ways, or as something new. It constantly moves between sameness and variation. Habits and forms recur forever with a difference—even if seemingly identical or indistinguishable, they return as always new, or always differing. As a dynamic becoming, rhythm makes us remember but it is also amnesiac, so it makes us forget, only to later come back afresh and anew, yet this return is every time different (cf. Henriques et al. 2014, 4). It is therefore about making and unmaking life routines, an artistic life force, a constant movement, a life itself.

Matter incessantly vibrates and moves; it is active, productive, and generative, and undergoes constant transformations, entering in new assemblages or affecting and being affected by always new bodies. As explained in the previous section of this chapter, this process of entering in relations (or intra-acting) recruits from both the virtual and the actual, turning each event into a singular, dynamic, and unprecedented occurrence. Such a view remains in line with the new materialist manner of thinking. A variety of approaches gathered under the umbrella of new materialism—although often quite different from each other and forged in distinctive contexts, circumstances, or within diverse disciplines of science—seem to be guided by a similar logic, which is one of connectivity (contrasting the divisive logic of oppositions, inherent in the dominant ways Western culture refers to the world). Centering on vibrant agency and productivity of material-semiotic processes, new materialist philosophical movement is preoccupied with exploring how different kinds of bodies (organic, technological, social, linguistic, etc.) collide, dash with, and combine, and investigates how knowledge on these becomings emerges and is put into practice.

Taking inspiration from vitalist philosophies, new materialism conceives of the politics of life as vibrant becoming-other, a constant differing understood in terms of a bundle of non teleological, rhizomatic, unpredictable, and open procedures generating impulsive, often surprising effects. Consequently, not only materiality but also movement and rhythm should be seen as concepts crucial for grasping the new materialist processes of rhizomatic *becoming-with-other-bodies*, or of what I call later in this section—the *un/learning.*

Whereas in my argumentation movement is defined in terms of a constant duration of time, rhythm is understood—along with Deleuzian philosophy—as both a vibration and a force of the virtual, a virtuality itself (see Manning 2009, 2014, Henriques et al. 2014). Conceived as vibration, rhythm eludes conscious reach—"its excess or resistive capacities can be summarized to lie in its movements outside the (technologically enhanced) conscious spectrum of (human) perceptual faculties" (Henriques et al. 2014, 18). It is preindividual and cannot be subdued to a simple visual (or other sensual) detection or straightforward classificatory ordering. As vibratory force, rhythm remains inherent to all kinds of matter, turning it into a vital and active agent in forming assemblages and relations. It is a force that on a permanent basis reorganizes materialities, rearranges substances, and structures them anew. This applies to all kinds of bodies, even though in many cases, these metamorphoses remain imperceptible to the human sensory apparatus. Rhythm, therefore, triggers molecular becomings of matter, occurring at different levels of intensity and different speeds; as referring to affect, it is a connective force.

Related to understanding of rhythm as a vibration is its framing as a virtuality itself, which also remains in line with Deleuze and Guattari's approach. Accordingly, rhythm is seen as "the virtuality of (material) entities—a virtuality immanently (re-)constitutive of their actual properties" (Henriques et al. 2014, 22). It is the richness of possibilities, which the actual can never fully exhaust, but by which it is constantly informed—this can refer to the abundant archives of the past that shape what we experience as present, actualizing as intensities, affects, thoughts, and acts. Rhythm, in such formulation, constitutes a multiplicity of tendencies and potential becomings. Hence, in both understandings briefly sketched earlier,[2] rhythm is linked to potentiality and productivity. Yet, in this sense, the concept of rhythm can apply well to imperceptible movements and nonconscious dimensions of experience. It is an intensity, both actual and virtual, a zone of emergence, a difference in itself. As such, it also implies a whole wealth of theorizations and applications. Most important in the context of my argumentation is, however, how rhythm embodies politics of connectivity eluding at the same time strictly representational framing. As Henriques et al. suggest,

> Rhythm is a concept that moves between disciplines, focusing attention on, among other things, how our sensory worlds are mediated and organized, how we come to learn to move our bodies and become individuals, and how our

experiences might escape being captured in systems of representation or efficient production, standardization and control. (2014, 4)

When conceiving of rhythm in new materialist manners, it is important to differentiate between the rhythm and the rule. With introduction of strict rules and measurements, or of an ordered control, the original spontaneity and artlessness of rhythm get irretrievably lost. This is a point of view fostered by, for instance, Rudolph Bode, a well-known theoretician of rhythm and a pedagogue. As he explains, the word "rhythm" is derived from Greek ῥέω (rhéō), which stands for the expression "to flow." For Bode it means that "we can infer . . . that rhythm is imprinted with the quality of what flows, that is, of the continuum. . . . true rhythm is a continuum" (2014, 54). Yet this continuum cannot be rationally measured through application of any externally designed framework or classificatory system. As such, rhythm remains beyond the intellectual cognition, which can only impose regulation on it, turning it into a rule and, hence, also annihilating its original, intensive flow. The continuum of rhythm, for Bode, "*is not rationally graspable at all; it can only be looked at and experienced: therefore, rhythm has to be part of the irrational*" (2014, 55; original emphasis). From this he also concludes that, on account of being an irrational form, rhythm cannot be subjected to "*the judgmental, comparative, measuring functions of the intellect*" (Bode 2014, 55; original emphasis). The principle of rationality, or of what can be intellectually grasped and meticulously measured, is the rule or order rather than rhythm. These rational principles are, however, secondary and force the natural, primary, vital rhythm of life to recede and disappear. In its original form, rhythm is not intellectual but rather constitutes a part of life's totality. When ordered and turned into a rule, it becomes "an isolated experience," no longer a part of the overwhelming continuity of life; it gets eradicated and flattened. Hence, for Bode, it is a fundamental error to confuse the rhythm with the rule (2014, 58), as "*all rhythm is a function of continuously flowing time, and all regulation finds itself outside time*" (2014, 61; original emphasis). And regulation always requires a repression of the spontaneous rhythm of life itself. To translate this into a Deleuzian framework, it would imply that rhythm is composed of a multiplicity of molecular movements, whereas regulation would consist of an imposition of a molar structure on micro-movements, wherein the rhythmic qualities of matter/movements have to irrevocably recede: "*The existing rhythm is destroyed because ordered and measured acts of the will replace the impulses of the senses, which move rhythmically*" (Bode 2014, 64; original emphasis). According to such a point of view, the rhythm is seen as the governing law of the cosmos, where the latter is conceived in terms of an irrational "totality of life." Consequently, "rhythm is connected to the flow of life" (Bode 2014, 55).

To recapitulate, in a new materialist spirit, which acknowledges and appreciates vitality and agency of matter, rhythm is seen as a constant, often imperceptible vibration, a quality of all matter, its ability to produce and transform, the ability to intra-act. In Grosz's words, "Vibration is the common thread or rhythm running through the universe from its chaotic inorganic interminability to its most intimate forces of inscription on living bodies of all kinds and running back again" (2008, 54). Consequently, rhythm consists of constant transmissions of energy and activity, a permanent process of reorganization of substances, particles, and materials. It is intrinsic to all forms of matter; it makes matter flow and move, act and react, and affect and be affected. As such, it is closely related to the concept of intensity (or affect) distributed across the surfaces of the bodies as they move and collide. In such understanding, rhythm is a heterogeneous flow of energy, a constant variation affecting different bodies and mediums, a permanent machinistic becoming of bodies. Defined in terms of a series of vibrations, rhythm also refers to the virtuality of material bodies that actualizes as their temporary properties. In that sense, rhythm is a vibrating plentitude, which might move in different directions, informed by past and future alike.

Such understanding of rhythm is a salient context for emergence of the concept of *un/learning*, which rests on dynamic tensions between non-dualistically organized processes of *learning* and *unlearning*, where *unlearning* can, and should, be considered as a productive *learning* procedure. These two tendencies, importantly, are not organized in an oppositional way, but rather they are the two dimensions of one and the same process, that is, the constant differing or becoming-other. *Unlearning*, in this context, refers to forgetting old routines and rules, disavowing structured regulations imposed on the multiplicity of processes of knowledge production, in order to open up to the new, that is, to *learning* of the different logic of thinking or a different form of life. Such reformulation requires thinking in terms of fragility rather than pure efficiency, the latter so typical for Western culture oriented towards a progressive quest for might and control over the world conceptualized as external to, and put at the disposal of, a human being. In line with feminist (and new materialist!) ideas tending to disavow the well-established, exclusionary, and dualistic system of thought (i.e., a metaphysical fundament of Western culture), *un/learning* signals connectivity and entanglement with/in the environment. It emerges from a multiplicity of relations and encounters in which the bodies enter and by which they are thoroughly affected. Different from the more traditional process of subsequent acquisition of knowledge relying on structured definitions and straightforward classifications, *un/learning* is about a radical openness and exposure, that is, about returning the body back to its surroundings with which it remains in a symbiotic liaison—affecting and being affected, and thus constantly differing from itself.

As John Schostak and Jill Schostak underline, new materialist knowledge production encourages "raising questions that make the powerful feel uncomfortable, even threatened" and regaining "this political dimension [which] suggests the possible overthrow of a previously stable or at least dominant order of ways of knowing, thinking, believing, acting" (2008, 1). *Un/learning* subscribes to this logic and dismantles the dominant hierarchies involved in cognitive processes—rather than conceiving of an independent human subject as the master of knowledge production procedures, the new materialist approach focuses on the situated, embodied practices as well as both human and nonhuman agencies.[3] It involves complex relationalities generated in material-semiotic encounters. The process is collective, and always different, given the varying intensity of bodily encounters as well as different contexts in which they happen. There is a fluidity in this phenomenon—it is guided by the spontaneous rhythm of collective, vital becoming-other, a multiplicity of movements and metamorphoses, a constant transformation of the always-differing assemblages of bodies.

Un/learning demands a radical exposure, a condition of total vulnerability to the virtual potentialities that can actualize and inform the creative becoming-other, a constant movement that is generative of new habits, new concepts, and new transformations as well as of their multiple and complex rehearsals. It is also productive of new understandings and novel knowledges, remaining completely singular although always contingent on the material-semiotic circumstances in which they are generated. The process of *un/learning* is equally informed by its pasts and its futures (and their complex meanings) in their various, dynamic metamorphoses and different—often unexpected—actualizations. As Karen Barad explains,

> Time can't be fixed. The past is never closed, never finished once and for all, but there is no taking it back, setting time aright, putting the world back on its axis. There is no erasure finally. The trace of all reconfigurings is written into the enfolded materialisations of what was/is/to-come. (Barad 2010, 264)

The series of intensive encounters with other bodies, human and nonhuman, semiotic and material, temporary and stable, is what sets the process of becoming-other in motion. No longer can the body be understood as stasis, or a noun, but rather, it must be conceived of in dynamic terms, that is, as a multiplicity of movements, a collectivity with others, formed by relations and affective connections. This, however, demands a resensitization of (human) bodies as well as a disavowal of their alleged boundaries and well-defied contours. It is also necessary to *unlearn* the taken-for-granted perceptual habits and to *learn* to see differently, through the body, and together with other bodies. This is what the synaesthetic seeing is about. Sensitive encounters with (memorial) (installation) art may, in such context, facilitate this process as well as serve as a point of departure for developing a different understanding of politics of experience, liberating the latter from the constraints of a conscious subject and instead acknowledging the active role of sensuous bodies, as well as of "withness," in knowledge production procedures.

SYNAESTHETIC ENCOUNTERS WITH MEMORIAL INSTALLATION ART

Encounters with art are generatively instructive. Art reveals the whole complexity of experiential events that are productive of new knowledges understood in material-semiotic terms. Works of art, when approached in new materialist manners, are not so much to be deciphered, decoded, and interpreted as engaged with and responded to. They impress and touch us, intensifying affects and sensations which animate thoughtful becomings. It is not the representational dimension that testifies to the work of art's status as art. Art is not about signification. Rather, it is about making the sensible real and experiential. Encounters with art are also always singular. As Deleuze and Guattari explain, "The monument does not actualize the virtual event but incorporates or embodies it: it gives it a body, a life, a universe" (1997, 177). It is not enough to explore the textuality of works of art. Examination of their immersion in ideological discourses, textual implications they produce, or emotional investments they encourage is simply not sufficient. From the new materialist perspective, it seems more vital to focus on the possibilities of becoming they offer or their capacities to enter into relations with other bodies. It is equally interesting to reveal the virtualities they embody, occasionally remaining latent in their material form. The processes of becoming of artistic events, triggered by bodily encounters with works of art, are generative of effects—they foster new becomings and new transformations born out of creative linkages, transforming and transformed in the very process.

In the context of memorial art, the explorations of affective-intellectual operations of artistic installations or structures may also shed light on the nature of mnemonic processes, exposing their entanglements, instability, and vibrational metamorphoses. These transformations produce effects, also in terms of new knowledges and new further becomings. Oftentimes, the processes of opening to the new demand a disavowal of taken-for-granted assumptions and perceptual habits. Interactions with art, in such instances, are revealing, as art makes us vulnerable and exposed to sensations and affections, remaining beyond conscious control. It is exactly what *un/learning* is about. Yet a closer look at how art becomes and what it is capable of doing lets us acknowledge the relationality of all encounters as well as realize the importance of effects they can potentially generate. Noticeably, the work of art, or an artistic event, itself also emerges from a multiplicity of encounters and relations or from intense material collisions.

The analysis of these phenomena may lead us to conceiving of a new idea of the politics of experience (to which I will return in the final chapter of this book). For now, I will look at four examples of memorial installation art that help realize the synaesthetic character of seeing and the contingent nature of material-semiotic processes as well as to acknowledge the constant movement of the actual and the virtual in the rhythmic becoming of life.

Yad Layeled (Moshe Safdie, 1987)

Exceptional in its construction and emotional appeal, *The Children's Memorial Yad Layeled* currently functions as a part of the immense Yad Vashem complex erected in Jerusalem on the Mount of Remembrance (see chapter 2 for a more elaborate analysis of the museum). Constructed on the tallest point of the site, the memorial is built underground into the hill and its interior is hidden from the view of the entering visitors. Such organization actually has other functions too, as it prevents the entrance of the bright Israeli sunlight into the memorial cave. This is important for the effects the site produces. Designed by Moshe Safdie already in 1976, when the architect had been approached by the then Yad Vashem's director Itzhak Arad, the project was not constructed until 1987. This was when a couple of the Holocaust survivors Abraham and Edith Spiegel—impressed by the forcible convincingness of the memorial's design—decided to fund its construction in memory of their son Uziel who had perished during the Shoah. The problem of assuring financial measures for the memorial was partly connected to its challenging, even daring design, which did not resemble any of the more traditional memorials commemorating the Holocaust in Israel and worldwide. The construction of the memorial is persuasive and creates a deeply moving atmosphere. It seems to offer an experience of duration as well as reflects on the atemporal workings of memory, encouraging visitors to give up their everyday perceptual routines and open themselves to something new and irregular. In doing so, it generates sensation of fragility and exposure related to affectively experienced physical incertitude, when the habitual responses of the body have to be temporarily forgotten and the body is challenged with the experience of the indiscernible, unfathomable space.

The cold, white, granite pillars, with which the dark vestibule of the memorial violently contrasts, sever the entrance into the room. As Stephanie Shosh Rotem explains, "On the top of the hill Safdie placed stone columns of various heights in straight rows. . . . Next to the stones he planted trees that at the time were initially the same height as the stones but have since grown significantly taller, symbolizing the growth denied the children/columns" (2013, 52). This strategy triggers experience of movement, or time duration, which simultaneously operates in different dimensions and affects bodies in distinctive manners—they undergo various becomings and transformations. Basked in the bright sunlight, visitors approach a dark interior without knowing what to expect inside. On their entry, they are suddenly thrown into a mysterious, shady space, where nothing can be discerned. For one moment there is inevitably panic and dread, a complete confusion where and how to proceed inside, as steering through the irresistible darkness of the inscrutable space seems completely unpredictable, if not entirely impossible. The site does not offer any navigational hints or directions to follow. The encircling obscurity seems to be totally overwhelming. Yet the effects that the space produces are impressive.

Inside the memorial room visitors get immersed in the dim lights of thousands of *yahrtzeit* candles (usually used by Jews for celebrating the anniversary of death of the loved ones) that—gently moving—illuminate the memorial's interior in a subtle way. The stunning scenery with countless glittering lights is created by a tricky illusion—in fact there are only four candles lit within the space. Encased in special glass and surrounded by mirrors that do not reflect visitors, they create a wondrous visually capturing sensation. Actually, delicately moving small lights are the only discernible elements of the room and the only visual detail offered to those who entered the space. Visitors are able to neither visually locate the memorial's walls nor distinguish its shape. The spatial organization of the site remains a mystery, immersed in deep obscurity. The candles, or rather innumerous reflections of the four small flames, delicately light up the darkness above, below, and on all sides of visitors, which produces the bodily impression of being suspended in this overwhelming space. The physical situation is likely to create confusion and a feeling of loss as well as of being thrown into an unknown and unspecified environment where nothing seems to be familiar and recognizable. Obviously, there is something cosmic or unearthly about this chamber, which produces a perplexing sensation of spatial infinitude and eternal duration, of being somewhere and nowhere at the same time. This impression is magnified through the strategy of lowering the temperature within the memorial cave—the cold of the underground structure meaningfully contrasts with the warmth of the outside, taking visitors to a different world, while this difference is underlined through bodily sensation of coldness and humidity.

The mysterious encounter with the memorial is likely to produce an undetermined feeling of tension between presumed presence and perceived non-presence as nothing can be visually fixed within the room—neither the physical organization of the space nor the bodies of other visitors. The presence of others may be inferred but not discerned. Minor noises can be heard, yet their source remains unknown. However, the sensation of the presence of unrecognizable others is paralyzing, as it can be felt and experienced, although not grasped in visual terms. Inside the cave, people tend to move slowly, if at all, since their bodies seem to perceive the space as a non-space, a void, or a duration of unfathomable nothingness, with no distinguishable elements and no points of reference on which they could rely. This causes freezing hesitation and doubt. Every step becomes tentative as there are no spatial clues indicating how and where to proceed. The physical encounter with the memorial triggers the feeling of fragility and uncertainty, while encouraging realization of the vulnerability of life and its constant flimsy becoming. The body gets spatially lost or at least totally disoriented. Forced to rely on their haptic skills and compelled to examine the space in a proprioceptive fashion, visitors' bodies become exposed and are made susceptible to the unpredictable, perceptually unknown environment.

The sensation of duration in the memorial is amplified by the monotonous sound of listing of names, ages, and hometowns of children murdered during the Shoah. Once in the room, visitors are constantly bombarded with this dreary litany slowly read in an ad infinitum manner. The tediously recited list is very long—it takes three years to reach the end, and then the reading starts again. It never finishes. The persistent sound of the names intensifies the feeling of an ungraspable duration that would never stop. It is as if the memorized events dwelled in the past, present, and future at the same time. This complex entanglement can be felt bodily, encouraging reflection on the virtual character of memory itself as well as on how it informs the actual and anticipates what is to come. There is a constant movement of memory, a rhythm of life that remains uncontainable within the representational structures and symbols, a constant becoming of different dimensions of temporality.

The affective appeal of the memorial is intense and memorable because its operations rely on throwing visitors away from their ordinary perceptual routines and taken-for-granted schemes. This mostly concerns the bodily habitudes and automatic propensities. Such exertion makes them realize the learned or acquired nature of impulses and reactions to stimuli and forces their temporary suspension. In these unusual circumstances, visitors get induced into the process of *un/learning*, that is, of forgetting the automatic, unreflexive mechanisms of perception; instead, they need to expose their bodies to the completely novel surroundings, intensely working on their senses and triggering bodily-intellectual becomings. Therefore, although initially, on entrance, the memorial freezes visitors' bodies with its obscurity and dimness, causing a feeling of perplexity and confusion, its material organization also encourages them to unlearn everyday perceptual habits and invites a more proprioceptive or visceral response to the site's visually imperceptible spatial organization. Consequently, it operates through the indiscernible, which introduces the body in the state of suspension, causing vacillation in every movement. In an intensive corporeal material-semiotic encounter, the memorial character of the space actualizes.

The Garden of Exile (Daniel Libeskind, 2001)

The memorial space of the artistically arranged *Garden of Exile*, a part of JMB, is designed by Daniel Libeskind, an architect of the famous museum building (see chapter 2 for the analysis of the latter). *The Garden* constitutes an integral part of one of the museal routes, called the Axis of Emigration, commencing in the extension's underground lobby and ending in this tricky, confusing site. *The Garden* itself consists of a set of forty-nine pillars, planted on an outstandingly regular grid. The immense columns are filled with soil and serve as a support for olive trees growing on the top of them. The trees are physically unreachable for visitors, planted high on the top of the concrete pillars. Even though their branches seem to offer a garden-like snug shadow to sightseers and may potentially create an ambiance of coziness, the site is inhospitable and tends to disquiet visitors instead of giving them comforting rest and relief. The weird structure of the whole space—as seen from the distance—looks wildly crooked and strikingly disturbing. All the pillars seem to lean down towards one side as if they were situated diagonally vis-à-vis the ground. Surprisingly, however, when visitors find themselves within the memorial site, they suddenly discover that the columns are not diagonal but they are placed at a 90-degree angle to the ground. The striking look of *The Garden* is achieved by other means—not the columns but the ground itself is tilted in two angles. This produces a bizarre effect of contortion, so rare and physically discomforting. The unusual positioning of the ground and the columns can only be sensed physically on entering the memorial space. Once in *The Garden*, visitors' bodies suddenly realize and corporeally feel that the ground violently bends. Another architectural detail of the site is also noticeable, namely the ground is paved with stones of varying sizes, which makes walking through the memorial space uncomfortably hard and demanding. The march through *The Garden* is uncertain as steps are taken unsteadily and in a hesitant way. The perspective gets shaky and disorienting, which is due to both the tilted ground and the perpendicularly planted pillars. If one looks up, the offered view is disquieting and unexpected, as the pillars seem to be falling, even though they stand still and are absolutely vertical to the ground. The surface on which visitors are invited to walk produces uncomfortable physical results. If humid, the soil becomes slippery and the moving through the memorial might turn even more arduous and risky. The materiality of water or moisture affects the materiality of the ground and the materiality of visitors' walking. The entangled movements of different material bodies produce effects of distortion and incertitude. Every time a foot clashes with the irregular surface of the soil, walkers may become less assured of their physical steadiness as well as of the continuity of their passage.

Libeskind's *Garden of Exile* operates though the complex entanglement of the material and the semiotic, which co-form and co-constitute each other, remaining in constant and continuous movement. The qualities of the memorial also emerge in movement as visitors pass through the stony landscape and have their navigation affected by its disturbingly organized structure. Such a material arrangement of the space obviously prevents any sustained degree of comfort and stability for visitors as they slowly meander among the pillars and proprioceptively absorb its unusual construction. The semiotic qualities of the memorial emerge out of a physical contact of the visitor's body and the architectural space. The fact that it is difficult to hold balance in *The Garden of Exile* is likely to stimulate the overwhelming feeling of precariousness that might facilitate realization of vulnerability of life. Even though holding balance in any regular space demands a whole configuration of micro-movements (as explained earlier in this chapter), in this memorial terrain, visitors are invited to realize this fact in a more complete way, as their positionings vis-à-vis the tilted, irregular surface of the ground demand constant physical adjustments and corrections. It is a perpetual movement, or rather a multiplicity of movements. Hence, the character of the site is generated through the corporeal experience, the enfleshed sensation of its materiality and how it acts on visitors' bodies, entering in dynamic machine-like assemblages with them. At the same time, however, the materiality of this space is constituted culturally, through meaning-making structures and symbolic connotations that visitors produce in confrontation with it and with the help of their individual previous experiences and knowledges (i.e., the virtual). Certainly, the material-semiotic sensorial apparatus, as well as its abstract/virtual dimensions, is an inseparable element of the whole multifaceted encounter of the visitor and the memorial space of *The Garden*. Taking these complex processes and vibrating movements so crucial to the operation of this memorial into account, it may be argued that *The Garden of Exile* could serve as an illustrative instance of how matter and meaning remain inseparable. As Karen Barad writes, "Meaning is not an ideality; meaning is material. And matter isn't what exists separately from meaning. Mattering is a matter of what comes to matter and what doesn't" (2014, 175).

On a more representational level, the complex and multidimensional intra-action of the visitor's body and the unfamiliar terrain of *The Garden of Exile* invites displacing sensations, so different from what gardens usually offer. The thought gets vividly animated by the physical sensations experienced on site. It seems that nothing is as it should be here: the ground does not provide any comforting stability, the shadow of the unreachable trees is luridly disquieting, the perspective nauseates, the walk through the space is brutally exhausting. The unexpected, physical effects of the place could possibly translate into visitors' uncertainty and doubt, disrupting any sense of their well-being as well as depriving them of the feeling of secure predictability and sheltered comfort. Consequently, the encounter with the memorial seems to be fraught with alienation and estrangement. Again, the seemingly systematic and predictable physical organization of the space produces disturbing effects, violently forcing a more proprioceptive response to the disruptive nature of this material-semiotic encounter. The unsettling character of the site is experienced at the level of the visitors' skeleton and muscles, which helps realizing how the human body relies on usual perceptual routines and how inadequate they are in cases of such troubling physical arrangements. These habits have to be *unlearnt*, and the body must open itself to the novelty of this newly encountered material-semiotic environment.

Also the materials used for the erection of *The Garden of Exile* sustain the culturally triggered meanings of unfriendliness and isolation; the bodily solitude unleashes production of devastating feelings of alienation and despair. These sensations are connected to, or even generated in, a set of physical movements of bodies. These intra-actions involve visitors and the pillars cutting them off the familiar surrounding as well as visitors' encounters with the astonishingly violent geometry of the site, whose pebbled ground unexpectedly tilts. The memorial process generated on site, however, also involves cultural meanings ascribed to (and sustained with) the materials used in the construction of the place, the spatial organization of *The Garden*, the vibrating and unstable assemblages of sensory impulses produced within it, the physical movements of the body through the site, the micro-movements of the memorial itself, and the discomfort the navigation through the surprising stony structure possibly incites. Hence, the memorial character of the site, as well as the memory work performed by visitors, emerges out of a number of dynamic relationalities and intense bodily transactions. It is itself a relation consisting of a multiplicity of micro-collisions or micro-perceptions involved in the event of an encounter, a constantly reconfiguring assemblage of (micro)movements that triggers passionate *un/learning*, turning the involved bodies into vulnerable entities with fluid and always fluctuating boundaries temporarily produced as effects of relations and encounters. The actualization of these contours, as well as the production of affective-intellectual knowledges, is informed by the rhythmic pulsation of the virtual. Therefore, the knowledge that visitors bring with them to the site (including the meaning-making structures; the previous bodily encounters; the sensory memory; the knowledge of the Shoah; their more immediate national, ethnic, or racial contexts; and their particular situations and positionings) actively participates in the process of generating the memorial event. These experiences, and virtual or abstract futures they anticipate, are never identical or even similar to each other. As bodies are different (and constantly differing) and continuously enter into new relations, the composition of the material-semiotic elements of the generated experience is always vibrantly moving and undergoing incessant reconfigurings. The process of evoking the memorial character of the space is therefore a matter of both *con*-sensus (or feeling along with others, which is located in particular cultural contexts) and complete singularity, a procedure that is both social/collective and singular/always different.

Shalekhet (Menashe Kadishman, 2001)

As *The Garden of Exile*, the installation *Shalekhet* is also a part of JMB. Devoted to the victims of all crimes of war, and not exclusively to those perished during the Shoah, it is placed downstairs, in one of the voids of the building. It is the only void in the museum that can actually be accessed by visitors. The space is somber and murky, lit up by a single ray of light entering it through the slit in its ceiling, which—in terms of a produced atmosphere—corresponds with the rest of the building's interior (see chapter 2 for more details). The construction of this evocative installation seems to be very simple. The artist decided to cover the whole floor of the void with over 10,000 faces coarsely formed from iron plates; they are scattered randomly over the whole space, densely concealing the floor in four or five layers. The disks' features are cut out: two eyes, a nose, and an open, horrified mouth. They seem to be frozen in a moment of emitting a painful scream, which fits within the sonic nature of this particular processual work of art. The idea of the installation is to invite visitors to walk onto the iron faces and explore the room wherein it is situated. It does not mean, however, that many of them actually step on the disks and take a couple of paces. There is a lot of hesitation and doubt, but when they eventually decide to follow the artist's intended instructions, their walk causes constant and disturbing noise and the plates cling and clang, rattling vibrantly under visitors' steps. The layers of the disks make the surface uneven and shaky, which affects the manner in which visitors walk on them. Even if their march is careful and attentive, the faces shift about under their feet, producing disquieting, horrifying sounds. The laud clanging suddenly fills the whole exhibition space, which contrasts with the quietude of the rest of the museum, where people usually hardly talk and if they do, it is at most a whisper. The noise gets violent and foreboding, resulting from a series of movements and bumping impingements of different bodies.

The experienced sound is a dispersed vibration triggered by the movement of the disks, the latter caused by visitors' movement. It is a series of encounters and a series of vehement bodily collisions. It means that the soundscape of the installation works through movement and actually needs the moving bodies of visitors to get activated and produce vibrant sonic effects. These pulsating movements enter into encounters with the memorial void's somber and repellent walls and—in form of screaming reverberations—are likely to produce the dim and gloomy feeling of isolation and estrangement that subsequently reenters visitors' bodies as sonic waves, eliciting discomforting restlessness and murky disorientation. These overwhelming intensities affect the surfaces of all bodies involved; they are haptically sensed. Experienced bodily, the movement of the installation-visitor assemblage is also bodily produced, since the sounds are born in an inventive machine-like intra-action of a visitor's body-in-movement and the space-in-movement. They simultaneously affect and are affected by each other, which is a procedure that leaves micro-traces on all entities involved in this generative series of collisions. Consequently, the synaesthetic relational process is jointly manufactured in a creative encounter of the visitor's body, the architecture of the site, and the elements placed within the space. Vibratory sounds of the movements of the assemblage of bodies add another dimension to these workings. The generated event relies on activation of a number of sensual dimensions of experience—the latter is not solely visual but rather involves a joint effervescent operation of different senses.

Importantly, as a physical vibration, or a series of movements, sound exceeds the body—whether organic or technological—that acts as its source. Yet it cannot merely be considered as a medium establishing relations between the already-existing primary individual entities that it relates. When approached from a new materialist point of view, these relations are generative and regenerative of the relating entities' very individuality. The bodies participating in the encounter are therefore only provisional; in fact, they constantly emerge and reemerge out of the relations, to which they immensely contribute. The sonic assemblages are therefore productive of the constitution of the relating bodies. The sound is a processual factor initiating relationalities wherein the involved entities undergo incessant transformations, that is, wherein they relentlessly and continuously become-other.

As signaled earlier, the intensity of the synaesthetic experience could not be fully acknowledged when approached from a purely visual perspective. The installation works through sonic energies being generated in the passionate and multidirectional impingement of visitors' bodies and the work of art, which together form a dynamic ecosystem, full of sensual interactions and movements. It works through vibrations and—in assemblage-like fashion—animates corporeal-intellectual flow of energies and forces. Moreover, it encourages awareness about how it is not only the signifying but also the sensorial aspect of artistic and mediatized expressions that are mediated by past perceptions, and how the virtuality of sense perception means that the form of the object—like a sonic wave—is, as Brian Massumi writes, "the way a whole set of active, embodied, potentials appears in present experience" (2011, 42). The virtual stands here for the involvement of both past events and the yet-undetermined future in any perception that particular bodies have in a given here and now. Consequently, the past enriches the attributes of that which bodies actually encounter. This occurs in the form of associations to the "archives" of the involved perceivers' previous experiences and through the ways the past always conditions their very capacities to sense, feel, and experience as well as process these very impressions. The future, on the other hand, involves the variation these experiential "events" will undergo, as relations to what is sensed and experienced evolve or new encounters dynamically affecting them take place. In the sonic encounter, the virtual arises into actuality.

As Eldritch Priest explains, "Perception itself always has a virtual dimension to it, a nonsensuous dimension whose qualitative autonomy gives thought its characteristic flow" (2013, 52). Thought is nonsensuous—it is felt abstractly (cf. Massumi 2011, 109). Massumi evinces that "when we pause to think, this is what we're doing: continuing life abstractly" (2011, 118). When the rhythm of experience, or of life, is taken from the body and turned into linguistic representation that imposes forms on it, it turns into abstraction and gets removed from the original flow of life. Yet the representational layer may intensify the original perception by producing meanings and significations. This adds and rehearses the primal experience but is also nourished by the original affects and intensities. Always moving, always transforming. Accordingly, perceptual events are passing, and any experience of an event, as Massumi argues (2011), is an experience of the process of passing. As such, they are assemblages of what has just been, of what is now, and of what is about to be. Abstraction, in Massumi's understanding, is co-constitutive of the concrete, as much as the virtual informs the actual. In the case of the installation *Shalekhet*, which works through relational engagements, the complex entanglement of the political/symbolic and the material/aesthetic is noticeable. They work with and through each other—as an assemblage of different bodies undergoing constant reconfigurings and reorganizations. The singular meanings visitors produce in the encounter with the memorial space are generated through the relational involvement of a number of bodies, as well as thanks to the abstraction stored in these bodies, actualized in the moment of creating a linkage. The visitor's body and the soundscape of the installation perform together to produce a meaningful and intense virtual-actual memorial event, always singular in its fleeting, temporary nature.

The Drowned and the Saved (Richard Serra, 1992/1997)

Richard Serra's sculpture, whose title *The Drowned and the Saved* bears a symbolic reference to the memoir work of an Italian Holocaust survivor Primo Levi, was initially commissioned by and installed at the Stommeln Synagogue in Pulheim, Germany, in 1992. The site was one of the very few German synagogues to survive the infamous *Kristallnacht* of 1938, so this location strongly determined the semiotic meaning of the work of art. Moreover, untypically for the artist, the installation was accompanied by a personal story of Serra, published in the exhibition catalogue, wherein he claimed his Jewish identity as well as the experience of living in fear of disclosing it to others imposed on him by his mother. The work, therefore, functions in a multimodal form—as a site-specific construction marked by the identity of its author. In 1997 the piece was purchased by the Diocesan Museum in Cologne and subsequently moved to the impressive building of the Kolumba Museum. As a consequence, the sculpture is now situated in the roofless former sacristy of a Catholic Church Sankt Kolumba (which, between 1943 and 1945, was destroyed except for the outside walls). Even though Serra usually avoids any direct referencing to the Holocaust (and his own biography) in his artistic production, the title of this particular sculpture is very telling. Levi's collection of essays, entitled identically to Serra's work of art, seems to debate the precarious fragility and moving instability of mnemonic processes, remaining always in entangled relationship with the present and the future and counterbalanced by the inclination to forget, repress, or erase painful recollections. It may be argued that the sculpture embodies this perpetual tension, or a condition of vulnerable volatility and wavering. Unsurprisingly, given the artistic preferences of the sculptor, the work operates through its immense, yet fragile materiality sustained by a constant movement of forces of gravity and fraction, which make possible the sculpture's seemingly immobile lasting. As in the case of every equilibrium, its motionless positioning requires a multiplicity of movements—to achieve still balance, after all, is to defy every occurring movement and every acting force with a counteraction. Thus, stillness is not the lack but an abundance of vibrational movements.

Serra's installation consists of two identical, L-shaped beams, placed upside down and mutually supporting each other. Joined, they create a form resembling angled, squared-off, inverted letter U. Its size is confusing—too big to serve as a bench, too small to pass for an arch. In the context of its surroundings, it may resemble an altar or a *bimah* (cf. Godfrey 2007, 21), yet its form seems to be too modest and humble to be used for this purpose. Each of the pieces that the sculpture is composed of has the same shape with a horizontal arm longer than the vertical one. So conceived, none of them could stand upright on its own. Without the second piece, each of the arms would inevitably fall down. The two blocks of steel, however, face each other, one propping up the other, so that they remain in perfect stability, ideally counterbalanced by each other's weight. On the verge of disintegration and collapse, the construction seems to be impossible to thrive. It is full of contradictions—it does not exclusively involve the acting forces, but also it plays out the contrast between its heavy materiality and its implied fragile structure.

There is an interesting connection between the precarious construction of the installation and the title it was given. The latter seems to imply the opposition between the drowned and the saved, but also—simultaneously—evokes their mutual dependency, eliciting a compulsory relentless linkage between the two. The two blocks of steel also rely on each other for their very existence in their current shape and position. But they simultaneously confront each other, in a constant tension that translates into perfect equilibrium. Such constellation is coercive and full of intense micro-movements that make the perceived fleeting balance possible. A multiplicity of vibrations and acting forces contribute to the apparent heaviness of the seemingly motionless installation. A perfect immobility and stillness. A contradiction functioning against the usual routines. A shape contingent on itself. One part relying on the other, one side preventing the other from falling down. As Mark Godfrey describes it, "The sculpture dramatises principles of balance, weight, load and gravity" (2007, 20). Dividing the site wherein it is located into the space above and the space below, as well as forming a barrier almost in the middle of the room, the sculpture incarnates the idea of a perfect equilibrium, yet itself appears to remain shaky and unstable. It works through its located materiality rather than through representational means, although it has a representational layer too. It seems to materialize the shuddering yet enduring nature of memory, pointing to its fragility and susceptibility as well as highlighting its contingent character. As Hal Foster notices, the work of art evokes processes of spanning and passing, as both these movements seem to be intimated in it (1998a). There is a virtual potentiality of the sculpture's collapse inscribed in its construction, which elicits an imminent danger or at least incertitude about its future; there is also a reliance on forces of gravity, which turns the form in a countergravitational structure. Since the operating forces of gravity remain in equilibrium (as the two arms of the arch are identical in shape and weight), the installation is held in arrested motion; nevertheless, it demands a multiplicity of movements and requires a constant activity of forces. Noticeably, the sculpture appears exceptionally heavy, but the weight of the two immense blocks seems to be annihilated—again, by the force of gravity acted against itself. The amount of energy remains the same, so the construction stays in balance. This evokes contradictions and the precarious nature of the becoming of movement, as well as the fragility of its potential effects. The produced impression is that the work is not what it once were, even a second earlier; neither is it yet what it will become. It experiences a constant, enduring movement.

The Drowned and the Saved embodies a tense condition of uncertainty and perpetual menace. As contingent on the permanent operation of forces and movements, the sculpture elicits sensations of visceral unease and insecurity. It undeviatingly materializes painful, even impossible contradictions and ambiguities, pushing spectators towards a physical, somatic participation in the artistic event it generates. The construction disavows visitors' purely optical relation with it, encouraging a bodily response as well as reflection on the memorial experience such an encounter produces. Visitors are forced to confront the weight of the insecure, potentially unstable piece and realize the perpetual operation of forces that keep it in perceptually experienced stillness. Full of contrasts and contradictions working together and through one another, Serra's work of art imposes the necessity to disavow the habitual assumptions and taken-for-granted knowledges and expectations, and to see differently. It requires suspension of perceptual rules, playing out the solidity as entangled with fragility, heaviness as connected to susceptibility, and motion as not oppositional to immobility. There is a complex relationality between the actual and the virtual in its almost impossible construction, which encourages coming to terms with the unusual and the unexpected that cannot be contained within the traditional, well-established frameworks and subdued to straightforward rules and regulations. Embodying the nature of the convoluted processes of remembering and forgetting—entangling past, present, and future—the solid installation remains dynamic and lively, always in actual-virtual flux and constantly changing. No longer can stillness be seen as antithetical to movement, which puts under question the whole logic of thinking in oppositional terms. Such oversimplification of the richness of the rhythm of life and the durational movement of becoming does not do justice to multiplicity, or excess of transformational processes that never come to an end. The classificatory, regulative inclinations have to be unlearned in order for perception to be able to open up to the new. Learning a different logic of thinking—in terms of connectivities and withnesses rather than oppositions and dichotomies—is necessary to acknowledge the relational nature of life (and of memory) with all the processes that it produces and by which it is itself produced.

THE LOGIC OF RELATIONALITY: CONCLUDING REMARKS

The bodies are fluid; their boundaries fluctuate. When they encounter other bodies or impinge on them, they experience reconfigurations, which—even if minor and imperceptible—leave traces on their surfaces (the latter reemerge in this process) and affect their trajectories of becomings. There are no neutral encounters—in each such event there is an activity of forces and movements involved, and they never return as the same. The process of becoming of bodies implicates constant differing, or—quite simply—perpetual becoming-other. Even though always different from oneself, it is still the same body, dissolving stringent opposition between difference and sameness (cf. Deleuze 2011). Bodies, consequently, have to be (re)conceived as verbs, as perpetual processes, as dynamic assemblages entering into relations with other bodies. Only in relations do they exist; only through relations do they become. Such understanding implies the logic of relationality and withness, or of complex entanglements of bodies and their movements, of co-constitutive liaisons and intimacies, which are always productive of something new or unexpected, yet always located in a given "here and now." Importantly, this here and now is of material-semiotic nature and implies constant dynamism and permanent redrawing of its flowing boundaries. Each entanglement of bodies, or each encounter, is productive of new transformations generating new qualities of the involved entities. As in the case of rocks evoked in the story told by Manuel DeLanda quoted in the opening of this chapter, the perpetual work performed by different bodies tends to consolidate their temporary spatial relations into more or less stable structures and constellations. Their nature, however, is only temporary—it is a fleeting actualization of virtual potentialities that the involved entities have always already possessed. This testifies to the vulnerable condition of virtual-actual bodies, which are susceptible to forces acting on them as well as to confrontation with other bodies. These encounters set them in further motion, triggering their continuous rhizomatic metamorphoses. Worth noticing is the fact that the logic proposed in this chapter is completely post-anthropocentric, as it does not differentiate between different kinds of bodies (e.g., human and nonhuman) acknowledging their agencies and capacities for engagement in actions. As such, it subscribes to the inclusive, Deleuzian understanding of the body according to which the body can be anything (see chapter 1).

Participation in artistic events, generated jointly by viewers/visitors and the works of art, clearly exposes the precarious, temporary nature of bodies and their becomings. Since art unswervingly acts on the corporeal dimension and directly impacts the nervous system, it reveals the susceptible condition of their boundaries and pictures the entangled (and embodied!) nature of knowledge production processes. The latter seem to be always collective—it is a becoming contingent on other bodies, or—as I called it earlier—*becoming-with-other-bodies*. Importantly, an analysis of inventive encounters with art and how they are productive of affects and intensities, as well as how these sensations animate intellectual thought, can serve as a point of departure for reflection on the new conception of politics of experience. This is extremely vital from a feminist point of view, especially taking into consideration the feminist critical attitude towards the dominant ways of producing knowledge, given the Western culture's total disregard, or dismissal, of the role of the body in cognitive processes.

Drawing on notions of connectivity and withness, and focusing on the prolific logic of relationality, in the last chapter of this book, I will explore the feminist politics of *sym*pathy, framed as an ethico-onto-epistemological position or location wherefrom knowledges can be produced along with others. Such reconceptualization, I argue, is absolutely necessary if we want to transcend the discriminatory, anthropocentric, and exclusionary ways of thinking implying ocularcentric, controlling manners of imposing scientific categorizations on the objects of knowledge (i.e., of representation). Instead, the feminist politics of connectivity points to the complex network of relationalities, revealing how we are embedded in the world and how the world is embedded in us. This urges us to rethink the accountable ethics of responsibility (or rather response-ability), taking into consideration the entangled nature of our becoming with/in the world.

NOTES

1. Manning writes critically about phenomenology, supporting her view with a cursory analysis of Maurice Merleau-Ponty's late reflections, pointing that it is impossible for phenomenology to think the subject as divorced from the notion of intentionality. Even though I support Manning's clear explanation of Alfred N. Whitehead's process philosophy, I disagree with her interpretation of phenomenology. In this regard I am convinced by critical responses to Manning's article (2014) pointing to more diverse understandings of intentionality by other phenomenologists (e.g., Emmanuel Levinas and Michel Henry). Jody McNeilly points out that "historically it can be seen that intentionality is not a necessary or fixed tenet of phenomenology" (2014, 210) and evidences that "the body can be approached phenomenologically with or without a notion of intentionality. It is misleading to think that there is only one idea of intentionality and subjectivity informing phenomenology" (2014, 213). Similarly critical towards Manning's argumentation, and especially her presupposition of movement, is Maxine Sheets-Johnstone (2014), on whose works Manning originally draws. Sheets-Johnstone points to the fact that the kinaesthetic dimension of movement is missing from Manning's theorizations. As mentioned earlier, I mostly agree with these critical responses, yet I still think that Manning's reading of Whitehead is clear and useful; hence, I draw on it in my argumentation.

2. For a more elaborate understanding of rhythm in a new materialist spirit, see Henriques et al. (2014) as well as the whole special issue of *Body & Society* 20 (3 and 4), edited by the authors of this introductory text.

3. The question of agency needs to be approached critically. As Bruno Latour underlines, defining agency as connected to, or implying, intentionality remains within the anthropocentric logic of thinking and tends to "humanize" all matter (cf. Latour 2005; I have already mentioned this issue in the introductory part of this book). It is therefore necessary to focus on the human-nonhuman collectivities, centering on the metamorphous dynamics of these relations and connectivities. This, however, urges us to disavow the anthropocentric cognitive framework and work out a different, more inclusive, logic of thinking.

Chapter 5

Affective Connections: Feminist Politics of *Sym*pathy

FROM ENCOUNTERS WITH ART TO FEMINIST KNOWLEDGE PRODUCTION

"See with a feeling eye: feel with a seeing hand"—this short excerpt from Johann Wolfgang von Goethe's (2007) beautiful poem seems to capture the complexity of a synaesthetic experience conceived often as a point of departure for knowledge production processes. The latter are exceptionally important for sensitive feminist philosophies advancing a more equal, more inclusive, and less discriminatory politics. In order to do so, however (as I explained in the introduction to this book), it is necessary to find new ways of thinking, new figurations, and new strategies of developing critique as well as to reinvent the concepts and theories that might offer potential for creative change. Since, as mentioned earlier, in Deleuze and Guattari's view (1997), art, science, and philosophy are the three daughters of Chaos, or the three modes of thinking, in this chapter, I would like to underline that as three daughters of the same parent they are also sisters connected with deep ties of kinship. It is therefore possible to think them together as they are not incompatible but rather constitute a meaningful juncture. Given this "familial" entwinement, in the previous three chapters I offered reflections on the operations of memorial *works of art* (understood in new materialist terms), which served as illustrations for my theoretical deliberations and ideas. Hence, there were many connections between art and philosophy in the earlier parts of this book. In this chapter, I would like to focus more extensively on the links between artistic and scientific processes, pointing to the important material-semiotic aspects of knowledge production practices as well as highlighting their communal and embodied character. Consequently, my analyses of encounters with art—always situated in specific ideological, cultural, and material contexts—are considered as starting points for reflections on the politics of experience constituting an important basis for generating knowledges.

As my investigations presented earlier in this book revealed, the creative encounters with memorial art, or art related to trauma—conceived as active material-semiotic agents producing certain effects—can contribute to the emergence of more complex relationalities or forms of affinity and connection. Importantly, these encounters happen on a bodily-intellectual level and, in inventive ways, trigger further becomings of entities involved. My objective in this chapter is to point to the usefulness of such formulations for feminist politics, especially as far as knowledge production practices are concerned. As I want to make clear, the procedures of generating (scientific) knowledges are collective by their nature. They are not performed in isolation from the surrounding reality but rather are the products of the rhizomatic relations with/in the environment. These connections are synaesthetic as they involve certain sensuous proximity as well as synthetic operations of corporeal and intellectual cognitive faculties. They are also about a creative active-passive production with often unexpected results. Therefore, in fostering my thinking of the new materialist politics of *sym*pathy, I will look both into the idea of togetherness that this concept entails and to the notion of passivity, which involves an evacuation of the figure of the self being in control of its agencies and actions. I believe that the earlier thoughts developed in this volume and focusing on how art operates—how it absorbs us through its generative, affective qualities—can help us think about relationality and passivity. Aesthetic experience, one connected to artistic events and one not necessarily related to them, requires a certain manner of self-surrender or being acted on. Encounters with art expose our vulnerability to its intensive functioning that reach us through our bodies, often in involuntary or nonconsensual ways. This is especially visible in the case of trauma art or artistic production related to difficult occurrences, catastrophes, or genocidal events. Such works of art reveal the complex interweaving of past, present, and future, operating in actual-virtual manners and remaining in constant, unpredictable movements. Moreover, as Simon O'Sullivan reminds, art should be understood as machinic—it operates "on a variety of signifying but also asignifying registers" (2006, 6) and allows us to acknowledge the entangled nature of encounters with others. We do not become immune to the already-interpreted and deconstructed work of art—it still affects us and impacts us in immediate, bodily ways, divulging our vulnerability and irresistible fragility as well as situating us in a position of being acted on. Such condition requires both receptivity and answerability. These responses, however, remain beyond purely representational realm and testify to the material, relational becoming of bodies. The synaesthetic actual-virtual operations of memorial *works of art*, whose short analyses I offered in previous chapters, lay bare the material-semiotic nature of always-singular encounters, revealing the complex processes of affecting and being affected in the intensive events of manufacturing knowledge. For this reason, I believe that the examination of functioning of such artistic installations, coupled with consideration of the bodily-intellectual character of mnemonic processes (evidenced by the instances of trauma and traumatic memory), can serve as an interesting starting point for rethinking the politics of experience as well as reflecting on the complex character of knowledge production practices.

The main objective of this chapter is to advance a new materialist concept of *sym*pathy, grounded in the logic of connectivity, which I consider vital from a feminist point of view. Even though the historical connotations that the term generates are not necessarily favorable, my aim is to divorce this idea from the negative loading and reframe its meaning by situating it within a new materialist framework. In order to do so, I will succinctly map the evolution of thinking about sympathy, empathy, and compassion, relating it briefly to the feminist and postcolonial critiques and pointing out some concerns that they have raised. Nevertheless, my goal is also to emphasize the possibilities the concept of *sym*pathy creates for feminist politics of solidarity and connectivity. By doing so, I will first focus on one of the word-forming elements of the term, that is *sym-*, pointing to the intimacy of the "with" that it embodies and commenting on the potential that it has in the context of relational logic. Later on, I will elaborate on the idea of "passive syntheses" worked out by Gilles Deleuze while connecting it to the notion of passivity inscribed in the concept of sym*pathy*. Important for my argumentation, Deleuze's philosophy of subjectivity—conceived as both active and passive, acting and being acted on—fundamentally revises the dominant ways of thinking about the subject of knowledge as the most powerful, yet invisible figure in the processes of knowledge production. Claims inspired by Deleuzian philosophy, I believe, subscribe to the philosophical ideas of new materialism, offering an alternative formulation of subjectivity, which relies on the evacuation of the concept of a powerful, coherent, and agential "I." My further argumentation underlines a radical potentiality of passivity, understood as an interesting ethico-onto-epistemological position wherefrom knowledge is generated *together with other bodies* (both human and more-than-human) in the process of constant becoming. This takes me to reflections on vulnerability and susceptibility as inherent in the new materialist conceptions of subjectivity and serving as figurations to think about the entangled coexistence of different bodies remaining in dynamic, never-ending, machine-like relations with each other and through one another. What I want to point out is that it is not possible to approach objects, processes, bodies, and phenomena as isolated events or occurrences. Rather, it is necessary to look how they are entangled and connected with other bodies, whatever their shape, form, ontological status, level of liveliness, dynamics of metamorphoses, and so on. The logic of relationality, which I advocate for in this book, forces us to acknowledge that indeed, as Donna Haraway notices, "nothing comes without its world" (1997, 137) or without its consequences. Hence, it is essential to do justice to the complexity of relations in which we are involved, which we recreate, and by which we are reconfigured.

APPROACHING "SYMPATHY" THROUGH A FEMINIST LENS

An interest in the idea of feeling what others feel, or understanding their situation by putting oneself in their shoes, has quite a long history, and it has generated a substantial amount of theoretical work. These debates, however, have never been univocal. On the one hand, the lines of critique focused on ethical problems that attempts at grasping positions of others might entail. Yet, on the other hand, they indicated probable advantages a strategy of imagining situatedness of others could possibly possess. The concepts fostered by philosophers and sociologists have traditionally raised a lot of reservations and doubts, also on the part of feminist and postcolonial scholars, and especially those interested in knowledge production processes. Epistemologists have for long reflected on how (or whether at all) to speak for less-powerful or discriminated-against others (whose abilities to speak for themselves are often seriously restricted), how to know their locations and study their contexts, or how to claim knowledge of issues that do not directly affect researchers. Certainly, the dominant model of producing scientific theories based on empirical research offers a ready-to-apply solution, arguing that the more distanced position researchers adopt, the more objective knowledge they produce. The principles of a noninterference and emotional detachment have been seen as necessary attributes of a reliable research process. This way of thinking, as I explained in the introduction to this book, has paved the way for the ocularcentric (scientific) culture resting on the means of vision (observation) as the most objective (since operating from a distance) sense and scientific instrument. Politics of sympathy, empathy, connectivity, or withness in such a context seem to be completely antithetical to the dominant academic models as they put emphasis on an emotional bondage with and encourage an affective investment in the issues and topics under research.

Even though feminist and postcolonial scholars point to the problems the traditional model of producing knowledge engenders, and attempt at developing alternative ways of thinking, they are at the same time aware of the difficulties and challenges these new theorizations pose. Since this chapter aims at discussing the new materialist politics of *sym*pathy, in this section, I would like to take a closer look at how the concept of sympathy has been approached historically and what kind of critiques it has generated. As mentioned earlier, my intention is to divorce this notion from the negative connotation it has acquired over the decades, pointing instead to the potential its reformulation in new materialist terms may possibly offer for feminist politics.

Taking into consideration the ferocious debates surrounding such terms as "empathy," "sympathy," and "compassion," it seems necessary to explore serious reservations they incite and varied hesitations they evoke. It is, however, not an easy task, especially bearing in mind the historical zigzagging metamorphoses of meanings associated with these concepts as well as mixed ethical implications these positions produce. Nevertheless, to offer a setting for my further argumentation, I will briefly trace these transitions, looking at the possible problems each of the subsequent (re)formulations generated. It is also crucial in this context to carefully map feminist critiques that these theorizations incited and point out how these critical voices have triggered subsequent—more informed and more sensitive—reconceptualizations and revisions. What needs to be made clear is the fact that certain ambivalence in the ways feminists approach these terms is discernible, which testifies to their uncertain status—appealing and problematic at the same time. On the one hand, this hesitation has translated into almost complete abandonment of the concepts of sympathy and compassion, as they are considered too hierarchically conceived and too much infused with ideological power. On the other hand, however, the notion of empathy has recently generated renewed interest among feminists, who, nevertheless, remain attentive to the concept's ethical and epistemological implications and methodological consequences. Therefore, it seems that the possibilities it offers for the development of a more up-to-date politics of solidarity still remain important in current historical circumstances, yet the concept needs a lot of critical attention and sensitive (re)conceptualization.

Acknowledging critical voices and being aware of the problems the politics of sympathy (or empathy) might possibly pose, I still consider them vitally important from a feminist point of view and remaining in line with many of the postulates articulated in feminist critiques of the dominant models of knowledge production. I also believe that their reformulation informed by new materialist philosophies could provide the new logic of thinking, that is, one more focused on relationality and entanglement of different (f)actors possessing important agencies. Moreover, the idea of connectivity can potentially serve as an alternative to the traditional—that is, anthropocentric, ocularcentric, representational—models of generating scientific "truths," especially given connectivity's reliance on the politics of life as a movement of becoming (explained in the previous chapter of this book). However, before discussing the ethico-onto-epistemological reverberations of such position, it is necessary to explore historical contexts in which concepts of sympathy, empathy, and compassion have been forged and wherein they acquired their dominant (yet not completely coherent) meanings.

From the fourteenth to the beginning of the seventeenth century, the term "compassion" was used to refer to both "suffering together with another" and "an emotion felt on behalf of another who suffers" (Garber 2004, 20). As such, it has typically related to situations involving negative experiences and emotions and has been used to depict the difficult situations of others as indirectly experienced by those located in a more privileged position (even though those positions could be temporary and fleeting and not necessarily fixed within the sociocultural structures of power). A similar term, "sympathy," from the seventeenth century onward has been employed to describe the "act of feeling what another was feeling throughout a full range of passions" (Foster 2010, 128), that is, these feelings have no longer been necessarily limited to suffering, misery, or pain, but potentially could apply to situations of joy and pleasure. Thus, the term implied a situation of sharing emotions and experiences of whatever kind without necessarily equipping these sensations with positive or negative valance. The idea of "shareability" is inscribed in the concept itself. Taking into consideration the construction of the term, the original Greek word-forming expression *sym-* (or *syn-*, meaning "with, together") refers to a connection with another, that is, "feeling with," "co-experiencing," or "participating in someone else's passions." Actually, the term "compassion" has a very similar construction (and meaning), as the prefix *com* (or *con*), from Latin, also invokes "withness" or "connectivity." Interestingly, however, in many languages, "sympathy" is used in reference to a wider range of feelings, whereas the employment of "compassion" remains limited to more negative contexts and sorrowful experiences (I will briefly come back to this issue later in this chapter). Therefore, although initially these two terms tended to describe situations of solidarity and understanding regardless of the emotional loading of the events to which they referred, in the course of time they started to be considered as appropriate responses exclusively to someone else's difficult conditions. Rarely have they been used in more affirmative contexts and situations, even though—in etymological terms—"feeling with" does not limit itself to negative experiences and troubling circumstances.

Taking into consideration critiques developed in the early twentieth century and focusing on the unequal status of some social groups versus others, the terms "sympathy" and "compassion" have started to be seen solely as implying patronizing positions of commiserating with other people, co-feeling their pain, or pitying for them. As such, they have been perceived as implicitly invoking a moral judgment as well as presupposing a certain social hierarchy. This criticism coincided with the emergence of the term "empathy," which connoted not merely the process of sharing other's feelings but also, importantly, a "cognitive understanding of them" (Foster 2010, 163). Such a conceptualization introduced a more "rational" approach to what the other is feeling. Empathy implies a possibility of cognitively sharing another's experiences, of adopting locations identical to those of other people, and, logically, of perceiving (and knowing) the world through their eyes. Noticeably, although empathy—different from sympathy or compassion—has been seen as morally neutral, it remained perceived as solely an imaginative position (Nussbaum 2003, 302). Consequently, the term "empathy" has started to be used as a substitute for the hitherto-employed, yet increasingly seen as problematic, terms "sympathy" or "compassion," as more justifiable on ethical grounds. As Marjorie Garber clarifies, the meaning of the term "empathy," especially in its early twentieth-century understanding, derives from *Einfühlung* coined by German aestheticians to "denote the power of projecting one's personality into the object of contemplation" (Garber 2004, 24). Accordingly, empathy signaled a more inclusive position, encompassing passions for inanimate objects (Currie 2011, 82), hence not referring merely to humans. The term, in such understanding, relates to aesthetic aspects of experience, that is, involving sensuous interactions. As Amy Coplan and Peter Goldie explain, empathy might connote "inner resonance that is based on a natural instinct" and should be seen as a process that pushes us to "imitate the movements and expressions we perceive in physical and social objects" (2011, xii). Again, the "feelings into" are conceived here in relation to both other people and objects, the latter both animate and inanimate. Nonetheless, such an understanding of empathy (or formerly sympathy) is rather minor; their prevailing meanings refer to feelings of people for other people and as such subscribe to a rather anthropocentric logic, so typical for the hierarchically organized Western culture.

From a feminist point of view, the problematic aspects of empathy and sympathy are connected to the question whether this kind of engagement can be dialogical and multidirectional, or rather it should be seen as a position available to (or falsely assumed by) only those who are socially privileged. The questions that need to be addressed in this context are numerous: Who can afford to emphasize/sympathize with others? What kind of ethical and moral assumptions do these positions require and what sort of implications do they produce? Do they sustain or undermine the already-existing social hierarchies reinforcing rather than challenging the status quo?[1] Obviously, those empathizing with others are usually located in privileged positions and feel sorry for the worse situation of those empathized with, which means that this very feeling establishes, or at least sustains, certain relations of power structuring social life. This is an aspect vital from the feminist and postcolonial points of view, especially as far as the analysis of cultural positionings and social stratifications is concerned.

Political circumstances of the emergence of the concepts of sympathy and empathy are also problematic. Susan Foster, for instance, urges to situate the increased interest in them in the context of the "colonial expansion" (2010, 11), as well as hierarchical structures associated therewith, and encourages to acknowledge the social stratifications already in place that made the positions of "the sympathizer" and "the sympathized with" possible. In regard to these "roles," the opposition between the active and the passive element of this (binary) pair, where the former is valued and appreciated while the latter is seen as subordinated and negatively loaded, is noticeable. This is especially important in light of the original analyses of sympathy elaborated by Adam Smith (2006 [1759]) and David Hume (2004 [1777]) based on clear distinctions between nations, races, classes, and genders. Accordingly, those living in comfort, educated, and privileged (i.e., men rather than women, whites rather than nonwhites, bourgeois rather than representatives of lower classes, colonizers rather than colonized) were capable of greater sympathy than those who had to devote their time to attend to their primary needs. Such problematic distribution of capacities to sympathize (or empathize) with others tended to reestablish the existent asymmetries and turned those in privileged positions into "more human" or "more compassionate" subjects, and, as such, also more valuable. This way of thinking is obviously completely antithetical to the arguments fostered by feminist and postcolonial voices.

Moreover, as many critical scholars emphasize, in analyzing empathy, we have to acknowledge the limitedness of the ability to imaginatively adopt the position of others as well as accept the circumscriptions of the capabilities to experience what others experience (for further discussions, see, e.g., Bartky 1996, Spelman 1997). Donna Haraway (1988), in her polemical discussion with Sandra Harding (1986) focusing on the feminist knowledge production, indicates the risks of romanticizing the experiences of the subordinated and specifies the dangers of appropriating their positions (through starting knowledge from marginalized lives, as Harding proposes)[2] for the purpose of those in power. Such strategy strengthens the already well-established systems of distribution of privileges and reinforces the position of dominant groups in society and within the academia. This means that even certain feminist critiques bear risks of being partly distorted by dominant views, which might make them blind to their important ethical implications. Similar concerns are raised by Chandra Mohanty (1988, 2003) and Gayatri Spivak (1988), both developing rather critical views on the dominant systems of knowledge production, which—although including marginal/subaltern voices on a declarative level—still tend to subordinate them to the dominant episteme. There is always a serious danger in the process of speaking for others or by making them speak for themselves by employing the language of the dominant group.

Such policy symbolically mutes the experience of "the others" of Western culture, since it remains inexpressible in its diversity and difference in the Western vocabularies and meaning-making structures. Analogically, Sara Ahmed argues that while assuming that one can feel what another feels, we fail to acknowledge the differences "in history, power, and experience" (2004a, 29) that structure and motivate these distinct positions, which might lead to sustaining (or even deepening) social gaps rather than to bridging them. In similar vein, Carolyn Pedwell pays special attention to the dynamics between the empathizer/sympathizer and the empathized/sympathized with, that is, to the dichotomy that tends to reify (often unwillingly) the dominant relations of power or obscure how one is tacitly complicit in their operations (2012, 2013).

The debate on the possibility of feeling what others feel or understanding their positions is far from being unambiguous. Although feminist (and other) critiques of sympathy and empathy are immense and well founded, they often acknowledge the transformative powers of sympathizing/empathizing with others as well as tremendous potentials these engagements might offer for the feminist politics of solidarity. Working out of new concepts to think these topics is urgent, given the interest in the issues of connectivity, which have recently acquired new currency in feminist debates. Certainly, new formulations of these ideas have to be attentive to the aforementioned problems that these terms and positions pose, as well as they need to take into account the important limits of the possible affective-emotional investments (Berlant 1998, 648), whether it concerns epistemological locations, social justice, transnational politics, or the arts. Certain feminist scholars argue that empathy is an integral element of the processes of feminist knowledge production based on the mutual dialogical understanding encouraged by infusing the knowledge claims with emotions that they generate, as this makes them more accountable and responsible (e.g., Collins 1990).[3] If approached carefully, empathy can also provide a fundamental basis for transnational solidarities (e.g., Meyers 1994, Chabot Davis 2004, Gray 2011). Yet such forms of empathy necessarily have to be situated (in Haraway's 1988 understanding of the term) and take into consideration different locations occupied in social and transnational hierarchies by both empathizers and those who are empathized with. In that sense, as Pedwell argues, we need to disavow those conceptualizations of empathy that are primarily concerned with accuracy and equivalence and think instead about "the possibilities of empathy and/as translation," that is, "as a complex and ongoing set of translational processes involving conflict, negotiation and imagination with potentially transformative, though unpredictable, implications" (2014, 128). In a slightly different manner, Jill Bennett, in her study of responses to trauma art, promotes "a critical and self-reflexive *empathy* as the most appropriate form of engagement with trauma imagery" (2005, 8; original emphasis). She debates this issue in the context of traumatic memory and analyses the experiences that such artistic production generates (2005, 8). Bennett relates her understanding of "emphatic vision" to Dominick LaCapra's concept of "empathic unsettlement" (2001) that describes "the aesthetic experience of simultaneously *feeling for* another and becoming aware of a distinction between one's own perceptions and the experience of the other" (Bennett 2005, 17; original emphasis). Similar conceptualization is offered by Geoffrey Hartman (2000), who—although assuming that empathy is an indispensable and requisite response—argues that it cannot be uncritically trusted nor taken for granted. As he explains, "Art expands the sympathetic imagination while teaching us about the limits of sympathy" (2000, 122). The awareness of these serious limitations is important and may contribute to sharpening of the analyses developed in empathetic ways. Nikos Papastergiadis works out an analogous argumentation: empathy, in his formulation, is understood in terms of "going closer to be able to see, but also never forgetting where you are coming from" (Papastergiadis and Zournazi 2002). This view acknowledges the general unshareability of feelings experienced by different people situated in distinct social, political, and cultural positions, while simultaneously appreciating the potential of trying to get closer to others and understanding the dissimilar circumstances in which they are located. These more recent views are undoubtedly clued up on the former critiques and, consequently, tend to develop more sensitive and careful approaches.

In what follows I will offer a reconceptualization of the term "sympathy," by situating it within the new materialist philosophical framework. This proposition draws heavily on the concept of "passive syntheses" as developed by Gilles Deleuze as well as focuses on the notion of passivity as an interesting ethico-onto-epistemological position. My argumentation is informed by ideas, thoughts, and reflections presented in the prior chapters of this book and worked out in reference to the aesthetic experience triggered by an encounter with memorial, or "dark" (installation) art. These events, as mentioned earlier, can constitute a starting point for thinking further about the politics of experience in a more general sense and stimulate critical inquiry of the issues of connectivity and relationality as important aspects of sharing life with/in the world with other bodies and processes.

LOSING ONESELF: AFFECTING AND BEING AFFECTED

As explained earlier in this book, the dominant Western model of knowledge production relies on the figure of an active and independent subject of knowledge who is in power of representing the reality that surrounds him (!).

Feminist critiques have thoroughly exposed the maleness of such construction, pointing to the circumstances—both political and philosophical—in which the figure emerged and consolidated as well as explaining how such a structure contributed to further marginalization of women (and other "others") as far as the realms of science and knowledge are concerned. As Alessandra Tenesini (1999) clearly elucidates, tracing multidirectional developments of feminist epistemologies, the mainstream models of manufacturing scientific truths are in fact "malestream" in their construction and, consequently, produce biased knowledge, while the situatedness of the latter is never acknowledged or accounted for. What passes for universal is, therefore, very particular in its assumed construction and generated outcomes. Thus, it is necessary for feminist and postcolonial thinkers to develop new ways of producing knowledge that would disavow the existing discriminatory manners of thinking, offering instead something new and reliable. One way of doing this was to turn back to the body, an element disregarded or considered auxiliary in dominant philosophies, and typically associated with femininity (as opposed to "masculine" mind). Consequently, the "crisis of reason," as Elizabeth Grosz calls it (1993), has been triggered by the revival of the belief in agential and cognitive faculties of the body, which indicated its cardinal role in how we experience the world and make these experiences meaningful. The body, for feminists, is also conceived as the most immediate, primary location from which one experiences the world. The most significant differences, as well as how they impact everyday life, are also marked on the body. The body is lively—the body/mind split is therefore a completely artificial, or abstract, construction and can never be fully effectuated. The concept of synaesthetic perception, elaborated on in chapter 1, as well as further analyses of how it operates within the material-semiotic encounters with art, clearly expose the complex, dynamic entanglement of the bodily and the intellectual in the processes of generating knowledge.

New materialism, however, wants to go further, by pointing to agential qualities of all matter (both human and nonhuman, organic and inorganic, etc.) and acknowledging its crucial role in the material-semiotic procedures of advancing scientific claims. Accordingly, knowledge is understood as embodied, yet not exclusively in human bodies but also in all the involved objects, instruments, practices, technologies, methodological approaches, research techniques, languages, and so on, which all *matter* in the process. By adopting such a point of view, this philosophical strand tends to develop post-representational (or more-than-representational), post-ocularcentric, and post-anthropocentric ways of producing knowledges, necessarily underlining the material-discursive character of thusly conceived procedures. Situating my argumentation within this philosophical ferment, I would like to foster an embodied manner of producing knowledge based on an idea of subjectivity as a constant process of *becoming-with-other-bodies* (as elaborated on in the previous chapter of this book). Such a construction gives away the dominant conception of the subject of knowledge (which owes a lot to Immanuel Kant's philosophical theories) and focuses instead on the material-semiotic character of becoming. It also dismantles the oppositional logic of thinking in terms of hierarchically organized binary pairs. This especially applies to the juxtaposition of the concepts of activity and passivity. By drawing on Deleuze's monistic philosophy and his elaboration of passive syntheses, my objective is to expose the falsity and artificiality of the so-construed opposition, revealing the tremendous inventive productivity of both active and passive syntheses.

In the Kantian model of subjectivity, relying on the concept of an active subject of knowledge/seeing/observation, all the powers of identity formation (i.e., of active synthesis) are reserved to the always already-unified and transcendent entity (the "I"), which constitutes the underlying principle of the whole system of cognition (i.e., of Western metaphysics), yet it is erased from the results of his (!) undertakings. This is the model that paved the way for the prevailing Western ideas of subjectivity that have served as funding tenets for humanism and anthropocentrism, both granting extraordinary status and exceptional agencies to human beings, situating them apart (or rather above!) all other earthly critters. The human subject is, consequently, seen as qualitatively different from all other beings, either animate or inanimate. His (!) exceptionality translates into his special status as well as agencies and control he is able to perform and exert. In his innovative reversal of the Kantian logic, Deleuze (2011) argues for a more thorough examination of not only how the subject produces empirical identities through active syntheses but also how this process is itself the effect of differential passive syntheses that participate in the subject's becoming as well as in the overall becoming of the world/life. There is a deep entanglement of beings, objects, processes, and relations remaining in a constant flux and experiencing perpetual transformations. Rhythmic becoming, therefore, is in the Deleuzian philosophy understood as inherent to all forms of life, where life is conceived in totally inclusive terms, encompassing organic, inorganic, material, semiotic, human, mineral, technological, and other forms. Moreover, as explained in detail in chapter 4, this process is completely relational, and as such, it is a dynamic and unpredictable bundle of procedures of affecting and being affected in continuous, never-ending ways. Deleuze focuses not only on the role of the subject in the processes of subjectivity production but also, importantly, on how it itself is produced in the interminable passive processes of becoming with the world/others, or of being produced in the everlasting set of encounters with distinct and diversely moving bodies. As he further elaborates, passive syntheses are serial rather than singular—they are a series of "contractions," bodily, desiring, and unconscious (as all substance performs contractions). These movements unify a set of experiences into the habit through simultaneously retaining a part of it and forgetting the other one. Habits, however, require constant updating, that is, the contractions of experiences have to be ongoing (and always different!). It is not about sustaining the same but rather about a constant modification and transformation, that is, about *un/learning*.

As Deleuze explains, a habit

> concerns not only the sensory-motor habits that we have (psychologically), but also, before these, the primary habits that we are; the thousands of passive syntheses of which we are organically composed. It is simultaneously through contraction that we are habits, but through contemplation that we contract. We are contemplations, we are imaginations, we are generalities, claims and satisfactions. (2011, 95)

Consequently, a series of experiences are related to each other within the same body, which means, for instance, that the experience of one sense is always related to a series of contractions of other senses; they are synthetic and synaesthetic. Logically, conceiving of sensual experiences as separate from each other is simply a reduction, an artificial regulation that has been formulated within the Western system of thinking preoccupied entirely with the processes of "classi*fix*ation" (van der Tuin 2014a). The senses work together and their nature is bodily-intellectual. The rhythmic becoming of sensual perception (and of bodies) is, by definition, unregulated and unconstrained. If an external, molar structure is imposed on it, what we get is an oversimplification of the original richness of experience that tells us nothing about the abundant wealth of life as a relational movement.

Within the Deleuzian logic each body is rhizomatically related to other bodies (similarly differential), meaning that the series of syntheses of bodies can resonate or clash. Let me briefly remind here that Deleuze thinks of bodies in totally inclusive manners—for him "a body can be anything" (1988a, 127)—and all of them possess agential capacities to enter into productive, affective relations with other bodies. If we adopt this logic, we need to disavow the ways of thinking in oppositional terms prevailing in Western culture. Accordingly, the clash, or disintegration of a body (or of a machine which it temporarily forms with other bodies), is not seen as a negative, damaging process but rather as a production wherefrom something new, and with totally new qualities, emerges, setting in motion new transformational processes. It is a qualitative change reconfiguring the always-dynamic relations and triggering new potentialities and new flows. There is no destruction and there is no end. Just becoming.

Consequently, the subject formation takes place within the field emerging out of the serial passive syntheses being effectuated at all different levels simultaneously, where the production of subjectivity can be either an integration or a resolution of this field. Occasionally, it is both at the same time; a constant reorganization and a perpetual metamorphosis. These are the conditions in which something new is produced, emerging from the encounters in which a body participates. Such an elaboration of subject's becoming remains in line with Haraway's claim that "beings do not pre-exist their relatings" (2003, 6). Rather, they constantly emerge and reemerge out of them. Bodies are entirely relational; they are produced within relations and affected by other bodies—in the material-semiotic process of constant differing. They are situated at the entanglement of their past, present, and future. Similarly, in Deleuze's words,

> Every organism, in its receptive and perceptual elements, but also in its vicera, is a sum of contractions, of retentions and expectations. At the level of this primary vital sensibility, the lived present constitutes a past and a future in time. Need is the manner in which this future appears, as the organic form of expectation. The retained past appears in the form of cellular heredity. Furthermore, by combining with the perceptual syntheses built upon them, these organic syntheses are redeployed in the active syntheses of a psycho-organic memory and intelligence (instinct and learning). (2011, 93)

Passive syntheses, therefore, take place at different levels as well as they combine and interfere with active syntheses. As Deleuze continues, "Each contraction, each passive synthesis, constitutes a sign which is interpreted or deployed in active syntheses" (2011, 94). Whereas passive synthesis can be exemplified by habit (or constitutes our habit of living), which incarnates past and gestures to the future in the present, the active force of memory, or the virtual, sustains relationships between distant events. The process is therefore both receptive and productive, or passive and active, at the same time. These, however, are not real oppositions but provisional descriptions of different equally generative processes of becoming. The relational entanglement signals a multidimensional continuity between the subject and the world as they are both produced through their mutual collisions and intra-actions. We cannot say where one entity finishes and another one begins, as they constantly reemerge and redefine their fleeting, temporary boundaries always affected and reconfigured by new passionate encounters. This becoming is about the distribution of affective intensities across the surfaces of bodies. It is, as Ian Buchanan explains, "an intense 'I feel' that cannot be reduced to an identification, nor confused with a representation (though these may in fact help us to grasp its affect, but only ever in a weak sense)" (2000, 28). This "I feel" corresponds to a "profound and well-nigh telluric sympathy between the body and the earth, their mutual becoming" (Buchanan 2000, 29) as they differ together and through one another. Crucially, in Deleuzian framework, the sensation is not an end in itself but rather an important catalyst to a further critical inquiry (hence its capital role in knowledge production!). As it grasps us and forces to engage deeply yet involuntarily (as explained in chapter 1), affect should be considered an important spark that prompts thought or triggers inventive *un/learning*. For Deleuze, without the primary affect, which is understood in terms of "material impression," there would be no thought, no intellectual becoming. The aesthetic bodily encounter (which happens "through our senses") constitutes, therefore, a field of emergence for thoughtful metamorphoses (1972, 161; see also Massumi 2002a). There is no thought without a bodily encounter, as the former is contingent on the latter. Neither is there an intellectual production without an affective collision.

Such philosophy of becoming, informed by new materialist ideas and focusing on the embodied and relational processes of *un/learning*, reconnects human beings to the world while depriving them of their hitherto-assumed monopoly for agency, power, and control. Moreover, it questions absoluteness of the subject and resensitizes the boundaries of the embodied self by opening it up to the world at large, with all its different connections, relations, and dis/continuities. Accordingly, bodies are conceived in terms of hybrids that form temporary machines with other bodies through different "intra-actions" (Barad 2003, 2007) happening on both micro- and macro-levels. Such processes necessarily bring back the questions of connectivity and entangled coexistence, which are about being open to experimental transformations or unexpected reconfigurations. They also redirect our attention to the passivity of becoming, that is, to the exposure and susceptibility to the world as well as to the multiplicity of other bodies that trigger vital bodily-intellectual transformations.

The concept of passive syntheses, as much as the idea of passive becoming, brings us back to the major term of this chapter's argumentation. In the previous section, while approaching the term "sympathy," I mostly focused on the prefix *sym-* (or *com-*, for "compassion") implying connection and togetherness, which seems exceptionally relevant in the context of relationality of life and the multiplicity of encounters of which it is composed. However, the concept of "sympathy" gets even more appealing when looked at through its other co-forming element. The terms *pathos* (from Greek) or *passio* (from Latin) are equally important for my line of thinking. *Passion* and *passivity* are similar in their construction, as they both share the word-forming element *pass-*. It derives directly from Latin *passivus*, that is, capable of feeling of suffering (Greek *pathos* and Latin *passio* actually originally meant "suffering"). Whereas in the fifteenth century the term *passive* started to be used in opposition to *active*, since the early seventeenth century, its sense has connoted the state of enduring suffering without resistance (i.e., *passively*). The term "passion," nevertheless, also around this time, started to refer to the feelings of strong liking, enthusiasm, or predilection. Thus, there is certain ambivalence in its meaning and connotation as it refers to passive endurance of the possibly unpleasant experiences, yet it also connotes the state of being passively absorbed and taken by something fascinating, captivating, and charming. Even though seemingly distant from each other as far as their signifying dimensions are concerned, both contexts in which the term is used are about annihilation of resistance and defiance. And both are about getting lost in something or about losing oneself. *Un/learning*, therefore, is about losing what one has already become in the process of constant differing.

Passivity entails exposure and fragility as well as willingness and readiness to enter into relations, which might generate unpredictable outcomes. Such logic of connectivity, grounded in the concept of productive passive syntheses, unavoidably implies being sensitive and attentive to vulnerability of life and susceptibility of becoming. It is also about allowing oneself to get uncovered and open for different others. This philosophy is not exclusively about ontology but rather points to, as Michel Serres (Serres and Zournazi 2002) brilliantly notices, "desmology," which—coming from the Greek term *desmos* meaning "connection" or "link"—is preoccupied with linkages, liaisons, and connections between things/bodies, a "togetherness" of becoming rather than focusing on the static, sedimented state of them. As I will explain in the next section, I consider such theory of subjectivity a starting point for developing a new materialist sense of relationality and withness, so crucial for the feminist politics and ethico-onto-epistemologies.

THE LOGIC OF CONNECTIVITY—THE NEW MATERIALIST POLITICS OF *SYM*PATHY

Bearing the aforementioned ideas in mind, it is time to return to the main line of my argumentation, that is, to the new materialist politics of *sym*pathy. In this context, worth noticing is the fact that most, if not all, feminist conceptualizations mentioned in the section tracing evolutions and problems of the idea of feeling what others feel rely on the concept of empathy, almost entirely abandoning the term "sympathy" as (historically) more problematic and loaded with pejorative connotations. Somewhat against this predominant tendency, I advocate for a conceptual shift from *em*pathy to *sym*pathy. What I want to point out is that by going back to the etymological origins of these terms (which I have already partly done earlier) and locating them within a broader, that is, not exclusively English-language-dominated, context, we can notice a serious potential in the recently disregarded concept. Although the term "sympathy" has already been thoroughly critiqued (and I briefly mapped these critiques earlier), I think it is useful and productive to come back to its original meaning, *while* refining it in new materialist terms. Referring to etymologies of the terms "empathy" and "sympathy" will be again particularly useful for my formulation. Since I elaborated on the meanings of "sympathy" earlier, my intention here is just to succinctly remind that, whereas Greek ἐν (*en* [or *em*]) refers to "in, at," *σύν* (*sun* [or *syn*/*sym*]) stands for "with, together" and implies connections or assemblage. Different from *em*pathy, *sym*pathy—as defined within the new materialist context—connotes togetherness or withness rather than being *in*, or speaking *from*, the position of others. The latter formulations, or ideas loosely drawing on such a positioning, have already evoked an immense feminist criticism, skeptical towards the possibility (even theoretical) of assuming someone else's location and knowing their feelings, political interests, needs, and ways of thinking. Differently, *sym*pathy seems not to be loaded with problems of that kind, as it encourages the position of being next to someone else and speaking *with others* yet from *one's own location* rather than *for others* and from *their location*. Logically, it implies a particular ethical, political, and onto-epistemological situatedness and should be understood as a way of referring to, or better, connecting with, others, conceived of in terms of "thinking/feeling" *with* them. This has its significance in the context of feminist epistemological debates focusing on how to make the experiences of others visible without, at the same time, pretending to experience *as if* we were in their positions, or speaking *for* them, which is hardly unmediated, yet the effects of these mediations can never be fully accounted for. In this context, the new materialist manners of speaking, experiencing, or generating knowledge *with* someone/something, understood as a multidimensional, embodied, and relational process, might be a more productive strategy.

*Sym*pathy—withness and passivity. Keeping all these aforementioned metamorphoses in mind, I want to abandon, or disavow, the predominant connotations that the term "sympathy" produces in the current English-speaking context where it refers to situations of feeling affected by the pain and suffering of others. If we look at what the term connotes in French or certain Slavic languages, for instance, we can broaden its meaning as it then refers, first, to affinity and accord between people and, second, to the process of sharing sentiments with others (these feelings, significantly, are not necessarily painful or connected to suffering). In order to explain my interest in and predilection towards the term "*sym*pathy," I need to offer a brief digression revealing my own situatedness, which motivates my choices and preferences. The concept of *sym*pathy that I advocate for in this book is obviously located in the linguistic context in which I was raised, studied, and worked. This includes three languages: Polish (which is my mother tongue), French (which is the first foreign language in which I achieved fluency and in which I studied at the BA level), and English (which is the language in which I did both my MA degree and my PhD degree and, subsequently, in which I have worked since then). *Sym*pathy is therefore located at the intersection of these three languages and bears in its becomings significant imprints of meanings derived from all of them. Let me concisely clarify these connotations. Basically, there are three ways in which the word *sympathie* is used in French. First, it refers to a natural, spontaneous, and warm penchant or fondness towards somebody or something; second, it is employed to express participation in someone's joy or pain; third, it serves to depict benevolence or favorable attitude towards somebody or something. In Polish, the term *sympatia* can be used to express a friendly and positive attitude towards somebody or something as well as to connote a person one likes or has fallen in love with. In this last linguistic context, it is therefore employed exclusively in an affirmative way and to denote positive feelings. English "compassion" or "sympathy" translates into Polish as *współczucie*, which literally means "co-feeling." Hence, the term "sympathy" in these linguistic situations is used more inclusively to refer to the feeling of a broad range of passions, including more affirmative—and thus productive—applications. Therefore, *sym*pathy, apart from signaling connectivity and withness and assuming an intensive passive absorption and fragile openness, may potentially remain in line with a new materialist diffractive and affirmative attitude as far as manners of running a critique are concerned. Thusly construed, the concept invokes constant, transformative, and often unpredictable material-semiotic *becoming with the world/the others*.

The new materialist figuration of *sym*pathy is necessarily grounded in the earlier-described procedures of *passive syntheses*. The contractions/contemplations that these processes imply are sensorial and bodily as well as semiotic and intellectual. They are about rhythmic vibrations of bodies, or matter, in their different forms and transformations. The passive becoming *with* the world is about various entanglements that co-form each other. As elaborated on in chapter 4, a relation, in a new materialist understanding, does not describe a process that connects preexisting individual entities. It is rather about an emergence—relations are (re)generative of the relating bodies' very individuality. The entities are therefore only conditional; they constantly emerge and reemerge out of intra-actions, in which they participate; they are movements. Intra-activity is about deep, multidimensional and multidirectional interdependency in a mutual correlation understood as a condition for dynamic existence of natural-cultural entities remaining in the process of constant becoming. Intra-actions are necessarily material-semiotic, and they are about proximity, collision, clash, assemblage, meaning, *mattering*, transformation, co-constitution, flow of energy, affect, emotion, destruction, production, differing, and so on. The process of passive/active becoming (i.e., *un/learning*) is simultaneously effectuated at both bodily and mental levels, draws on memory (intellectual and corporeal), and refers to the natural and the cultural in their different, moving (re)configurations and translations. Worth noticing once again is that *un/learning*, in such formulation, always implies withness and connectivity; it is about acknowledging of *becoming with/in the world* and recognizing that we are implicated in the world in the same way as the world is implicated in us. Such an understanding of *becoming* can be creatively employed for an advancement of feminist politics and knowledges. The *sym*pathy between the body and the earth is a form of multidirectional, dynamic connection and a deep co-forming relationship. The acknowledgment of our entanglement with the world, of ourselves being produced by it and it being produced by us, can serve as a point of departure for enhancement, or recognition, of capacities to connect with other (not only human) bodies. Through these different forms of connectedness with others, something new is produced. This newness in not about a sum of characteristics that bodies possess, but rather, it is about an emergence of something with entirely new qualities as well as with new virtual potentials informed by the past and future alike. It is about the rhythm of becoming—sometimes amnesiac and sometimes bringing back memories and actualizing pasts. The virtuality of perception signals a constant involvement of both past events and the yet-undetermined future in any given located present. The past certainly informs the attributes of that which bodies encounter and actualizes itself in these encounters while being contingent on them. The archives of the experience of the perceiving bodies enrich new encounters and new relationalities as well as co-form the capacities of the very bodies to experience, vaguely anticipating what is to come. The future, on the other hand, is a potentiality of variations that these processes might possibly undergo, a vibrating virtuality on the threshold of actualization, which does not necessarily have to actualize. *Sym*pathy, therefore, is a constant pulsation of the virtual and the actual, their dynamic entanglements and intersections; it is about an incessant rhythmic movement between the molar and the molecular, or the expressible and the inexpressible; it is about reversibility between proximity and distance; it is also about *un/learning*. Its logic is one of withness and intimacy, yet also one whose effects might be unpredictable or capricious.

Thusly understood *sym*pathetic becoming-other is based on the logic of encounters with other bodies (which is simultaneously generative of the entities that are involved in the relations), resonating with some already-existent feminist approaches, while bypassing problems that empathetic situatedness may entail. Importantly, these encounters are, by definition, *aesthetic*, conceived in reference to the original Greek understanding of the term and pointing to sensuous aspects of perception (as explained in chapter 1). Certainly, it is not accidental that I preceded the discussion of the concept with analyses of the nature of remembering, aesthetic aspects of memorial and trauma art, "dark" experiences, and embodied forms of memory and knowledge. Experiencing art and participating in synaesthetic artistic events born out of the material-semiotic assemblage of bodies and processes—as my case studies revealed—help us realize the fluid boundaries of subjectivity and make us aware of our vulnerability. Trauma art seems to be especially interesting in this regard as its operations are so much infused with affects and intensities with (re)traumatizing potentials. These encounters let us get closer to the experiences of others, without necessarily aspiring to fully understanding or even "feeling" them. Rather, they are about remaining in proximity, or being deeply affected by them, without assuming the resemblance of these sensations and interpretations to the ones experienced and created by others. Such strategy encourages speaking from one's own position yet always *with* others, in their tremendously fluid richness and diversity.

Such thinking of *sym*pathy is premised on several feminist ideas stemming from many distinct philosophical inspirations and logics read diffractively and through one another. This also testifies to the necessity of working out the ways of being/becoming with others as well as acknowledges how bodies are co-formed by their relations with other bodies. This mutual co-constitution refers also to texts and theories—the practice of quotation, or of getting inspired by someone else's ideas, is exactly about diffractive coproduction and entanglement. In that sense, this new materialist formulation can be related to the concept of *aesthetic wit(h)nessing*, which emerged from the artistic-intellectual production of Bracha Ettinger (2006), heavily influenced by psychoanalytical thinking. Even though Deleuzian ideas share next to nothing with psychoanalysis, Ettinger's concept is worth mentioning here, especially on account of the fact that it is conceived in close reference to the encounter with (trauma) art. In an interesting and creative manner, Ettinger's formulation draws on the term "witnessing," which already implies certain proximity if not togetherness. Yet, as Grizelda Pollock explains,

> she [Ettinger] expands a word's conceptual range from the legal and testimonial meaning of bearing witness to the crime against the other, to being with, but not assimilated to, and to being beside the other in a gesture that is much more than mere ethical solidarity. There is risk; but there is also a sharing. . . . Ettinger is proposing an aesthetic wit(h)nessing: a means of being with and remembering for the other through the artistic act and through an aesthetic encounter. Art becomes a keeper of historical memory for the injured other by creating the site for a novel trans-subjective and transhistorical process that is simultaneously witness and wit(h)ness. (2010, 831)

Witnessing embodies being with the other while the other is undergoing something. It is already a relation joining the two seemingly unrelated entities within an event, even though experienced differently and producing distinct effects. The status of a witness already signals withness, or—quite simply—being with. By developing this position Ettinger seems to call for a necessity to cultivate capacities to get engaged with, or even exposed to, what is happening to both others and us. This engagement must be ethical as well as aesthetic, since art—as working through intensities and affects—has a power to leave (in)tangible imprints on the involved bodies, changing their material-semiotic becomings. Ettinger's formulation implies the shareability of pain and trauma. As Pollock elaborates, "We cannot but bear it, transport it, and potentially create a future precisely by such sharing," which demands exposure and fragility rather than the strategy of "anxiously policing the boundaries of difference which are the hallmark of the phallic model" (2010, 837), the latter symptomatic of the prevailing logic of Western culture. Certainly, there are limits to the degree a (traumatic) experience can be shared, also through the artistic means. It remains inextricably and ineradicably other, yet still can be participated in, although in completely situated and singular ways. Never the same and never experienced similarly. Not even close to. Nevertheless, there is some proximity, although understood in different terms, that is, connoting togetherness, responsiveness, and willingness to *be with*, which translates in certain—necessarily partial and located—knowledges, enacted differently by each body involved.

In a similar spirit, when writing about how we respond to the pain that is not our own, Judith Butler claims that

> when any of us are affected by the sufferings of others, it is not only that we put ourselves in their place or that they usurp our own place; perhaps it is the moment in which a certain *chiasmic link* comes to the fore and I become somehow implicated in lives that are clearly not the same as my own. (Butler 2012, 149; my emphasis)

Butler seems to be fully aware of the limits and constraints the strategies of placing oneself in positions of others might entail. It is not possible to experience something from the location of someone else or to see with someone else's eyes. It does not mean, however, that the lives of different bodies are not related to each other. Quite the contrary, Butler urges to realize these mutual implications in one another's life and to acknowledge the entangled relationalities and connections between them. Rather than adopting a "critical distance," so encouraged by the dominant positivist models of doing science and approaching others, such formulation assumes the impossibility of being apart while admitting that being connected to something or someone, or being implicated in the life of others, is not the same as living through their experiences or fully understanding their views, agencies, entanglements, positionings, and so on. The links forged between different bodies and relations affect everybody involved, changing their locations and being generative of their knowledges. In her analysis of Emmanuel Levinas's ethical (and religious) philosophy, Butler pays special attention to the term "sensibility" that Levinas applies to depict "that region of responsiveness that precedes the ego, a kind of response that therefore is and is not my response" (2012, 136). It means that the ego does not antedate the ability to respond but rather is temporarily cocreated by these very responses—this is "a form of responsiveness that implies a dispossession of the egological" (2012, 136). To rewrite this claim in a new materialist or Deleuzian spirit, the entity does not predate the relations in which it enters and to which it is responsive; rather, it emerges out of these connections and materializes merely as a provisional body with always fluid boundaries. This fluidity and openness signals the precarious state of the body/machine and testifies to its vulnerable openness to further reconfigurations.

The conditions of being connected to others are those of responsiveness and vulnerability, which makes us susceptible to being affected by others. Being receptive means that one cannot fully predict or control the ways of being acted on as well as the manners in which to respond to these relational processes. Such formulation implies the conditions of injurability, where—as Butler explains—answerability and injurability must be seen as inextricably bound with one another (2012, 142). Moreover, in her words, "precarity exposes our sociality, the fragile and necessary dimensions of our interdependency" (2012, 148). It means that bodies are always and invariably joined with and depended on other bodies. Even though Butler writes about these conditions in relations to human bodies, in new materialist account, the category of bodies is seen as far more encompassing. The entanglements involving nonhuman bodies are, however, equally vital and intensive and could be acted out across time and space—they involve the reversibility of here and there, now and then, thus enacting multilocality and cross-temporality of connections (which I partly explained in chapter 3).

As evidenced in their theorizations, both Ettinger and Butler in the works referenced earlier develop their argumentations by referring to situations of distress, suffering, or trauma, yet obviously similar relationalities are at place if we consider situations of joy or happiness. As Butler briefly contends,

> The bounded and living appearance of the body is the condition of being exposed to the other, exposed to solicitation, seduction, passion, injury, exposed in ways that sustain us but also in ways that can destroy us. In this sense the exposure of the body points to its precariousness. (2012, 141)

Hence, every encounter with the other is about radical openness made possible by the porosity of becoming. These various collisions and entanglements cannot be seen as representational, communicative, or expressive. Rather, they imply a relational transaction, an impingement that leaves material-semiotic marks on every participating body; each is simultaneously acting and being acted on, while forces and affects involved alter the trajectories of the becoming entities and fuel their further metamorphoses. This signals the politics of connectivity and withness, based on conditions of tenuous exposure. Therefore, the new materialist concept of *sym*pathy is grounded in the ideas of *vulnerability* and *susceptibility* to human as well as more-than-human others. There is withness in it, but there is also a radical passivity at the heart of it.

PASSIVITY AND RESPONSE-ABILITY: THE RISKS OF EXPOSURE

My thinking of vulnerability as a promising ethico-onto-epistemological position is inspired, among others, by the relatively recent work of Marianne Hirsch (2014). Unlike her, however, I situate this idea within the new materialist philosophy and partly reframe its understanding so that it could be conceived of in terms of intra-actions (Barad 2003, 2007). While being aware of the historical problems that the term "vulnerability" connotes, Hirsch argues that if we think of it "as a radical openness toward surprising possibilities, we might be able to engage it more creatively—as a space to work from and not only as something to be overcome" (2014, 337). And she further explains that vulnerability is not seen here as a "plea for protection that potentially signals weakness and perpetuates disempowerment" (2014, 338). Rather, I argue, it should be conceived as an acknowledgment of being related to others in a way that leaves memorable marks on our material-semiotic becomings. As Paul Harrison (2008) evinces, as soon as vulnerability is no longer cast as a position of disempowerment or disadvantage and framed as something to be urgently transcended, a less anthropocentric notion of care as well as of the politics of caring becomes imaginable. This subscribes fully to new materialist politics of entanglement. No longer is care necessarily tied to the utmost goal of self-preservation, signaling instead an unlimited compassion, that is, thinking-with or feeling-with others. For Harrison, the condition of vulnerability is shared among all mortal entities. It means, therefore, that acknowledging our own precarious construction lets us become aware of the fragility of *life at risk*. Reading this proposition through Barad's ideas, I think of vulnerability as a radical susceptibility to new intra-actions, a thorough openness of bodily-intellectual boundaries, and a state of being ready to *passively* absorb and therefore to be produced and to produce ourselves. These boundaries, therefore, do not serve as established and well-defined contours of predetermined individual entities but rather emerge out of the intra-actions; they are, by definition, relational, susceptible to each other, porous, and permeable. The bodies are agential—they generate but also, important, are generated through their relations with other bodies. As far as the latter process is concerned, the bodies have to be conceived in fundamentally passive terms.

Remaining within the affirmative new materialist spirit, passivity—in my formulation—is not associated with negativity or immobile stagnation. Even though neovitalist approaches inspired by Baruch Spinoza's theory of affectivity (so influential for Deleuze and Guattari's philosophy on which I heavily draw) connect it predominantly to the physics of motion (cf. Braidotti 2006b) and place emphasis on the constant activation of the body, my conceptualization of passivity does not conceive of it as antithetical to activity. Passivity, accordingly, is also about becoming, but this form of metamorphosis is triggered by the events of being acted on rather than acting. It stems from Deleuze's theorization of passive syntheses (elaborated on earlier), which are not opposed to movement. This seems to be especially vital as far as the *sym*pathetic feminist knowledge production is concerned—situated, attentive, accountable, partial, and relying on the democratic organization of relations among all agents involved. This form of intimate engagement (i.e., the state of being affected or acted on) that the sensitive knowledge production processes entail relies therefore "on the withdrawal of the self, a passivity that enables an active listening, an opening to surprises" (Schrader 2015, 9). As such, it is not necessarily a process grounded in goal-oriented ethics, being more about radical exposure and openness to unexpected becomings and reconfigurings. Consequently, what we need is special attention being paid to what Astrid Schrader calls "a fundamental passivity in caring knowledge practices" (2015, 4), as it sheds new light on a feminist conceptualization of scientific processes.

Drawing on Jacques Derrida, Schrader (2015) advocates for the politics of passivity as a necessary precondition for care about human and more-than-human-others. As she explains, Derrida (2002, 2008) claims that "there is a passivity at the heart of subjectivity which refers to mortality, a vulnerability shared among all living beings, a non-power at the heart of knowledge/power that all scientific witnessing entails" (2015, 4). This "radical passivity" is—for Derrida—"central to an experience of compassion" (2015, 5), which for Schrader implies a less-anthropocentric notion of care, enabled by learning to become affected or to be vulnerable. Acknowledging passivity as a condition that is shared with other (not only human) bodies, and situating it at the core of knowledge production procedures, translates into strengthening of capacities for *sym*pathy—of being intimately *with* and letting be affected and impinged on by the other. It introduces a manner of witnessing (or *wit(h)nessing*) entailing a passionate response, rather than being grounded in values of scientific certainty and academic truths. Undoubtedly, what we care about is contingent on what we encounter in either random or imposed ways. Moreover, such a manner of developing care for and about others promises to unfix the taken-for-granted dynamics between the subject and object of knowledge, or observer and observed, while opening these processes to unexpected becomings, where becoming is understood in both active and passive terms. This approach tends to redefine the dominant knowledge production practices, turning them into more accountable, feminism-informed *becoming-with-other-bodies* in a bundle of entangled material-semiotic passionate processes, necessitating careful engagement as well as affective investment.

As María Puig de la Bellacasa underlines, "Relations of thinking and knowing require care" (2012, 198), for "not only do relations involve care, care is itself relational" (2012, 198). This testifies to the situatedness of knowledge as well as of the processes of thinking—"they are inconceivable without a multitude of relations that also make possible the world we think with" (2012, 198). Accordingly, the procedures of relating and caring resonate with each other as caring is about creating relations, investing in something, whether it happens in volitional or involuntary ways. It therefore seems that, for Puig de la Bellacasa, care is understood as "an ontological requirement of relational worlds" (2012, 199). Yet even though relationality is always there, and "is all there is" (Puig de la Bellacasa 2012, 204), the feminist knowledge production based on the politics of care is not about erasing differences and tensions. In fact, thinking-with, or—in a more Deleuzian fashion—*becoming-with-other-bodies*, does not translate into "a world without conflict and dissension" where all divergences and discords are smoothed out (Puig de la Bellacasa 2012, 204). This would be far too simple, or even too simplistic and remaining within the reductionist spirit of positivism and representationalism drawing on strict divisions, straightforward classifications, and overgeneralizations. Care, for Puig de la Bellacasa, performs connections as much as disconnections, and these relational processes all have important consequences. They are about doings. As she clarifies, "Thinking with care is a response led by awareness of the efforts it takes to cultivate relatedness in collective and accountable knowledge construction without negating dissent" (2012, 205), especially because building alliances and strengthening connections affect the positions and trajectories of the bodies involved, yet they do not necessarily have to erase their divergences and discrepancies. All entities are affected, all are acted on, and all change differently. This requires a thorough acknowledgment of vulnerability and precarious condition of both human and more-than-human bodies.

In the process of new materialist *un/learning,* we necessarily need to allow ourselves to be vulnerable and susceptible as we practice openness, interconnection, imagination, and constant movement, as we acknowledge our own implication and complicity. As Hirsch suggests, the acceptance of vulnerability can be seen to provide a form of "passive power," or as a way to be "more connected to others" (2014, 338–39). Recognizing vulnerability is yet not about identification with someone or something (that would signal the risky strategy of appropriating another's position) but rather about shuttling between "affiliation and disaffiliation" (Hirsch 2014, 339). In a similar way, Butler writes about a "limited but necessary reversibility of proximity and distance" (2012, 137), yet she also notices that "receptivity is not only a precondition for action but one of its constituent features" (2012, 136). It is therefore not about agency, or not solely about it, but rather also about passive absorbing as much as about attentiveness and responsiveness to the processes, in which we are implicated. Consequently, it is about putting ourselves and the world at risk: risking new assemblages and clashes, risking dissolution or surprising, or even painful, metamorphoses. The radical openness is actually about becoming vulnerable and becoming precarious, that is, about *becoming-other* in a rhythmic movement oscillating between the past, present, and future; recruiting from the virtual and actual alike; actively absorbing in a passive susceptibility to life, and with unexpected consequences and outcomes. This corresponds well with Barad's claims, especially when she writes:

> To address the past (and future), to speak with ghosts, is not to entertain or reconstruct some narrative of the way it was, but to respond, to be responsible, to take responsibility for that which we inherit (from the past and the future), for the entangled relationalities of inheritance that "we" are, to acknowledge and be responsive to the noncontemporaneity of the present, to put oneself at risk, to risk oneself (which is never one or self), to open oneself up to indeterminacy in moving towards what is to-come. (2010, 264)

Exposure is risky. And it lays bare the relationality of life—the complex, bounded interdependency and connection. It can potentially be injuriously destructive, painful, and traumatizing. Yet even in such instances it triggers production and as such remains affirmative and transformational. Thus, thinking about the new materialist concept of *sym*pathy in ethico-onto-epistemological terms translates into thinking about it in reference to both producing and being produced by what one encounters. What is so tempting in this concept, in my opinion, is its reliance on passivity, as consideration of passivity lets us acknowledge our vulnerability and susceptibility, that is, our exposure and openness to the world. Relationality, movement, collectivity, and entanglement seem to be crucial terms for grasping the complex net of partial connections, often—as Haraway reminds—"fraught with contradictions, disagreements, and refusals—and made up of mundane practices that are nevertheless consequential" (2015, 258). *Sym*pathy, in that sense, can be considered closely connected to the work of *sym-poiesis*, as elaborated on by Haraway (2013, 2015), that is, of making together, which is about an active-passive or material-semiotic involvement or *un/learning*. This obviously requires certain "response-ability" understood as "not something you have toward some kind of demand made on you by the world or by an ethical system or by a political commitment" (Haraway 2015, 258). For her, response-ability "is not something that you just respond to, as if it's there already. Rather, it's the cultivation of the capacity of response in the context of living and dying in worlds for which one is for, with others" (Haraway 2015, 258; see also Haraway 2013). Consequently, the *sym-poietic* practice "figures response-ability as becoming-with, and it's rooted in the riskiness of play. . . . in taking chances with one another, not in prohibition" (Haraway 2015, 261). My elaboration of the concept of *sym*pathy is therefore also about acknowledging the fact of our bodies being active agents as much as being porous and vulnerable to passive exposure, as being made collectively, with other diversified bodies, and not always in a consensual way. As such they are movements (or verbs) rather than static entities. In fact, for Haraway, "reality is an active verb" (2003, 6), always in movement and always transforming. Consequently, *sym*pathy, understood here as a constant *becoming-other* or *un/learning*, is also a position from which knowledges are produced collectively *with* others rather than *on* or *for* others. The latter could result in usurping the positions of others by claiming to be able to speak for them (based on empathetically assuming their locations), that is, in devouring their fundamental otherness. And such manner of appropriating experiences of others precludes affirmation of their difference and disrupts the ethico-onto-epistemological logic of new materialism. Therefore, my formulation of *sym*pathy does not stand for advocacy for someone or something, but signals a condition of entanglement, of being implicated in the life of others. It does not advance claims to identification with others, assuming their positions, or fully understanding their points of view. It is simply about being, or "thinking/feeling," with them. *Sym*pathy is also about responsiveness to other bodies—human and more-than-human. And the condition of receptivity, shared by all bodies, encourages a *sym*pathetic connection that helps us imagine others' vulnerability and exposure, a precarious condition that defines us all and to which we all contribute. New materialist politics of *sym*pathy is about the collectivity, or togetherness, of *becoming*—as well as about how we all are implicated in the *becoming* of others and how they are implicated in ours. These relations are about vitality and generativity as much as about potentiality for destruction and a radical recomposition. Yet, similar to Haraway's *sym-poietic* practices, they might offer a chance for inventive "re-worlding" (2015, 261).

MATERIAL-SEMIOTIC CONNECTIONS: CONCLUDING REMARKS

Even though it seems that issues of connectivity, solidarity, and togetherness have recently acquired new currency in feminist scholarship and academic practice, in fact the feminist interest in such topics as vulnerability, fragility, and necessity to care for and about others has a relatively long history. The politics of care, so crucial for the new materialist manners of knowledge production, has been a long-standing topic of feminist and postcolonial investigations. Interestingly, the critiques raised in connection to this theme have typically pointed to the invisibility of the practices of care. Since they have traditionally been performed by women (and other "others" of the Western culture), they further contributed to the nonrecognition of their status as citizens and equal participants in social, cultural, and political life of communities. The better they have been performed, the more invisible they have remained. New materialism, however, postulates the necessity to expose what has hitherto stayed unnoticeable, or to disclose all the processes and practices that make possible their final results. This applies to the material aspects of representational strategies (which I explained in a more extensive way in the introduction to this book) as well as to all material components of processes in which we are all involved on an everyday basis. If we care for and about these procedures, we could more thoroughly grasp their material-semiotic effects. Such a reflection is vitally important in the context of knowledge production. It is necessary not only to reveal the material, meticulous labors of care (remaining hidden in the dominant models of generating scientific truths) but also to encourage more care and, consequently, more accountability in these processes. In that sense, the material-semiotic synaesthetic workings of the senses, as exemplified in the quotation from Goethe's poem with which I began this chapter, are closely related to the material practices and the politics of caring. Both require proximity and exposure, both demand affective investment, both are completely relational, and both are fundamentally material in their operations.

Caring is also context-specific as it can take different forms and generate various entanglements and connections. However, as Puig de la Bellacasa warns, we need to be cautious about the risky vicinity between the notion of "care" and the notion of "accuracy." After all, the latter term derives from the former—*accurare* means "to take care of," while the term "accurate" connotes the meaning of being "prepared with care," or "exact." As she notices,

> The notion of doing something with care led to that of "being exact." The tempting proximity between these terms reveals . . . the ambition to control and judge what/who/how we care for. This controlling aim echoes what happens with

> purposes of collecting knowledge practices under normative epistemologies that tend to erase the specificities of knowing practices. (Puig de la Bellacasa 2012, 211)

It is therefore necessary to be attentive to the potential dangers care might possibly pose in the context of doing science and manufacturing knowledge, as it runs the risk of translating into the leading principles of the traditional epistemological models based on representationalism and classificatory controlling patterns. Instead, there is a need to develop other, careful, ways of thinking that would help us react to the metamorphous nature of our historicity and to be able to respond to the challenges it poses. This is an important context for deliberating the politics of relationality occurring in reference to ethics, onto-epistemologies, politics, and art, while simultaneously drawing attention to problems connected to the operating social hierarchies and indicating risks for their (often-unwilling) reification.

My argumentation in this chapter intended to offer another voice in these debates. Since I focused on issues of vulnerability and fragility, which I find indispensable for the feminist knowledge production, I started my deliberations with the theorizations and analyses of material-semiotic encounters with works of art, focusing on their complex, multidimensional operations as well as memorable effects they are capable of producing. This, however, requires openness and exposure, a willingness to acknowledge that we can be acted on by other bodies and that these processes can generate unexpected results. They also trigger production of situated, singular, and dynamic knowledges, whose shapes and effects often cannot be predicted in advance. The politics of relationality, by definition, relies on the concept of withness or togetherness. Relation is about being/becoming *with* or about being responsive to what happens to us. The new materialist concept of *sym*pathy that I developed in this chapter serves as a figuration to approach these complex processes, as well as points to the necessity of caring for others in their different forms and shapes. It is a manner of connecting with other bodies and an ethico-onto-epistemological position wherefrom knowledges are produced and advanced. This concept is grounded in Deleuze's vitalist understandings of life as vibrating movement of becoming-other, yet it also recognizes the radical passivity of becoming, a necessary condition of self-surrender which makes our condition fragile and precarious as well as helps us imagine similar conditions of other bodies and their susceptibility to our actions. This is the character of dynamic and eternal *becoming-with-other-bodies*, which nevertheless always happens in very particular material-semiotic contexts and is vitally affected by them. As Judith Butler notices, "The body cannot be relieved of its locatedness, its exposure" (2012, 141). And she continues by saying—in truly relational mode—that "to find that one's life is also the life of others, even as this life is distinct and must be distinct, means that one's boundary is at once a limit and a site of adjacency, a mode of spatial and temporal nearness and even boundedness" (2012, 141). In order to grasp the spirit of such new materialist politics of connectivity and withness, it is necessary to disavow thinking in terms of autonomous and mighty subject of knowledge capable of producing objective claims from an isolated, detached position of an external observer. "Egological thinking" (Butler 2012, 136) has to be dismantled and replaced with more "ecological" attitudes, paying attention to relationality and interdependence in the necessarily entangled coexistence that we continuously share with other bodies.

NOTES

1. For further discussion, see, for example, Sandra Bartky (1996), Daryl Koehn (1998), and Lauren Berlant (2004).

2. Standpoint theory is—as explained by Sandra Harding (1986, 1993)—one of the three basic paradigms of feminist epistemologies. Harding places it along feminist empiricism and feminist postmodernism. She herself is a proponent of this epistemological system and one of the pioneers in the field of feminist philosophies of science. The list of other standpoint theorists includes Dorothy Smith, Nancy Hartsock, Hilary Rose, and Patricia Hill Collins. Standpoint theory considers women's lived experiences, and particularly those connected to everyday work of caring for others, as a necessary starting point for formulating knowledge claims. This constitutes an important standpoint wherefrom accountable knowledges could be produced. Feminists working within this epistemological paradigm underline that knowledge is always socially situated, but this situatedness is often not fully acknowledged (as it is the case with the dominant masculine model of knowledge production). It is vitally important to them to take this situatedness into consideration when formulating scientific ideas. In a somewhat Marxist spirit, standpoint theory focuses on the special situatedness of the marginalized groups, underlining that such positioning makes it possible for them to see better or to get more aware of things and phenomena that are not discernible from the position of the privileged. For these reasons every research should start with a social inquiry of power relations and hierarchical structures ordering everyday life. Yet the more accountable manner to run a strongly objective research (and the notion of "strong objectivity" was also developed by Harding 1993) is to start it from the lives of the marginalized. One of the most controversial, and most thoroughly critiqued, claims made by standpoint theory is that one does not necessarily have to belong to the marginalized group in order to be capable of adopting a standpoint pertaining to it. Nevertheless, as Harding explains, there are people in the margins that would never be able to speak for themselves. Standpoint theory, in such an account, is seen as having a potential for giving them voice and making their experiences visible to many, and especially to those located within the Western academia.

3. Drawing on experiences of black women in the United States, Patricia Hill Collins (1990) offers a model of Afrocentric feminist epistemology, which includes

four basic tenets. Thusly produced, knowledge has to be based on the lived concrete experience, which serves as a criterion of meaning. Collins advocates for the use of dialogue in assessing knowledge claims instead of favoring more confrontationally organized disputes and arguments. The model promotes the ethics of caring, which testifies to the emotional investment in the research topics as well as the ethics of personal accountability underlining researchers' situatedness and connections between their ideas developed within the academic contexts and the manners in which they live their lives.

Coda

In his philosophical exercise in phenomenology, Edward S. Casey debates the role of the embodiment in mnemonic processes and practices. As he writes, "Body memory is . . . the natural center of any sensitive account of remembering" (2000, 148). For him, "There is no memory without body memory" (2000, 172). Yet by formulating such claims he does not mean to say that "whenever we remember, we are in fact directly engaging in body memory. . . . Rather . . . we could not remember . . . without having capacity for body memory" (2000, 172). Such arguments point to the cardinal role of embodiment in processes of remembering and forgetting, underlining in fact the bodily, affective aspects of sensory corporeal realm as constitutive of the ways we tend to remember and make these memories meaningful. My elaboration of the concept of *synaesthetic perception* that I offered in chapter 1 of this book partly relies on such understanding. It intends to do justice to the complexity of perceptual processes occurring at the overlap of the bodily and the intellectual, revealing the affective-cognitive nature of both perception and practices of knowledge production. Knowing is embodied in the materiality—this refers to both the materiality of (organic and inorganic) bodies entering into fleeting relations or assemblages and the materiality of the context in which perception happens. Semiotic, in that sense, is also partly material and produces material effects.

The turn to affect as well as the increased interest in issues of matter and materiality, which have occurred relatively recently within the field of cultural studies, offer novel ways of thinking about our involvement with/in the world, fostering more affirmative attitudes and manners of developing critique. As I pointed out earlier, affect is about production and productivity. It is typically related to the physics of motion (cf. Braidotti 2006a) and creation of intensities and sensations. Affects are born out of encounters of differently understood bodies. And each encounter differs from others as bodies are not stable or frozen entities, but constantly unfolding processes and reconfigurations—movements and flows. Consequently, the concept of affect, understood in line with Deleuze and Guattari's philosophy, enables approaching the idea of difference in affirmative manners, focusing on its productive transformations in the procedure of constant differing. This constitutes a point of departure for formulating more productive critiques, divorcing them from the logic of negativity so deeply inscribed in the Western metaphysics. Such reformulation offers radical potentials for feminist argumentations as well as for situated practices of knowledge production that are so dear to feminist goals and agendas. As I made clear in the introduction to this volume, persistent sticking to purely representational modes of delivering a critique, and of thinking in general, translates into a substantial impasse as far as emancipatory and creative fashions of inventing concepts are concerned. In order to overcome these difficulties, a new "image of thought" is necessary, one which would not perpetuate the existing problems and discriminatory intellectual schemes inscribed in the logic of either/or but instead encouraging a resourceful production. It is vitally important for feminists to divorce the idea of difference from its negative valance and pejorative connotation it generates in the dominant culture, as much as it is critically necessary to learn to think *difference in itself* rather than always subordinating it to something else (i.e., conceptualizing it as *difference from*). The negative conceiving of difference—inscribed in the prevailing paradigms of the mechanism of representation (that I explained in the introduction)—has been located at the heart of the hierarchically organized discriminatory politics, placing women (and other "others") in subordinated positions and framing them as "deviations" from the norm of sameness (which typically stood for "Western-white-English-speaking-maleness").

What Deleuze and Guattari's philosophy has to offer to feminist struggles is envisaging difference outside the regime of sameness. Instead of the dominance of the system of doubleness and otherness, enabled by notions of subjectification and signification, their approach fosters recognition of difference beyond the logic of the same, that is, of major illusions of representations: identity, analogy, resemblance, and opposition. The turn to affect seems therefore to offer promising ways for overcoming these difficulties and triggering more affirmative, yet context-informed, politics and knowledges. Affect is always different and so is the becoming of bodies. Because of the relational nature of affect and its reliance on connectivity, it bears a promise for creating inventive alliances and fostering manners of thinking in terms of continuities and connections. Such strategies offer new perspectives for the feminist politics of solidarity as well as for situated practices of knowledge production. The latter remain necessarily contextual, partial, and temporary.

As Elizabeth Grosz clarifies, "Deleuze thinks difference primarily as force, as *affirmation*, as action, as precisely effectivity" (2001, 62; original emphasis). Accordingly, thought is here understood as an

> active force, positive desire, which *makes* a difference. . . . Deleuze's project thus involves the reenergization of thought, the affirmation of life and change, and an attempt to work around those forces of antiproduction that aim to restrict innovation and prevent change: to free lines, points, concepts, events, from the structures and constraints that bind them to the same, to the one, to the self-identical. (Grosz 2001, 62; original emphasis)

Being affirmative in itself, the concept of affect also encourages a novel way of positively envisioning creative and pleasurable involvements with the visual, forcing a bodily perceptual production, which is not necessarily easily transferable into the representational realm. This has significant reverberations for feminist approaches to art and the visual, which—when enclosed within their ideological renderings connected to the sphere of widely understood images and texts—have struggled for long with conceptualizing the women's (or feminist) pleasure. Can we refer in terms of pleasure to something that is derived from an interaction with the ideology-infused, and as such discriminatory and oppressive, dominant visual culture? If we acknowledge an affective nature of perception, no longer do these pleasures have to be understood in negative terms (as oppositional, resistant, referring to masquerade, masochism, masculinization, etc.). By focusing on purely aesthetic (rather than representational) aspects of the visual culture, the interaction (or intra-action) with it may be conceptualized in affirmative manners as a constant production, a perpetual material-semiotic unfolding, a life itself. This, however, has to be cautious and wary in order not to fall into the trap of affirming the existing, undeniably oppressive, status quo. Instead, it is about sharpening the critique while acknowledging the complex, sometimes illogical, character of perceptual processes.

Such experimental fashion of approaching art and artistic production derives from Deleuze and Guattari's writings about art as being a way of thinking, operating through affects and sensations. This radically reposits more traditional ways of understanding art and aesthetic experience. Noticeably, the discipline of art history has for long tended to refer to art through representation (i.e., by *reading* the objects of art, regardless of the adopted methodology). Deconstruction, with its entwinement with postmodern thought, is not very different from the more traditional approaches to art and artistic objects, even though it acknowledges (or even deepens!) a crisis of representation. By rendering all art a product of ideological meaning-making schemes, derivative of practices of representation, deconstruction encloses art within the realm of negativity, from which there seems to be no escape. Yet, when approached through its asignifying registers, art is no longer seen as exclusively related to representational structures. If we admit that art operates through affects, we open ourselves to the possibility of more affirmative renditions of visual culture. As Simon O'Sullivan notices, in this context, the concept of affect has to be thought in twofold ways: "as the effect of art on the body and as that which constitutes the art object. In both cases affect is orientated against an overemphasis on signifying regimes, but also against habit and opinion" (2006, 6). As he further clarifies, adopting such a perspective is necessary if we work to "correct the overemphasis on ideological critique and semiotic approaches to art by attending to the affective dimension of the art experience. We might see this as a return to a notion of the aesthetic albeit a specifically immanent one" (2006, 7). A modus operandi of such approach is "affirmation and creation rather than negation and critique" (O'Sullivan 2006, 9), which remains in total accord with the new materialist spirit and its understanding of a *work of art* (elaborated on in chapter 1).

Approaching art through the concept of synaesthetic perception (which, nevertheless, does not apply exclusively to art) presents us with another way of thinking art in general, that is, as O'Sullivan insists, "beyond the 'horizon of the signifier,' beyond textuality, but not through the return to traditional aesthetic theory or indeed the previous artist-centred models" (2006, 4). In line with the new materialist ideas, "this involves a further turn from the linguistic, a turn towards matter and to the expressive potentialities of the latter" (O'Sullivan 2006, 4). The synaesthetic understanding of experience, as referring to the bodily and the intellectual as well as to the conjunctive use of senses, resonates with such an approach and highlights the singularity of each perceptual event (as always different and differing). As I intended to make clear in the course of my argumentation, such an account enables focusing on the aesthetics of encounter, often unreadable and unrepresentable, yet still present there and always active. Accordingly, a *work of art* is not simply a physical object or space functioning solely within the representational structures of meaning. Rather, it is something whose qualities emerge out of the encounter. As such, these material-semiotic events are relational in their nature.

Deleuze and Guattari teach as how to think of art as a world of affects, or a universe of forces, which is capable of producing unexpected effects. A similar perspective is inscribed in the new materialist rendition of art. Accordingly, the process of encountering art is not external to the participating entities. Never do the involved bodies preexist the relation—the relation itself is their ontology. The process of encountering the work of art happens on a molecular level, beyond subjectivity, where subjects become bundles of events or assemblages of affects and sensations—"a set of liberated singularities, words, names, fingernails, things, animals, little events" (Deleuze 1995, 7). From this we can conclude that art has a unique power to return us back to the world, to reconnect and entangle us with it, and to make it in a truly post-anthropocentric manner (as an anthropocentric philosophical attitude has made people estranged from the world and situated them aside from all other critters and inanimate objects). Given its agential capacities and constant movement that defines it, no longer is art perceived as solely an object, but rather it constitutes a zone of the emergence for creative forces. It is an affective event experienced in a direct fashion or given in the experience, independently of such categories as the perceiving subject and the perceived object. The juxtaposition of the two gets dethroned and eradicated—the process of encountering is about relations and linkages organized rhizomatically in a nonhierarchical manner. Perception is far more complex than its purely visual renditions assume. It involves the sensory apparatus conceived of as an entangled perceiving machine located in particular, always moving and always changing contexts. Such formulation of perception gives away the ocularcentric rudiments of Western metaphysics and especially of Western scientific culture.

Encounters with art generate outcomes. Art is a bloc of sensations capable of producing effects. Knowledge, or formation of ideas, in such an account, arises from affects and not from signifying structures into which primary sensations are shaped on the representational (or emotional) level. The latter, as I made clear in chapter 1 (following Massumi 2002a), is more about the process of "capturing" or "freezing" the event in the well-established linguistic schemes, that is, subordinating it—through "recognition"—to what is already known. It is about "giving a name" to the event, whereas in fact, rather than referring to something else, the event is entirely immanent to itself. Certainly, affects cannot be read in any straightforward ways; they can only be experienced. As a bundle of affects, art has a potential for producing new affects, which in Deleuzian terms would be understood as the effects a body has on another body and its duration/movement (Deleuze 1998, 139). What needs to be kept in mind is that affects happen on the level of matter, being immanent to it. As extra-discursive, they remain non-recognizable in representational terms.

Since art is a manner of thinking (generated through production of sensations and intensities), it can be instrumental in promoting certain modes of a critical inquiry as well as in opening up and resensitizing us to the broadly understood others. As Deleuze notices, "The work of art is born from signs as much as it generates them" (Deleuze 2008, 62). The experience of art articulates the embodied nature of knowing and exposes the material-semiotic fashions of thinking triggered by participation in artistic perceptual events. Responses to the world, to other bodies, to the material operations of art are to be seen as manners of processing information. This happens also in direct, sensory, bodily activities, which are not immediately being turned into consciously worked-out concepts. All these processes, obviously, are located in cultural (semiotic and representational) contexts contributing immensely to the shapes perceptual events might temporarily take. It is therefore not accidental that in my investigations, I decided to focus on a specific form of art, that is, one related to trauma or traumatic occurrences. Such art operates through the persuasive entanglement of the material and the semiotic as well as embodies the entwinement of past, present, and future.

In chapter 2, when I turned to the issue of the material nature of the processes of remembering, as well as to the production of knowledge triggered by an encounter with the architectural space of museums related to the trauma of Shoah, my intention was to expose the complexity of the processes of inter-/intra-acting with such material-semiotic sites. My analyses focused on historical, cultural, and political contexts of functioning of these museums and on their material organization. These two aspects, constituting each other and remaining in tight entanglement, translate into certain experiences, although the latter are also contingent on the specificity of bodies encountering these spaces. Hence, the memory work encouraged by these inventive intra-actions is always singular and different, informed by the individual "histories" and "memories" (and, thus, knowledges) enclosed within the colliding bodies and processes as well as emerging from them. This translates into always new perceptual events, enriching the archives of the bodies and producing effects in forms of new experiential qualities and new knowledges. My objective was also to point to the necessity to work out critical vocabularies to address the effects affective-emotional encounters might possibly generate, especially taking into consideration the fact that—as demonstrated in my analyses of case studies—these operations are frequently harnessed for political purposes. Bearing in mind that workings of affects often happen on the imperceptible level, it is imperative to realize and process their effects, even though they are never easily controllable. Remaining, however, within a more affirmative spirit of new materialism, my objective in chapter 2 was also to demonstrate that the creative ways of encountering the lived experience of trauma can also trigger a deeper, and more intimate, understanding of these horrific events, while not pretending that these experiences are similar to the ones of those people whose stories are depicted in memorial spaces. These material-semiotic events—situated at the overlap of past, present, and future—are enabled by the material arrangement of new museums dedicated to the commemoration of traumatic occurrences and employing both affective and narrative means of functioning. Encounters of that kind might stimulate a more complex form of thoughtful and affective connections. Such politics is important from a feminist point of view, especially on account of the fact that feminist agenda includes goals focused on better and more thorough understanding of experiences of discrimination and oppression of any kind. The current debates center not exclusively on *what* knowledges should be spread but also on *how* to do it in inclusive, nondiscriminatory ways and in manners completely respectful and sensitive to those whom these experiences directly concern. In this context, a central role of the materiality of the body as much as of the encountered space is affirmed as crucial to understand the transmission of knowledges. It also triggers critical reflection on both the past and the ways it is used or rehearsed in the present.

Focusing on the relational material-semiotic experiences generated in memorial sites, I also exposed the falsity of the binary between the authenticity and inauthenticity as far as the engagements with these places are concerned. The logic that the more genuine the site, the more authentic experiences it produces is based on inadequate assumptions, which are the legacy of the representational system of thinking and the classificatory schemes deriving from it. Such a strategy of segregating the memorial sites by putting them into artificially created categories is futile as it does not take into consideration the singularity of the processes stimulated by the encounters of bodies, instead falsely assuming a univocal nature of these investments. A discussion tackling the so-called "dark sites" offers a point of departure for these investigations as they are considered a "special" category of tourist attractions, remaining tinged with the logic of negativity. Another reason for zooming in on "dark tourism" is that this type of activity is nowadays strictly related to the commemoration of traumatic events and occurrences, which provides an interesting starting point for deliberating the bodily (material) nature of trauma as well as how it cooperates with (or, alternatively, eludes) the representational framing.

In my investigations of the material character of trauma, as well as of how body remembers in not necessarily representational ways, my objective was to expose the complex entanglement of the past, present, and future and how this complexity actualizes in unexpected moments and situations. It testifies to the virtual character of memory, especially as it is contained within the body, as a somatic imprint, or a "literal" trace (as Caruth and Van der Kolk prefer). My attempt to focus on the analytical category of trauma in affirmative ways is to offer a more productive approach to the "information" stored in the material flesh, or in matter in general, conceptualizing it as an active agent contributing significantly to the processes of generating knowledges and shaping everyday perceptual experiences. The virtuality of memory, so evident in the case of trauma, reveals its dynamic and unexpected character as well as atemporal functioning. The concept of trauma, conceived as an embodied and nonrepresentational form of remembering, manifests the agential capacities of matter as well as its active operations, which generate very tangible effects.

My dealing with trauma and traumatic memory constitutes also a point of departure for reflecting on the nature of perceptual inter-/intra-actions, or collisions with other inclusively understood bodies, that always leave memorable, yet not necessarily perceptible or representable, traces on entities involved. The latter, importantly, remain in constant transformation, reemerging from relations in which they constantly participate. When encountering *works of art*, or artistically arranged "dark" memory sites, the experiences generated within these encounters alter and reconfigure the involved bodies, affecting the provisional trajectories of their becomings and reworking their temporary composition. Some dimensions of such experiential events remain beyond consciousness; nevertheless, they still happen to produce intense results. Thinking about the unrepresentability of trauma helps us in this context realize the complex nature of perception and facilitates grasping its material-semiotic effects. The brief elaboration of case studies of works of art embodying trauma serves as an illustration of the ways in which traumatic experiences operate as well as offers a reflection on the nature of interaction with material artifacts equipped with important agencies. The unfolding of material process of perception, always situated in semiotic contexts, exposes the vitality of matter and its capacities for relational metamorphoses and transformations. The movements of matter, whose realization is made possible within the encounters with memorial works of art (and which make their memorial character possible), testify to its agential qualities (and its *mattering*!) and highlight its role in the embodied processes of knowledge production. This seems to be crucial for feminist politics, especially as far as the critiques of the dominant scientific models and their epistemological assumptions are concerned.

The concept of trauma, importantly, also poses the notion of the body. Certainly, this is especially vital in the context of the new materialist approach that this book fosters. But the notion of the body, and how it knows and experiences, has for long been present in feminist investigations as well as in feminist attempts to develop more situated or located epistemological perspectives. Feminists have for decades argued that the body is both the most immediate and the most important context for experience and that all differences are primarily bodily differences. Even though traditionally the notion of the body has been associated with femininity (as opposed to the masculine mind), especially given its reproductive functions, acknowledging the active role of the body and its agential capacities has for long figured as one of the goals on feminist agendas. This has been especially significant for the knowledge production practices, which usually tend to omit the important bodily cognitive faculties. The return of the body in the context of knowledge production remains therefore in line with feminist critiques. Hence, the concepts of trauma and embodied knowing associated therewith resonate with feminist agendas and foster non-oppositional manners of formulating argumentations and developing new figurations.

The extralinguistic aspects of the processes of remembering call for an extended understanding of "seeing," which is not grounded in a traditionally conceptualized procedure of registering the event and—via mediation of the subject and linguistic concepts that the subject produces—representing it to oneself. Synaesthetic perception is not about recognition, that is, about subordinating the new to the already known. Rather, it is about opening up to the unexpected, with all its possible risks, connections, and transformative potentials. This extended process of seeing with the whole body is thoroughly material—it engages senses, sensibilities, and affects; it is an immediate registering that eludes purely representational structuring. What Cathy Caruth (1996) calls an "unclaimed experience" in this context has to be conceived as a literal (or immediate) and nonrepresentational memory of trauma, an extralinguistic mark left on the body, an embodied memory of the painful occurrence. Importantly, synaesthetic perception is not exclusively about materiality of seeing. Instead, it points to the entangled nature of perceptual processes, revealing its material-semiotic nature. Thus, in chapter 3, I pay a lot of attention to Marianne Hirsch's concept of postmemory that is about both affective knowing and the representational mediation of these knowledges, which shapes how they are experienced or lived. These peculiar operations of postmemory correspond well with the new materialist optic that the book adopts as well as they offer an interesting transition to reflections on the procedures of transmitting trauma, which points to the politics of connective relationality. If considered inclusively, Hirsch's concept can be useful in grasping different (i.e., narrative and affective) operations both of remembrance sites and of memory (either personal or collective) and how memories can be passed on to others. Postmemory lets us creatively approach the issue of shareability of traumatic experiences, even though it does not assume a direct knowing of what others went through or felt. Rather, it highlights the idea of connectivity so important for the feminist politics of solidarity and withness.

By stressing the monistic nature of the synaesthetic perception, as well as by building the book around the logic of connectivity, which exposes the falsity and artificiality of thinking in terms of oppositions and divisions, my objective was to signal the potentialities new materialism offers for feminist politics. Disavowing ocularcentrism, representationalism, and anthropocentrism situated at the core of the traditional manners of producing knowledge, this philosophical ferment emphasizes the necessity of overcoming the logic of negativity (which contributes to the constant perpetuation of exclusionary, dualistic ways of thinking), arguing instead for a more affirmative and conciliatory approach. Philosophically, affect is always positive; it is about production, generation, and movement. It does not mean, however, that the experiences produced within the encounter with art related to trauma should be seen as purely affective and hence asocial. Neither is my intention to claim that affect and representation are unlinked from each other. Quite the contrary, by adopting a new materialist perspective, my argumentation reveals the intertwinement of the material and the discursive, as well as points to the fundamental instability of the entanglement in which they remain. Hence, it is of vital importance not only to work out critical vocabularies to approach these processes but also to operationalize these concepts and make them more "livable" in both academic and nonacademic situations. A strategy of connecting different argumentations as well as distinct ways of formulating claims and ideas offers insights into new possibilities or tensions that can be productive and generative. Such a diffractive way of thinking gives away confrontational logic, focusing instead on patterns of resonance and interference as much as on the processes of overlapping of critiques, which stimulates invention of new perspectives and new images of thought. The approach fostered within this volume is inspired by diffractive methodology and draws on works of many (feminist) scholars from different disciplinary backgrounds and contexts. In an affirmative spirit of new materialism, I productively read their ideas through one another instead of juxtaposing these argumentations against each other. Also—in a cartographic manner—I intend to find connections and alliances among different thinkers and their concepts, rather than reading them separately as representing distinct paradigms and logics. Together with affirmative critiques, a methodology adopted in my argumentation tends to disavow a binarized logic of exclusion being at the origins of patriarchal system of domination from its very inception. It also provides a point of departure for formulating a novel, non-dualistic account of (embodied) perception, which—as explained earlier—is, from a feminist point of view, a very promising strategy.

By disengaging difference from its negative connotations, and conceptualizing it in and of itself, the Deleuze and Guattari's philosophy invokes the notion of becoming as alternative to the concept of a unified subjectivity. This allows them to think multiplicity beyond the paradigm of mere doubling, or proliferation/repetition of the same. Combined with a relational ontology, such formulation challenges the notion of the liberal humanist subject of knowledge (and representation) who exists prior to and independently of any object of study (observation). Rendition of subjectivity in terms of constant becoming, and situating it in the context of material-semiotic encounters with others (i.e., *becoming-with-other-bodies*), opens up possibilities for conceiving a vulnerable politics of relationality, so vitally important for feminist ethico-onto-epistemological agendas. My reflections on rhythm and movement as crucial for understanding the logic of connectivity offered in chapter 4, supplemented with a brief analysis of the Whiteheadian process philosophy, point to the fluidity of inclusively understood bodies and the provisional nature of their boundaries. Understanding bodies as constant movement of *becoming-other* (i.e., of constant *differing* triggered by encounters with other bodies) exposes their fragile nature, which makes them susceptible to changes and transformations.

Given the metamorphous and conditional character of subjectivity, the processes of becoming with others involve a constant *un/learning*, inscribed in the politics of permanent differing. Such logic requires an active withdrawal of the historical self, a dissolution of boundaries, or an acknowledgment of their temporary and porous nature. This is about constant change and perpetual recomposition of bodies. The processes of *learning* and *unlearning*, implied by the philosophy of becoming, are seen here as mutually co-constitutive. The same can be said about the phenomena of knowing/remembering and forgetting. Gaston Bachelard writes that "knowing must . . . be accompanied by an equal capacity to forget knowing. Non-knowing is not a form of ignorance. . . . This is the price that must be paid for an oeuvre to be . . . a sort of pure beginning, which makes its creation an exercise in freedom" (1969, xxix). My goal in chapter 4 was to point to how our perceptual routines and bodily-intellectual habits have to be suspended, or even thoroughly reworked, in an inventive encounter with a material-semiotic work of art. Artistic installations dedicated to the commemoration of the trauma of Shoah serve as illustrative cases of how such transformations and "adjustments" have to be necessarily made when human bodies collide with their untypical materiality located in particular semiotic circumstances. The dynamic operations of these works of art, and how they dash with visitors' bodies, let us better grasp the acquired nature of habits that have to be partly undone when such artistically arranged memorial space is encountered. The material-semiotic experiences generated within these perceptual events leave memorable traces on the entities involved, affecting their trajectories and reconfiguring their *mattering* materialities. Such processes translate into new imperceptible knowledges, or information stored within matter that shapes both the bodies and their capacities for experiencing or forming new relational connectivities in what is to come. Thus, the logic of relationality, exposed by and in encounters with art related to trauma, as discussed in chapter 4, facilitates thinking in terms of constant differing (understood in productive, affirmative manners), embodied in the figuration of *becoming-with-other-bodies*. This signals an important conceptual transition from politics of *ego*logism (cf. Butler 2012) to relational onto-epistemology of *eco*logism (or withness).

The synaesthetic approach to perception, the agential rendition of materiality, the entangled nature of mnemonic processes, and the dynamic conception of subjectivity developed in the first four chapters of this book, respectively, all illustrated with the affective operations of works of art, constitute an important theoretical basis for the development of the concept of *sym*pathy elaborated on in chapter 5. It serves as a new materialist figuration for feminist ethico-onto-epistemologies, offering a perspective on the situated processes of knowledge production. Since feminist and other critical scholars have revealed and thoroughly discussed how scientific processes, or practices of asserting academic "truths," have always been enmeshed with power, it has become enormously important to focus on how to produce more accountable and nondiscriminatory knowledges. They would foster more sensitive and responsible ethico-politics, remaining respectable to difference and differing. My interests presented in this part of the book are closely related to the monistic spirit of new materialism; they advance the politics of connectivity, based on relational onto-epistemology. The concept of *sym*pathy seems to offer a prolific combination of the logic of withness and the politics of radical passivity grounded in the ideas of collective becoming of life, which involves producing and being produced at the same time in the everlasting bundle of passive-active syntheses. The *sym*pathetic and sensitive practices of knowledge production—resting on ideas of exposure, vulnerability, and fragility—assume the politics of caring, of getting involved in something, of being ready to be acted on (in material-semiotic terms) by other bodies, which coproduce with us (and with others). Such strategy embodies the spirit of relationality and togetherness, which translates into a willingness to create new assemblages, to enter into machinic relations with other bodies, to get absorbed in the processes of becoming. This is considered as a condition for knowledge production, which in fact never happens in isolation from other bodies. The processes of knowing are thoroughly material and translate in situated and partial claims, always temporary in nature and always open to new reconfigurations. Such understanding radically differs from the dominant models of generating scientific claims, relying on the oppositional manner of thinking, which converts into "objective" classificatory systems and hierarchical structures of ordering (of bodies, phenomena, processes, species, etc.), pretending to have a universal status. The new materialist politics of *sym*pathy is inclined to disavow the binarized system of thought positioned at the core of Western scientific cultures, advancing instead a logic of rhizomatic and fragile becoming, or openness to novel possibilities and unusual connections or alliances. It also argues that acknowledging the intellectual-affective nature of cognition as well as its collective character could stimulate a critical reflection on how we are entangled with the world and how much mutual susceptibility these entanglements involve. The experiential encounters with art—that registers and embodies affect—can in this context help us think about the complexity of processes of knowledge (co)production. This triggers (re)thinking of the politics of experience in a more general sense. The procedures of material-semiotic knowing, encompassing vulnerability and care in passive exposure to the others, are not about might, control, prediction, and classification embedded in the representational, ocularcentric, and anthropocentric organization of Western scientific culture. Rather, they are about total unpredictability and a collective flow, or—as Deleuze cleverly evinces—about remaining "attentive to the unknown knocking at our door" (1989, 193).

Bibliography

Abu-Lughod, Lila, and Catherine Lutz, eds. 1990. *Language and the Politics of Emotions*. Cambridge, MA: Cambridge University Press.

Aceti, Lanfranco. 2009. "The War Shaped Identities: Destruction as Cultural Inheritance." In *In Transition: Cultural Identities in the Age of Transnational and Transcultural Flux*, edited by Helene Black, 31–41. Ekaterinburg: NEME.

Agamben, Giorgio. 2005. "Die Zwei Gedächtnisse" [The Two Memories]. *Die Zeit*, May 4. Accessed October 16, 2012. http://www.zeit.de/2005/19/Mahnmal_2f_Agamben.

Ahmed, Sara. 2004a. "Affective Economies." *Social Text* 79 (22) (2): 117–39.

Ahmed, Sara. 2004b. *The Cultural Politics of Emotion*. Edinburgh: Edinburgh University Press.

Alaimo, Stacey. 2010. *Bodily Natures: Science, Environment, and the Material Self*. Indianapolis, IN: Indiana University Press.

Alaimo, Stacey, and Susan Hekman, eds. 2008. *Material Feminisms*. Indianapolis, IN: Indiana University Press.

Alexander, Jeffrey Charles. 2008. "Iconic Consciousness: The Material Feeling of Meaning." *Environment and Planning D: Society and Space* 26 (5): 782–94.

Althusser, Louis. 1971. "On Ideology and Ideological State Apparatuses: Notes towards an Investigation." In *Lenin and Philosophy*, translated by Ben Brewster, 127–86. London, UK: New Left Books.

Appel, Dora. 2002. *Memory Effects: The Holocaust and the Art of Secondary Witnessing*. New Brunswick, NJ: Rutgers University Press.

Arnold de Simine, Silke. 2012. "Memory Museum and Museum Text Intermediality in Daniel Libeskind's Jewish Museum and W.G. Sebald's Austerlitz." *Theory Culture & Society* 29 (1): 14–35.

Ashworth, G. J., Brian J. Graham, and J. E. Tunbridge. 2007. *Pluralizing Pasts: Heritage, Identity and Place in Multicultural Societies*. London, UK: Pluto.

Ashworth, Goeffrey J. 2002. "Holocaust Tourism: The Experience of Kraków-Kazimierz." *International Research in Geographical and Environmental Education* 11 (4): 363–67.

Ashworth, Goeffrey J. 2004. "Tourism and the Heritage of Atrocity: Managing the Heritage of South African Apartheid for Entertainment." In *New Horizons in Tourism: Strange Experiences and Stranger Practices*, edited by Tejvir Singh, 95–108. Oxfordshire, UK: CAB International Publishing.

Assmann, Aleida, and Ute Frevert. 1999. *Geschichtsvergessenheit/Geschichtsversessenheit: Vom Umgang mt deutschen Vergangenheiten nach 1945* [Historical Obsession/Historical Obsession: Dealing with German Past after 1945]. Stuttgart: Deutsche Verlagsanstalt.

Bachelard, Gaston. 1969. "Introduction." In *The Poetics of Space*, edited by Gaston Bachelard, xv–xxix. Boston, MA: Beacon Press.

Badiou, Alain. 2005. *Handbook of Inaesthetics*. Stanford, CA: Stanford University Press.

Baer, Ulrich. 2002. *Spectral Evidence: The Photography of Trauma*. Cambridge, MA: MIT Press.

Bærenholdt, Jøgen Ole, and Michael Haldrup. 2004. "On the Track of the Vikings." *Tourism Mobilities: Places to Play, Places in Play*, edited by John Urry and Mimi Sheller, 78–89. London, UK: Routledge.

Bærenholdt, Jøgen Ole, Michael Haldrup, Jonas Larsen, and John Urry. 2004. *Performing Tourist Places*. London, UK: Routledge.

Barad, Karen. 1996. "Meeting the Universe Halfway." In *Feminism, Science, and the Philosophy of Science*, edited by Lynn Hakinson Nelson and Jack Nelson, 161–94. Dordrecht: Kluwer Academic Publishers.

Barad, Karen. 2003. "Posthumanist Performativity: Toward an Understanding of How Matter Comes to Matter." *Signs: Journal of Women in Culture and Society* 28 (3): 801–31.

Barad, Karen. 2007. *Meeting the Universe Halfway: Quantum Physics and the Entanglement of Matter and Meaning*. Durham, NC: Duke University Press.

Barad, Karen. 2010. "Quantum Entanglements and Hauntological Relations of Inheritance: Dis/continuities, SpaceTime Enfoldings, and Justice-to-Come." *Derrida Today* 3 (2): 240–68.

Barad, Karen. 2014. "Diffracting Diffraction: Cutting Together-Apart." *Parallax* 20 (3): 168–87.

Barrett, Estelle, and Barbara Bolt eds. 2013. *Carnal Knowledge: Towards a "New Materialism" through the Arts*. London: I. B. Tauris.

Barrett, Lisa F. 2009. "Variety Is a Spice of Life: A Psychological Construction Approach to Understanding Variability in Emotion." *Cognition and Emotion* 23 (7): 1284–306.

Bartky, Sandra Lee. 1996. "Sympathy and Solidarity: On a Tightrope with Scheler." In *Feminists Rethink the Self*, edited by Diane T. Meyers, 177–96. Boulder, CO: Westview Press.

Baumgarten, Alexander. 2013. *Metaphysics. A Critical Translation with Kant's Elucidations, Selected Notes, and Related Materials*, translated and edited by Courtney D. Fugate and John Hymers. London and New York: Bloomsbury Publishing.

Beardsley, Monroe. 1982. *The Aesthetic Point of View*. Ithaca, NY: Cornell University Press.

Beauvoir, Simone de. 1953. *The Second Sex*. London, UK: Picador.

Beckstead, Zachary, Gabriel Twose, Emily Levesque-Gottlieb, and Julia Rizzo. 2011. "Collective Remembering through the Materiality and Organization of War Memorials." *Journal of Material Culture* 16 (2): 193–213.

Beech, John. 2000. "The Enigma of Holocaust Sites as Tourist Attractions: The Case of Buchenwald." *Managing Leisure* 5: 29–41.

Beier-de Haan, Rosmarie. 2006. "Re-Staging Histories and Identities." In *Companion to Museum Studies*, edited by Sharon Macdonald, 86–197. Oxford, UK: Blackwell.

Bendelow, Gillian, and Simon J. Williams, eds. 1998. *Emotions in Social Life: Critical Themes and Contemporary Issues*. London, UK: Routledge.

Benjamin, Walter. 1999. *The Arcades Project*, translated by Howard Eiland and Kevin McLaughlin. Cambridge, MA: Harvard University Press.

Bennett, Jane. 2010. *Vibrant Matter: A Political Ecology of Things*. Durham and London: Duke University Press.

Bennett, Jill. 2005. *Empathic Visions. Affect, Trauma and Contemporary Art*. Stanford, CA: Stanford University Press.

Berlant, Lauren. 1998. "Poor Eliza." *American Literature* 70 (3): 635–68.

Berlant, Lauren. 2004. "Introduction: Compassion (and Witholding)." In *Compassion: The Culture and Politics of an Emotion*, edited by Lauren Berlant, 1–14. London, UK: Routledge.

Billig, Michael. 1999. "Whose Terms? Whose Ordinariness? Rhetoric and Ideology in Conversation Analysis." *Discourse and Society* 10 (4): 543–58.

Biran, Avital, Yaniv Poria, and Gila Oren. 2011. "Sought Experiences at (Dark) Heritage Sites." *Annals of Tourism Research* 38 (3): 820–41.

Blackman, Lisa. 2012. *Immaterial Bodies: Affect, Embodiment, Mediation*. London, UK: Sage.

Blackman, Lisa, and Couze Venn. 2010. "Affect." *Body and Society* 16 (1): 7–28.

Blom, Thomas. 2000. "Morbid Tourism: A Postmodern Market Niche with an Example from Althorpe." *Norwegian Journal of Geography* 54: 29–36.

Bode, Rudolf. 2014. "Rhythm and Its Importance for Education." *Body & Society* 20 (3&4): 51–74.

Boivin, Nicole. 2008. *Material Cultures, Material Minds: The Impact of Things on Human Thought, Society, and Evolution*. Cambridge, MA: Cambridge University Press.

Bolt, Barbara. 2004a. *Art beyond Representation: The Performative Power of the Image*. London and New York: I.B. Tauris.

Bolt, Barbara. 2004b. "Painting Is Not a Representational Practice." In *Unframed: Practices and Politics of Women's Contemporary Painting*, edited by Rosemary Betterton, 41–61. London and New York: I.B. Tauris.

Bolt, Barbara. 2004c. "The Exegesis and the Shock of the New." *TEXT*, special issue, No. 3 (April). Accessed March 10, 2013. www.textjournal.com.au/speciss/issue3/bolt.htm.

Bolt, Barbara. 2009. "A Performative Paradigm for the Creative Arts?" *Working Papers in Art and Design* 5. Accessed March 20, 2013. https://www.herts.ac.uk/__data/assets/pdf_file/0015/12417/WPIAAD_vol5_bolt.pdf.

Bolt, Barbara. 2014. "Beyond Solipsism in Artistic Research: The Artwork and the Work of Art." In *Material Interventions. Applying Creative Arts Research*, edited by Estelle Barrett and Barbara Bolt, 22–37. London, UK: I.B.Tauris.

Bourdieu, Pierre. 2001. *Masculine Domination*. Stanford, CA: Stanford University Press.

Bowman, Michael S., and Phaedra C. Pezzullo. 2010. "What's So 'Dark' about 'Dark Tourism'?: Deaths, Tours, and Performance." *Tourist Studies* 9 (3): 187–202.

Braidotti, Rosi. 2000. "Teratologies." In *Deleuze and Feminist Theory*, edited by Ian Buchanan and Claire Colebrook. Edinburgh: Edinburgh University Press.

Braidotti, Rosi. 2002. *Metamorphoses: Towards a Materialist Theory of Becoming*. Cambridge, MA: Polity Press.

Braidotti, Rosi. 2006a. *Transpositions: On Nomadic Ethics*. Cambridge, MA: Polity Press.

Braidotti, Rosi. 2006b. "Affirmation versus Vulnerability: On Contemporary Ethical Debates." *Symposium: Canadian Journal of Continental Philosophy* 10 (1): 235–54.

Braidotti, Rosi. 2008. "In Spite of the Times. The Postsecular Turn in Feminism." *Theory, Culture & Society* 25 (6): 1–24.

Brennan, Teresa. 2004. *The Transmission of Affect*. Ithaca, NY: University of Cornell Press.

Buchanan, Ian. 2000. *Deleuzism. A Metacommentary*. Edinburgh: Edinburgh University Press.

Buell, Lawrence, Ursula K. Heise, and Karen Thornber. 2011. "Literature and Environment." *Annual Reviews of Environment and Resources* 36: 441–63.

Butler, Judith. 1990. *Gender Trouble: Feminism and the Subversion of Identity*. New York: Routledge.

Butler, Judith. 1993. *Bodies That Matter: On the Discursive Limits of "Sex*." New York: Routledge.

Butler, Judith. 1997. *Excitable Speech: A Politics of the Performative*. London and New York: Routledge.

Butler, Judith. 1999. "Gender Is Burning: Questions of Appropriation and Subversion." In *Feminist Film Theory. A Reader*, edited by Sue Thornham. New York: New York University Press.

Butler, Judith. 2010. "Performative Agency." *Journal of Cultural Economy* 3 (2): 147–61.

Butler, Judith. 2012. "Precarious Life, Vulnerability and the Ethics of Cohabitation." *The Journal of Speculative Philosophy* 26 (2): 134–51.

Callaghan, Mark. 2010. "Speak Out: Invisible Past, Invisible Future: A German's Alternative Response to the Holocaust." *ART TIMES* (November/December). Accessed March 13, 2016. http://www.arttimesjournal.com/speakout/Nov_Dec_10_Callaghan%20/Nov_Dec_10_Callaghan.html.

Carrier, Peter. 2005. *Holocaust Monuments and National Memory Cultures in France and Germany since 1989: The Origins and Political Function of the Vél'd'Hiv' in Paris and the Holocaust Monument in Berlin*. New York: Berghahn Books.

Carroll, Noël. 1986. "Art and Interaction." *Journal of Aesthetics and Art Criticism* 45 (1): 57–68.

Carroll, Noël. 2005. "Art and Recollection." *Journal of Aesthetic Education* 30 (2): 1–12.

Caruth, Cathy, ed. 1995a. *Trauma: Explorations in Memory*. Baltimore, MD, and London: Johns Hopkins University Press.

Caruth, Cathy. 1995b. "Trauma and Experience: Introduction." In *Trauma: Explorations in Memory*, edited by Cathy Caruth, 3–12. Baltimore, MD, and London: Johns Hopkins University Press.

Caruth, Cathy. 1996. *Unclaimed Experience: Trauma, Narrative, and History*. Baltimore, MD, and London: Johns Hopkins University Press.

Casey, Edward S. 2000. *Remembering: A Phenomenological Study*. Bloomington and Indianapolis, IN: Indiana University Press.

Chabot Davis, Kimberly. 2004. "Ophra's Book Club and the Politics of Cross-Racial Empathy." *International Journal of Cultural Studies* 7 (4): 399–419.

Classen, Constance. 1993. *Worlds of Sense: Exploring the Senses in History and across Cultures*. London and New York: Routledge.

Classen, Constance. 1998. *The Color of Angels: Cosmology, Gender and the Aesthetic Imagination*. London and New York: Routledge.

Classen, Constance. 2001. "The Social History of the Senses." In *Encyclopedia of European Social History*, edited by Peter N. Stearns. New York: Charles Scribner & Sons.

Classen, Constance. 2012. *The Deepest Sense: A Cultural History of Touch*. Urbana, IL: University of Illinois Press.

Classen, Constance, Dawid Howes, and Anthony Synnott. 1994. *Aroma: The Cultural History of Smell*. London and New York: Routledge.

Clough, Patricia T. 2008. "The Affective Turn: Political Economy, Biomedia and Bodies." *Theory, Culture & Society* 25 (1): 1–22.

Clough, Patricia T. 2009. "The New Empiricism: Affect and Sociological Method." *European Journal of Social Theory* 12: 43–61.

Clough, Patricia T., and Jean Halley, eds. 2007. *The Affective Turn: Theorizing the Social*. Durham, NC: Duke University Press.

Colebrook, Claire. 2005. *Philosophy and Post-Structuralist Theory: From Kant to Deleuze*. Edinburgh: Edinburgh University Press.

Colebrook, Claire. 2007. *Gilles Deleuze*. New York and London: Routledge.

Collins, Patricia Hill. 1990. *Black Feminist Thought: Knowledge, Consciousness and the Politics of Empowerment*. New York: Routledge.

Colman, Felicity. 2013. "The Matter of the Image: Notes on Practice-Philosophy." In *Bergson and the Art of Immanence*, edited by Charlotte DeMille and John Mullarkey. Edinburgh: Edinburgh University Press.

Coole, Diana, and Samantha Frost, eds. 2010a. *New Materialisms: Ontology, Agency, and Politics*. Durham, NC: Duke University Press.

Coole, Diana, and Samantha Frost. 2010b. "Introducing New Materialism." In *New Materialisms: Ontology, Agency, and Politics*, edited by Diana Coole and Samantha Frost, 1–43. Durham, NC: Duke University Press.

Coplan, Amy, and Peter Goldie, eds. 2011. *Empathy: Philosophical and Psychological Perspectives*. Oxford, UK: Oxford University Press.

Cosgrove, Denise. 1999. *Mappings*. London: Reaktion Books.

Cromby, John. 2007. "Toward a Psychology of Feeling." *International Journal of Critical Psychology* 21: 94–118.

Crouch, David. 2002. "Surrounded by Place: Embodied Encounters." In *Tourism. Between Place and Performance*, edited by Simon Coleman and Mike Crang, 207–18. Oxford: Berghahn.

Crouch, David. 2005. "Flirting with Space: Tourism Geographies a Sensuous/ Expressive Practice." In *Seductions of Place. Geographical Perspectives on Globalization and Touristed Landscapes*, edited by Carolyn Cartier and Alan A. Lew, 23–25. London and New York: Routledge.

Crouch, David, and Luke Desforges. 2003. "The Sensuous in the Tourist Encounter. Introduction: The Power of the Body in Tourist Studies." *Tourist Studies* 3 (1): 5–22.

Crouch, David, and Nina Lübbren. 2003. "Introduction." In *Visual Culture and Tourism*, edited by David Crouch and Nina Lübbren, 1–20. Oxford and New York: Berg.

Crysler, Greig, and Abidin Kusno. 1997. "Angels in the Temple." *Art Journal* 56 (1): 52–64.

Culberstone, Roberta. 1995. "Embodied Memory, Transcendence, and Telling: Recounting Trauma, Re-Establishing the Self." *New Literary History* 26 (1): 169–95.

Currie, Gregory. 2011. "Empathy for Objects." In *Empathy: Philosophical and Psychological Perspectives*, edited by Amy Coplan and Peter Goldie, 82–98. Oxford, UK: Oxford University Press.

Dann, Graham M. S. 1994. "Tourism: The Nostalgia Industry of the Future." In *Global Tourism: The Next Decade*, edited by William F. Theobald, 55–67. Oxford, UK: Butterworth Heinemann.

Dann, Graham M. S. 1998. *The Dark Side of Tourism*. Aix-en-Provence: Centre International de Recherches et d'Etudes Touristiques.

Danto, Arthur C. 1985. "The Vietnam Veterans Memorial." *The Nation* 31 (August): 152.

Davies, Douglas J. 1996. "Imagination Playing with Death: A Review of the Exhibition Midden in Het Leven Staan Wij in de Dood." *Mortality* 1: 323–26.

Dekel, Irit. 2009. "Ways of Looking: Observation and Transformation at the Holocaust Memorial, Berlin." *Memory Studies* 2 (1): 71–86.

Dekel, Irit. 2013. *Meditation at the Holocaust Memorial in Berlin*. London, UK: Palgrave.

DeLanda, Manuel. 1996. "The Geology of Morals: A Neo-Materialist Interpretation." Accessed September 20, 2013. http://www.t0.or.at/delanda/geology.htm.

DeLanda, Manuel. 2006. *A New Philosophy of Society: Assemblage Theory and Social Complexity*. London and New York: Continuum.

Delbo, Charlotte. 1965. *Aucun de nous reviendra*. Paris: Les Éditions de Minuit (English version: *Auschwitz and After*, translated by Rosette C. Lamont, introduction by Lawrence Langer. New Haven, CT: Yale University Press).

Delbo, Charlotte. 1970. *Une connaisance inutile*. Paris: Les Éditions de Minuit (English version: *Auschwitz and After*, translated by Rosette C. Lamont, introduction by Lawrence Langer. New Haven, CT: Yale University Press).

Delbo, Charlotte. 1971. *Mesure de nos jours*. Paris: Les Éditions de Minuit (English version: *Auschwitz and After*, translated by Rosette C. Lamont, introduction by Lawrence Langer. New Haven, CT: Yale University Press).

Delbo, Charlotte. 2001 (1990). *Days and Memory*, translated by Rosette Lamont. Evanston, IL: Northwestern University Press.
Deleuze, Gilles. 1968. *Spinoza et la problème de l'expression* [Spinoza and the Problem of Expression]. Paris: Les Editions de Minuit.
Deleuze, Gilles. 1972. *Proust and Signs*. New York: George Braziller.
Deleuze, Gilles. 1986. *Cinema 1. The Movement-Image*. Minneapolis, MN: University of Minnesota Press.
Deleuze, Gilles. 1988a. *Foucault*, translated by Séan Hand. Minneapolis, MN: University of Minnesota Press.
Deleuze, Gilles. 1988b. *Spinoza. Practical Philosophy*, translated by Robert Hurley. San Francisco, CA: City Light Books.
Deleuze, Gilles. 1989. "Qu'est-ce qu'un dispositif?" [What Is a Dispositif?] In *Michel Foucault philosophe* [Michel Foucault Philosopher], edited by François Ewald. Paris: Seuil.
Deleuze, Gilles. 1990. *The Logic of Sense*, translated by Mark Lester and Charles Stivale, edited by Constantin V. Boundas. London: Athlone Press.
Deleuze, Gilles. 1992. "What Is the Dispositif?" In *Michel Foucault Philosopher*, translated by T. J. Armstrong, 159–68. New York: Routledge.
Deleuze, Gilles. 1995. *Negotiations: 1972–1990*, translated by Martin Joughin. New York: Columbia University Press.
Deleuze, Gilles. 1998. *Essays Critical and Clinical*. London and New York: Verso.
Deleuze, Gilles. 2001. *Empiricism and Subjectivity: An Essay on Hume's Theory of Human Nature*. New York: Columbia University Press.
Deleuze, Gilles. 2008. *Proust and Signs*. New York and London: Continuum.
Deleuze, Gilles. 2011. *Difference and Repetition*, translated by Paul Patton. New York and London: Continuum.
Deleuze, Gilles, and Félix Guattari. 1983. *Anti-Oedipus. Capitalism and Schizophrenia*. Minneapolis, MN, and London: University of Minnesota Press.
Deleuze, Gilles, and Félix Guattari. 1987. *A Thousand Plateaus: Capitalism and Schizophrenia*. Minneapolis, MN, and London: University of Minnesota Press.
Deleuze, Gilles, and Félix Guattari. 1997. *What Is Philosophy?* London, UK: Verso.
Demasio, Antonio. 1995. *Descartes' Error: Emotion, Reason and the Human Brain*. London: Picador.
Demasio, Antonio. 1999. *The Feeling of What Happens: Body, Emotion, and the Making of Consciousness*. London: Vintage.
Demasio, Antonio. 2003. *Looking for Spinoza: Joy, Sorrow and the Feeling Brain*. London: Vintage.
Denzin, Norman K. 1984. *On Understanding Emotion*. San Francisco, CA: Jossey-Bass Publishers.
Derrida, Jacques. 2002. "The Animal That Therefore I Am (More to Follow)," translated by David Wills. *Critical Inquiry* 28 (2): 369–418.
Derrida, Jacques. 2008. *The Animal That Therefore I Am*, translated by David Wills. New York: Fordham University Press.
Dewey, John. 1934. *Art as Experience*. Balch, MI: University of Michigan Press.
Dolphijn, Rick, and Iris van der Tuin. 2010. "The Transversality of New Materialism." *Women: A Cultural Review* 21 (2): 153–71.

Dolphijn, Rick, and Iris van der Tuin. 2012. *New Materialism: Interviews & Cartographies*. Ann Arbor, MI: University of Michigan Press.

Domańska, Ewa. 2013. "Humanistyka ekologiczna" [Ecological Humanities]. *Teksty drugie* [Second Texts] 1–2: 13–32.

Domańska, Ewa. 2014a. "Historia ratownicza" [Rescue History]. *Teksty drugie* [Second Texts] 5: 12–26.

Domańska, Ewa. 2014b. "Humanistyka afirmatywna: płeć i władza po Butler i Foucaultcie" [Affirmative Humanities: Gender and Power after Butler and Foucault]. *Kultura Współczesna* [Contemporary Culture] 4: 117–29.

Drobnick, Jim. 2004. "Volatile Effects: Olfactory Dimensions of Art and Architecture." In *Empire of the Senses: The Sensual Culture Reader*, edited by David Howes. Oxford: Berg.

Edensor, Tim. 2001. "Performing Tourism, Staging Tourism, Reproducing Tourist Spaces and Practice." *Tourist Studies* 1 (1): 59–81.

Edmond, Jacob. 2014. "Diffracted Waves and World Literature." *Parallax* 20 (3): 245–57.

Eisenman, Peter. 2001. "Foreword." In *Architecture from the Outside*, by Elizabeth Grosz, xi–xiv. Cambridge, MA: MIT Press.

Ettinger, Bracha L. 2006. "Wit(h)nessing Trauma and the Matrixial Gaze." In *The Matrixial Borderspace/Bracha L. Ettinger*, edited by Brian Massumi, 123–56. Minneapolis, MN: University of Minnesota Press.

Featherstone, Mike. 2010. "Body, Image and Affect in Consumer Culture." *Body & Society* 16: 193–221.

Felman, Shoshana. 2002. *The Juridical Unconscious: Trials and Traumas in the Twentieth Century*. Cambridge, MA, and London: Harvard University Press.

Felman, Shoshana, and Dori Laub. 1992. *Testimony: Crises of Witnessing in Literature, Psychoanalysis and History*. New York and London: Routledge.

Fine, Ellen. 1998. "Transmission of Memory: The Post-Holocaust Generation in the Diaspora." In *Breaking Crystal: Writing and Memory after Auschwitz*, edited by Efraim Sicher, 185–200. Urbana and Chicago, IL: University of Illinois Press.

Flanzbaum, Hilene. 1999. *The Americanization of the Holocaust*. Baltimore, MD: Johns Hopkins University Press.

Foley, Malcolm, and J. John Lennon. 1996. "JFK and Dark Tourism—A Fascination with Assassination." *International Journal of Heritage Studies* 2 (4): 198–211.

Foster, Hal. 1998a. "The Un/Making of Sculpture." In *Richard Serra Sculpture: 1985–1998*, 13–31. Los Angeles, CA: Museum of Contemporary Art.

Foster, Hal. 1998b. *Richard Serra—Sculpture 1985–1998*. Los Angeles, CA: Museum of Contemporary Art.

Foster, Susan Leigh. 2010. *Choreographing Empathy: Kinesthesia in Performance*. London and New York: Routledge.

Foucault, Michel. 1977. *Discipline and Punish: The Birth of the Prison*. New York: Vintage Books.

Foucault, Michel. 1978. *The History of Sexuality, Vol. I: An Introduction*. New York: Vintage Books.

Foucault, Michel. 1980. *Power/Knowledge: Selected Interviews and Other Writings, 1972–1977*. New York: Vintage Books.

Foucault, Michel. 1982. "The Subject and Power." In *Beyond Structuralism and Hermeneutics*, edited by Hubert Dreyfus and Paul Rabinow, 208–26. Brighton: Harvester.

Fridlund, Alan. 1994. *Human Facial Expression: An Evolutionary View*. San Diego, CA: Academic Press.

Gadamer, Hans-Georg. 1982. *Truth and Method*. New York: Crossroad.

Garber, Marjorie. 2004. "Compassion." In *Compassion: The Culture and Politics of an Emotion*, edited by Lauren Berlant, 15–27. London: Routledge.

Geerts, Evelien, and Iris van der Tuin. 2013. "From Intersectionality to Interference." *Women's Studies International Forum* 48: 171–78.

Giardini, Federica. 1999. "Public Affects. Clues towards a Political Practice of Singularity." *European Journal of Women's Studies* 6: 149–59.

Godfrey, Mark. 2007. *Abstraction and the Holocaust*. New Haven, CT, and London, UK: Yale University Press.

Goethe, Johann Wolfgang von. 2007. "Roman Elegy V." In *Roman Elegies: And Other Poems & Epigrams*, translated by Michael Hamburger. Manchester: Carcanet Press.

Golańska, Dorota. 2015. "Affective Spaces, Sensuous Engagements: In Quest of a Synaesthetic Approach to 'Dark Memorials.'" *International Journal of Heritage Studies* 21 (8): 773–90.

Graham, Brian. 2002. "Heritage and Knowledge: Capital or Culture?" *Urban Studies* 39: 1003–17.

Graham, Brian, Gregory J. Ashworth, and John E. Tundbridge. 2000. *A Geography of Heritage: Power, Culture and Economy*. London, UK: Arnold.

Gray, Brenda. 2011. "Empathy, Emotion and Feminist Solidarities." In *Sexed Sentiments: Interdisciplinary Perspectives on Gender and Emotion*, edited by Willemijn Ruberg and Kristine Steenbergh, 207–32. Amsterdam and New York: Rodopi.

Griffiths, Paul E. 1997. *What Emotions Really Are: The Problem of Psychological Categories*. Chicago, IL: University of Chicago Press.

Grosz, Elizabeth. 1993. "Bodies and Knowledges: Feminism and the Crisis of Reason." In *Feminist Epistemologies*, edited by Linda Alcoff and Elizabeth Potter, 49–82. New York and London: Routledge 1993.

Grosz, Elizabeth. 1994. *Volatile Bodies. Toward a Corporeal Feminism*. Bloomington and Indianapolis, IN: Indiana University Press.

Grosz, Elizabeth. 2001. *Architecture from the Outside*. Cambridge, MA: MIT Press.

Grosz, Elizabeth. 2005. *Time Travels: Feminism, Nature, Power*. Sydney: Allen and Unwin.

Grosz, Elizabeth. 2008. *Chaos, Territory, Art: Deleuze and the Framing of the Earth*. New York: Columbia University Press.

Grosz, Elizabeth. 2011. *Becoming Undone*. Durham, NC: Duke University Press.

Grunewald, Ralph. 1992. "Architectural Symbolism and Other Features of the USHMM." Washington, DC, Internal Museum Document (March 23, 1992).

Guerin, Frances, and Roger Hallas, eds. 2007. *The Image and the Witness: Trauma, Memory and Visual Culture*. London: Wallflower Press.

Gutwein, Daniel. 2009. "The Privatization of the Holocaust: Memory, Historiography, and Politics." *Israel Studies* 14 (1): 36–64.

Hall, Carla. 1987. "Celebrating the Will to Remember: Arthur Rosenblatt and the Holocaust Museum." *Washington Post* (April 29): D1.

Hall, Stuart, ed. 1997. *Representation: Cultural Representations and Signifying Practices*. London: Sage.

Hapkemeyer, Andreas. 1999. "On the Principle of Dialog in Jochen Gerz's Works for Public Spaces." In *Jochen Gerz-Res Publica: Public Works 1968–99*, edited by Rosanna Albertini, Andreas Hapkemeyer, Marion Hohlfeldt, Helga Pakasaar, and Hans-Werner Schmidt. Ostfildern and New York: Hatje Cantz Publishers.

Haraway, Donna. 1988. "Situated Knowledges. The Science Question in Feminist and the Privilege of Partial Perspective." *Feminist Studies* 14 (3): 575–99.

Haraway, Donna. 1997. *Modest−Witness@Second−Millennium. FemaleMan−Meets−OncoMouse: Feminism and Technoscience*. London and New York: Routledge.

Haraway, Donna. 2003. *The Companion Species Manifesto*. Chicago, IL: Prickly Paradigm Press.

Haraway, Donna. 2013. "Sowing Worlds: A Seed Bag for Terraforming with Earth Others." In *Beyond the Cyborg: Adventures with Donna Haraway*, edited by Margaret Grebowicz and Helen Merrick, 137–46. New York: Columbia University Press.

Haraway, Donna, in conversation with Martha Kenney. 2015. "Anthropocene, Capitalocene, Chthulhocene." In *Art in the Anthropocene: Encounters among Aesthetics, Politics, Environments and Epistemologies*, edited by Heather Davis and Etienne Turpin, 255–70. London: Open Humanities Press.

Harding, Sandra. 1986. *The Science Question in Feminism*. New York: Cornell University Press.

Harding, Sandra. 1993. "Rethinking Standpoint Epistemology: What Is 'Strong Objectivity'?" In *Feminist Epistemologies*, edited by Linda Alcoff and Elizabeth Potter, 49–82. New York: Routledge.

Harel, Dorit. 2010. *Facts and Feelings: Dilemmas in Designing the Yad Vashem Holocaust History Museum, Jerusalem*. Jerusalem: Yad Vashem Publications.

Harrison, Paul. 2008. "Corporeal Remains: Vulnerability, Proximity, and Living on after the End of the World." *Environment and Planning A* 40 (2): 423–45.

Hartman, Geoffrey. 2000. "Tele-Suffering and Testimony in the Dot Com Era." In *Visual Culture and the Holocaust*, edited by Barbie Zelizer, 111–24. New Brunswick, NJ: Rutgers University Press.

Heckner, Elke. 2008. "Whose Trauma Is It? Identification and Secondary Witnessing in the Age of Postmemory." In *Visualizing the Holocaust: Documents, Aesthetics, Memory*, edited by David Bathrick, Brad Prager, and Michael D. Richardson, 62–85. Rochester, NY: Camden House.

Hemmings, Clare. 2005. "Invoking Affect: Cultural Theory and the Ontological Turn." *Cultural Studies* 19 (5): 548–67.

Henriques, Julian, Milla Tiainen, and Pasi Väliaho. 2014. "Rhythm Returns: Movement and Cultural Theory." *Body & Society* 20 (3 and 4): 3–29.

Herman, Judith Lewis. 1997. *Trauma and Recovery*. New York: Basic Books.

Hirsch, Joshua. 2004. *Afterimage: Film, Trauma, and the Holocaust*. Philadelphia, PA: Temple University Press.

Hirsch, Marianne. 1992–1993. "Family Pictures: Maus, Mourning, and Post-Memory," *Discourse* 15 (2) (Winter): 3–29.

Hirsch, Marianne. 1997. *Family Frames. Photography, Narrative and Postmemory*. Cambridge, MA: Harvard University Press.

Hirsch, Marianne. 2008. "The Generation of Postmemory." *Poetics Today* 29 (1): 103–28.

Hirsch, Marianne. 2012. *The Generation of Postmemory. Writing and Visual Culture after the Holocaust*. New York: Columbia University Press.

Hirsch, Marianne. 2014. "Connective Histories in Vulnerable Times." *PMLA* 129 (3): 330–48.

Hirsch, Marianne, and Leo Spitzer. 2011. *Ghosts of Home: The Afterlife of Czernowitz in Jewish Memory*. Berkeley, CA: University of California Press.

Hoffman, Eva. 2004. *After Such Knowledge: Memory, History, and the Legacy of the Holocaust*. New York: Public Affairs.

hoogland, reneé. 2009. "The Affective Turn and Visual Literacy." In *Teaching Visual Culture in an Interdisciplinary Classroom: Feminist (Re)Interpretations of the Field*, edited by Elżbieta H. Oleksy and Dorota Golańska, 163–74. Utrecht: Zuidam Uithof Drukkerijen.

Hornstein, Shelley, and Florence Jocobowits, eds. 2002. *Image and Remembrance: Representation and the Holocaust*. Bloomington, IN: Indiana University Press.

Howes, David, ed. 1991. *The Varieties of Sensory Experience: A Source Book in the Anthropology of the Senses*. Toronto: Toronto University Press.

Howes, David. 2003. *Sensual Relations: Engaging the Senses in Culture and Social Theory*. Ann Arbor, MI: University of Michigan Press.

Howes, David, ed. 2004. *Empire of the Senses: The Sensual Culture Reader*. Oxford, UK: Berg.

Howes, David. 2013. "The Social Life of the Senses." *Ars Vivendi Journal* 3: 4–23.

Hume, David. 2004 (1777). *An Enquiry Concerning the Principles of Morals*. Amherst, NY: Prometheus Books.

Hungerford, Amy. 2001. "Memorizing Memory." *Yale Journal of Criticism: Interpretation in the Humanities* 14 (1): 67–92.

Hüppauf, Bernd. 1997. "Emptying the Gaze: Framing Violence through the Viewfinder." *New German Critique* 72: 3–44.

Huyssen, Andreas. 1995. *Twilight Memories: Marking Time in a Culture of Amnesia*. New York: Routledge.

Iseminger, Gary. 2003. "Aesthetic Experience." In *The Oxford Handbook of Aesthetics*, edited by Jerrold Levinson, 99–117. Oxford and New York: Oxford University Press.

Iseminger, Gary. 2008. "Experiential Theories of Aesthetic Value." In *Aesthetic Experience*, edited by Richard Shusterman and Adele Tomlin, 79–97. New York and London: Routledge.

Jaggar, Alison M. 1996. "Love and Knowledge: Emotion in Feminist Epistemology." In *Women, Knowledge, and Reality: Explorations in Feminist Philosophy*, edited by Ann Garry and Marilyn Pearsall, 166–90. New York: Routledge.

James, William. 1884. "What Is an Emotion?" *Mind* 9: 188–205.

Jay, Martin. 1994. *Downcast Eyes: The Denigration of Vision in Twentieth-Century French Thought*. Berkeley, CA: University of California Press.

Johnson, Mark. 1987. *The Body in the Mind*. Chicago, IL: Chicago University Press.

Josephs, Ingrid. 2000. "Feeling as Movement from a Person-Centered Standpoint: Going beyond William Stern." *Theory and Psychology* 10 (6): 815–29.

Kaiser, Birgit M., and Kathrin Thiele. 2014. "Diffraction: Onto-Epistemology, Quantum Physics and the Critical Humanities." *Parallax* 20 (3): 165–67.

Kantsteiner, Wulf. 2006. *In Pursuit of German Memory: History, Television, and Politics after Auschwitz*. Athens, OH: Ohio University Press.

Kaplan, E. Ann, and Ban Wang. 2004. "Introduction: From Traumatic Paralysis to the Force Field of Modernity." In *Trauma and Cinema: Cross-Cultural Explorations*, edited by E. Ann Kaplan and Ban Wang, 1–22. Hong Kong: Hong Kong University Press.

Kaufman, Eleanor. 1998. "Falling from the Sky: Trauma in Perec's and Caruth's Unclaimed Experience." *Diacritics: A Review of Contemporary Criticism* 28 (4): 44–53.

Kear, Jonathan. 2009. "Spectres of the Past, Inhabitations of the Present: Jochen Gerz and the Problem of Commemoration." In *Memories and Representations of War: The Case of World War I and World War II*, edited by Elena Lamberti and Vita Fortunati, 193–214. Amsterdam and New York: Rodopi.

Kearney, Richard. 1994. *Modern Movements in European Philosophy*. Manchester and New York: Manchester University Press.

Kemper, Theodore D. 1990. *Research Agenda in the Sociology of Emotions*. Albany, NY: State University of New York Press.

Kerridge, Richard. 2012. "Contemporary Ecocriticism between Red and Green." In *Ecology and the Literature of the British Left: The Red and the Green*, edited by Johm Rignall, H. Gustav Klaus, and Valentine Cunningham. Farnham: Ashgate.

Kerridge, Richard. 2014. "Ecocritical Approaches to Literary Form and Genre: Urgency, Depth, Provisionality, Temporality." In *The Oxford Handbook of Ecocriticism*, edited by Greg Garrard. Oxford, UK: Oxford University Press.

Kimmelman, Michael. 1993. "Critic's Notebook: Making Art of the Holocaust: New Museum, New Works." *The New York Times* (April 23). Accessed February 13, 2017. http://www.nytimes.com/1993/04/23/us/critic-s-notebook-making-art-of-the-holocaust-new-museum-new-works.html?pagewanted=all.

Knudsen, Britta Timm. 2006. "Emotional Geography: Authenticity, Embodiment and Cultural Heritage." *Ethnologia Europaea/Journal of European Ethnology* 36 (2): 5–25.

Knudsen, Britta Timm. 2011. "Thanatourism: Withessing Difficult Pasts." *Tourist Studies* 11 (1): 55–72.

Knudsen, Britta Timm, and Anne Marit Waade, eds. 2002. *Re-Investing Authenticity. Tourism, Place and Emotions*. Leeds: View Channel Publications.

Koehn, Daryl. 1998. *Rethinking Feminist Ethics: Care, Trust and Empathy*. London: Routledge.

Krause, Sharon R. 2008. *Civil Passions: Moral Sentiment and Democratic Deliberation*. Princeton, NJ: Princeton University Press.

LaCapra, Dominick. 1998. *History and Memory after Auschwitz*. Ithaca, NY: Cornell University Press.

LaCapra, Dominick. 2001. *Writing History, Writing Trauma*. Baltimore, MD: Johns Hopkins University Press.

Lankford, E. Louis. 1998. "Aesthetic Experience in a Postmodern Age: Recovering the Aesthetics of E. F. Kaelin." *Journal of Aesthetic Education* 32: 23–30.

Latour, Bruno. 1987. *Science in Action*. Cambridge, MA: Harvard University Press.

Latour, Bruno. 1993. *We Have Never Been Modern*. Cambridge, MA: Harvard University Press.

Latour, Bruno. 2004. "Why Has Critique Run out of Steam? From Matters of Fact to Matters of Concern." *Critical Inquiry* 30: 225–49.

Latour, Bruno. 2005. *Reassembling the Social: An Introduction to Actor-Network Theory*. Oxford, UK: Oxford University Press.

Laurier, Eric, and Chris Philo. 2006. "Possible Geographies: A Passing Encounter in a Café." *Area* 38 (1): 353–63.

LeDoux, Joseph. 1996. *The Emotional Brain: The Mysterious Underpinnings of Emotional Life*. New York: Simon & Schuster.

Lennon, J. John, and Malcolm Foley. 2010. *Dark Tourism: The Attraction of Death and Disaster*. London, UK: Cengage Learning.

Levin, David M. 1988. *The Opening of Vision—Nihilism and the Postmodern Situation*. New York and London: Routledge.

Levin, David M. 1993. *Modernity and the Hegemony of Vision*. Berkeley, CA: University of California Press.

Lewis, Michael, and Jeannette M. Haviland, eds. 1993. *Handbook of Emotions*. New York: Guildford Press.

Leys, Ruth. 2000. *Trauma. A Genealogy*. Chicago, IL: University of Chicago Press.

Leys, Ruth. 2007. *From Guilt to Shame. Auschwitz and After*. Princeton, NJ, and Oxford, UK: Princeton University Press.

Leys, Ruth. 2011. "The Turn to Affect: A Critique." *Critical Inquiry* 37 (3): 434–72.

Libeskind, Daniel. 1991. "Between the Lines." In *Architecture in Transition: Between Deconstruction and New Modernism*, edited by Peter Noever. Prestel: Munich.

Libeskind, Daniel. 1992. *Erweiterungsbau des Berlin Museums mit Abteilung Jüdisches Museum* [Expansion of the Berlin Museum with Jewish Museum]. Berlin: Ernst & Sohn Verlag für Architektur.

Libeskind, Daniel. 1995. *1995 Raoul Wallenberg Lecture*. Ann Arbor, MI: College of Architecture and Urban Planning.

Libeskind, Daniel. 2000. *The Space of Encounter*. New York: Universe.

Libeskind, Daniel. 2001. *The Space of Encounter*. London, UK: Thames & Hudson.

Libeskind, Daniel, and Hélène Binet. 1999. *Jewish Museum Berlin*. Amsterdam and Dresden: G+B Arts International.

Lippard, Lucy R. 1999. *On the Beaten Track: Tourism, Art, and Place*. New York: The New Press.

Lisle, Debbie. 2004. "Gazing at Ground Zero: Tourism, Voyeurism and Spectacle." *Journal for Cultural Research* 8 (1): 3–21.

Löfgren, Orvar. 1999. *On Holiday: A History of Vacationing*. Berkeley, CA: University of California Press.

Logan, William, and Keir Reeves. 2009. "Introduction: Remembering Places of Pain and Shame." In *Places of Pain and Shame: Dealing with "Difficult Past,"* edited by William Logan and Keir Reeves, 1–14. London: Routledge.

Lupton, Deborah. 1998. *The Emotional Self: A Sociocultural Exploration*. London, UK: Sage.

Lutz, Catherine. 1988. *Unnatural Emotions: Everyday Sentiments on a Micronesian Atoll and Their Challenge to Western Theory*. Chicago, IL: University of Chicago Press.

Lyotard, Jean-François. 1991. "Critical Reflections." *Artforum* 24 (8): 92–93.

Maccannell, Dean. 1989. *The Tourist: A New Theory of the Leisure Class*. New York: Schocken Books.

Macdonald, Sharon. 2006. "Undesirable Heritage: Fascist Material Culture and Historical Consciousness in Nuremberg." *International Journal of Heritage Studies* 12 (1): 9–28.

Macdonald, Sharon. 2013. *Memorylands. Heritage and Identity in Europe Today*. New York: Routledge.

Manning, Erin. 2006. *Politics of Touch*. Minneapolis, MN: University of Minnesota Press.

Manning, Erin. 2009. *Relationscapes. Movement, Art, Philosophy*. Cambridge, MA: MIT Press.

Manning, Erin. 2013. *Always More Than One. Individuation's Dance*. Durham, NC: Duke University Press.

Manning, Erin. 2014. "Wondering the World Directly—Or, How Movement Outruns the Subject." *Body & Society* 20 (3 and 4): 162–88.

Marder, Michael. 2014a. *Plant-Thinking. A Philosophy of Vegetal Life*. New York: Columbia University Press.

Marder, Michael. 2014b. *The Philosopher's Plant: An Intellectual Herbarium*. New York: Columbia University Press.

Massumi, Brian. 2002a. *Parables for the Virtual*. Durham, NC: Duke University Press.

Massumi, Brian. 2002b. "Introduction: Like a Thought." In *A Shock to Thought: Expression after Deleuze and Guattari*, edited by Brian Massumi, xiii–xxxix. New York: Routledge.

Massumi, Brian, ed. 2002c. *A Shock to Thought: Expression after Deleuze and Guattari*. New York: Routledge.

Massumi, Brian. 2008. "The Thinking-Feeling of What Happens," *Inflexions* 1 (1): n.p.

Massumi, Brian. 2011. *Semblance and Event: Activist Philosophy and the Occurrent Arts*. Cambridge, MA: MIT Press.

Massumi, Brian. 2014. *What Animals Teach Us about Politics*. Durham, NC: Duke University Press.

McNeilly, Jody. 2014. "A Phenomenology of/with Total Movement: Response to Erin Manning." *Body & Society* 20 (3 and 4): 208–21.

McShine, Kynaston, Lynne Cooke, and John Rajchman. 2007. *Richard Serra Sculpture: Forty Years*. New York: Museum of Modern Art.

Meek, Allen. 2014. *Trauma and Media. Theories, Histories, and Images*. New York and London: Routledge.

Merleau-Ponty, Maurice. 1968. *The Visible and the Invisible*. Evanston, IL: Northwestern University Press.

Message, Kylie. 2006. *New Museums and the Making of Culture*. Oxford, UK: Berg.

Meyers, Diane T. 1994. *Subjection and Subjectivity*. London, UK: Routledge.

Miles, Malcolm. 2004. *Urban Avant-Gardes: Art, Architecture and Change*. London, UK: Routledge.

Miles, William F. S. 2002. "Auschwitz: Museum Interpretation and Darker Tourism." *Annals of Tourism Research* 29 (4): 1175–78.

Mintz, Alan. 2001. *Popular Culture and the Shaping of Holocaust Memory in America*. Seattle, WA: University of Washington Press.

Mohanty, Chandra T. 1988. "Under Western Eyes: Feminist Scholarship and Colonial Discourses." *Feminist Review* 30: 61–88.

Mohanty, Chandra T. 2003. *Feminism without Borders: Decolonizing Theory, Practicing Solidarity*. Durham, NC: Duke University Press.

Nathanson, Donald L. 1992. *Shame and Pride: Affect, Sex, and the Birth of the Self.* New York: W. W. Norton & Company.

Ngai, Sianne. 2005. *Ugly Feelings*. Cambridge, MA: Harvard University Press.

Novick, Peter. 2001. *The Holocaust and Collective Memory*. London, UK: Bloomsbury Publishing PLC.

Nussbaum, Martha. 2003. *Upheavals of Thought: The Intelligence of Emotions*. Cambridge, MA: Cambridge University Press.

Obrador Pons, Pau. 2003. "Being-on-Holiday. Tourist Dwelling, Bodies and Place." *Tourist Studies* 3 (1): 47–66.

Ockman, Joan. 2006. "A Place in the World for a World Displaced." In *Yad Vashem. Moshe Safdie—The Architecture of Memory*, by Joan Ockman, Moshe Safdie, Avner Shalev, and Elie Wiesel, 19–49. Jerusalem: Yad Vashem Publications.

Olkowski, Dorothea. 1999. *Gilles Deleuze and the Ruin of Representation*. Berkeley, CA: University of California Press.

O'Neill, Sean. 2002. "Soham Pleads with Trippers to Stay Away." *Daily Telegraph*. Accessed March 13, 2013. http://www.telegraph.co.uk/news/main.jhtml?xml=/news/2002/08/26/nfen26.xm-l&sSheet=/portal/2002/08/26/ixport.html.

Ong, Walter J. 1991. "The Shifting Sensorium." In *Varieties of Sensory Experience: A Sourcebook in the Anthropology of the Senses*, edited by David Howes, 25–30. Oxford, UK: Berg.

Opaschowski, Horst W. 2001. *Tourismus im 21. Jahehundert, das gekaufte paradies* [Tourism in the 21st Century, the Paradise Bought]. Hamburg: B.A.T. Freizeit-Forschungsinstitut GmbH.

O'Sullivan, Simon. 2001. "The Aesthetics of Affect. Thinking Art beyond Representation." *Angelaki. Journal of the Theoretical Humanities* 6 (3): 125–35.

O'Sullivan, Simon. 2006. *Art Encounters Deleuze and Guattari: Thinking beyond Representation*. London, UK: Palgrave.

Pallasmaa, Juhani. 2005. *The Eyes of the Skin. Architecture and the Senses*. Chichester: Wiley.

Papastergiadis, Nikos, and Mary Zournazi. 2002. "Faith without Certitudes: A Conversation with Nikos Papastergiadis." In *Hope: New Philosophies for Change*, edited by Mary Zournazi, 78–95. Annandale, NSW: Pluto Press.

Papoulias, Constantina, and Felicity Callard. 2010. "Biology's Gift: Interrogating the Turn to Affect." *Body & Society* 16 (1): 29–56.

Parikka, Jussi. 2007. *Digital Contagions. A Media Archeology of Computer Viruses*. New York: Peter Lang.

Parikka, Jussi. 2010. *Insect Media: An Archeology of Animals and Technology*. Minneapolis, MN: Minnesota University Press.

Pedwell, Carolyn. 2012. "Economies of Empathy: Obama, Neoliberalism and Social Justice." *Environment and Planning D: Society and Space* 30 (2): 163–79.

Pedwell, Carolyn. 2013. "Affect at the Margins: Alternative Empathies in a Small Place." *Emotion, Space and Society* 8: 18–26.

Pedwell, Carolyn. 2014. *Affective Relations. The Transnational Politics of Empathy*. London and New York: Palgrave Macmillan.

Pickford, Henry W. 2012. "Dialectical Reflections on Peter Eisenman's Memorial for the Murdered Jews of Europe." *Architectural Theory Review: Women, Practice, Architecture* 17 (2–3): 419–39.

Pickford, Henry W. 2013. *The Sense of Semblance: Philosophical Analyses of Holocaust Art*. New York: Fordham University Press.

Pieper, Katrin. 2006. *Die Musealisierung des Holocaust. Das Jüdische Museum Berlin und das U.S. Holocaust Memorial Museum in Washington D.C. Ein Vergleich* [The Musealization of the Holocaust: The Jewish Museum Berlin and the U.S. Holocaust Memorial Museum in Washington D.C.: A Comparison]. Köln: Böhlau.

Pile, Steve J. 2010. "Emotions and Affect in Recent Human Geography." *Transactions of the Institute of British Geographers* 35 (1): 5–20.

Pinotti, Andrea. 2015. "Mnemosyne and Amnesia, Social Memory and the Paradoxes." In *Socioaesthetics: Ambiance—Imaginary*, edited by Anders Michelsen and Frederic Tygstrup, 73–85. Leiden and Boston, MA: Brill.

Pollock, Griselda. 2003. "Holocaust Tourism: Being There, Looking Back and the Ethics of Spacial Memory." In *Visual Culture and Tourism*, edited by David Crouch and Nina Lübbren, 175–89. New York: Berg Publishers.

Pollock, Grizelda. 2010. "Aesthetic Wit(h)nessing in the Era of Trauma." *EurAmerica* 40 (4): 829–86.

Poria, Yaniv, Richard Butler, and David Airey. 2003. "The Core of Heritage Tourism: Distinguishing Heritage Tourists from Tourists in Heritage Places." *Annals of Tourism Research* 30 (1): 238–54.

Poria, Yaniv, Arie Reichel, and Avital Biran. 2006. "Heritage Site Management: Motivations and Expectations." *Annals of Tourism Research* 33 (1): 162–78.

Preece, Tanaya, and Garry Price. 2005. "Motivations of Participants in Dark Tourism: A Case Study of Port Arthur, Tasmania, Australia." In *Taking Tourism to the Limits: Issues, Concepts and Managerial Perspectives*, edited by Chris Ryan, Stephen J. Page, and Michelle Aicken, 191–98. Oxford, UK: Elsevier Ltd.

Priest, Eldritch. 2013. "Felt as Thought (or Musical Abstraction and the Semblance of Affect)." In *Sound, Music, Affect: Theorizing Sonic Experience*, edited by Marie

Thompson and Ian Biddle, 45–64. London, New Delhi, New York, and Sydney: Bloomsbury.

Probyn, Elspeth. 2005. *Blush: Faces of Shame*. Minneapolis, MN: University of Minnesota Press.

Puig de la Bellacasa, María. 2012. "'Nothing Comes without Its World': Thinking with Care." *The Sociological Review* 60 (2): 197–216.

Rauterberg, Hanno. 2005. "Building Site of Remembrance." In *Holocaust Memorial Berlin*, edited by Eisenman Architects, n.p. Germany: Lars Müller.

Reading, Ann. 2002. *A Social Inheritance of the Holocaust: Gender, Culture and Memory*. London, UK: Palgrave.

Reddy, William M. 2001. *The Navigation of Feeling. A Framework for the History of Emotions*. Cambridge, MA: Cambridge University Press.

Riley, Denise. 2005. *Impersonal Passion: Language as Affect*. Durham, NC: Duke University Press.

Rojek, Chris. 1993. *Ways of Escape*. Basingstoke, UK: Macmillan.

Rojek, Chris. 1994. "Leisure and the Dreamworld of Modernity." In *Leisure, Modernity, Postmodernity and Lifestyles*, edited by Ian Henry, 3–12. Brighton, UK: LSA.

Rojek, Chris. 1995. *Decentring Leisure. Rethinking Leisure Theory*. London, UK: Sage.

Rojek, Chris. 1997. "Indexing, Dragging and the Social Construction of Tourist Sights." In *Touring Cultures: Transformations of Travel and Theory*, edited by Chris Rojek and John Urry, 52–74. New York and London: Routledge.

Rothberg, Michael. 2000. *Traumatic Realism: The Demands of Holocaust Representation*. Minneapolis, MN: University of Minnesota Press.

Rothberg, Michael. 2009. *Multidirectional Memory: Remembering the Holocaust in the Age of Decolonization*. Stanford, CA: Stanford University Press.

Rowlands, Michael. 1999. "Remembering to Forget: Sublimation as Sacrifice in War Memorials." In *The Art of Forgetting*, edited by Adrian Forty and Susanne Küchler, 129–45. Oxford, UK: Berg.

Russell, James A. 2003. "Core Affect and the Psychological Construction of Emotion." *Psychological Review* 110 (1): 145–72.

Russell, James A., and José-Miguel Fernandez-Dols, eds. 1997. *The Psychology of Facial Expression*. Cambridge, MA: Cambridge University Press.

Ryan, Chris, and Rahul Kohli. 2006. "The Buried Village, New Zealand—An Example of Dark Tourism?" *Asia Pacific Journal of Tourism Research* 11 (3): 211–26.

Schostak, Jill, and John Schostak. 2008. *Radical Research. Designing, Developing and Writing Research to Make a Difference*. London and New York: Routledge.

Schrader, Astrid. 2015. "Abyssal Intimacies and Temporalities of Care: How (Not) to Care about Deformed Leaf Bugs in the Aftermath of Chernobyl." *Social Studies of Science* 45(5): 1–26. doi:10.1177/0306312715603249.

Seaton, A. V. 1996. "Guided by the Dark: From Thanatopsis to Thanatourism." *International Journal of Heritage Studies* 2: 234–44.

Seaton, A. V., and J. J. Lennon. 2004. "Thanatourism in the Early 21st Century: Moral Panics, Ulterior Motives and Alterior Desires." In *New Horizons in Tourism—Strange Experiences and Stranger Practices*, edited by Tejvir Singh, 63–82. Wallingford: CABI Publishing.

Sedgwick, Eve Kosofsky. 2003. *Touching Feeling: Affect, Pedagogy, Performativity*. Durham, NC: Duke University Press.

Sedgwick, Eve Kosofsky, and Adam Frank. 1995. "Shame in the Cybernetic Fold: Reading Silvan Tomkins." *Critical Inquiry* 21: 496–522.

Selwyn, Tom. 1996. "Introduction." *The Tourist Image. Myths and Myth Making in Tourism*, edited by Tom Selwyn. Chichester, UK: John Wiley and Sons.

Senie, Harriet F. 2001. "Perpetual Tension: Considering Richard Serra's Jewish Identity." In *Complex Identities: Jewish Consciousness and Modern Art*, edited by Matthew Baigell and Milly Heyd, 206–22. New Brunswick, NJ: Rutgers University Press.

Serres, Michel, and Mary Zournazi. 2002. "The Art of Living: A Conversation with Michel Serres." In *Hope: New Philosophies for Change*, edited by Mary Zournazi, 192–208. Annandale, NSW: Pluto Press.

Shalev, Avner. 2006. "Building a Holocaust Museum in Jerusalem." In *Yad Vashem. Moshe Safdie—The Architecture of Memory*, by Joan Ockman, Moshe Safdie, Avner Shalev, and Elie Wiesel, 50–60. Jerusalem: Yad Vashem Publications.

Sharpley, Richard. 2005. "Travels to the Edge of Darkness: Towards a Typology of Dark Tourism." In *Taking Tourism to the Limit: Issues, Concepts, and Managerial Perspectives*, edited by Chris Ryan, Stephen Page, and Michelle Aicken, 215–26. London: Elsevier.

Sharpley, Richard. 2009. "Shedding Light on Dark Tourism: An Introduction." In *The Darker Side of Travel. The Theory and Practice of Dark Tourism*, edited by Richard Sharpley and Philip Stone, 3–22. Bristol, Buffalo, and Toronto: Channel View Publications.

Sheets-Johnstone, Maxine. 2014. "Thinking in Movement: Response to Erin Manning." *Body & Society* 20 (3 and 4): 198–207.

Shiva, Vandana. 1997. *Biopiracy: The Plunder of Nature and Knowledge*. Boston, MA: South End Press.

Shosh Rotem, Stephanie. 2013. *Constructing Memory. Architectural Narratives of Holocaust Museums*. Frankfurt am Main: Peter Lang.

Shouse, Eric. 2005. "Feeling, Emotion, Affect." *M/C Journal* 8. Accessed August 27, 2014. http://journal.media-culture.org.au/0512/03-shouse.php.

Shusterman, Richard. 1997. "The End of Aesthetic Experience." *Journal of Aesthetics and Art Criticism* 55: 29–41.

Shusterman, Richard. 1999. "Somaesthetics: A Disciplinary Proposal." *The Journal of Aesthetics and Art Criticism* 57: 299–313.

Shusterman, Richard. 2000a. *Performing Live*. Ithaca, NY: Cornell University Press.

Shusterman, Richard. 2000b. *Pragmatic Aesthetics. Living Beauty, Rethinking Art*. Lanham, MD: Rowman & Littlefield.

Shusterman, Richard. 2008. "Aesthetic Experience: From Analysis to Eros." In *Aesthetic Experience*, edited by Richard Shusterman and Adele Tomlin, 45–58. New York and London: Routledge.

Shusterman, Richard, and Adele Tomlin, eds. 2008. *Aesthetic Experience*. New York and London: Routledge.

Slayton, Sharon L. 2006. "Hiroshima: Tourist Destination and Plea for Peace." Accessed December 4, 2009. http://www.grief-tourism.com/hiroshima-tourist-destination-plea-for-peace.

Smail, Daniel L. 2004. *On Deep History and the Brain*. Berkeley, CA: University of California Press.

Smith, Adam. 2006 (1759). *The Theory of Moral Sentiments*. Mineola, NY: Dover Publications Inc.

Smith, Daniel W. 1997. "Introduction." In *Essays Clinical and Critical*, by Gilles Deleuze. London and New York: Verso.

Smith, Laurajane. 2004. *Archeological Theory and the Politics of Cultural Heritage*. London, UK: Routledge.

Smith, Nell, and W. Glen Croy. 2005. "Presentation of Dark Tourism: The Waiora, the Buried Village." In *Taking Tourism to the Limits: Issues, Concepts, and Managerial Perspectives*, edited by Chris Ryan, Stephen Page, and Michelle Aicken, 199–213. Amsterdam: Elsevier.

Söderström, Ola. 2005. "Representation." In *Cultural Geography. A Critical Dictionary of Key Concepts*, edited by David Atkinson, Peter Jackson, David Sibley, and Neil Washbourne, 11–15. London and New York: Tauris.

Solomon, Robert C. 1995. *A Passion for Justice: Emotions and the Origins of the Social Contract*. Lanham, MD: Rowman and Littlefield.

Solomon, Robert C., ed. 2003. *What Is an Emotion? Classic and Contemporary Readings*. Oxford, UK: Oxford University Press.

Sontag, Susan. 2003. *Regarding the Pain of Others*. London, UK: Penguin.

Spelman, Elizabeth V. 1989. "Anger and Insubordination." In *Women, Knowledge, and Reality: Explorations in Feminist Philosophy*. Boston, MA: Unwin Hyman.

Spelman, Elizabeth. 1997. *Fruits of Sorrow: Framing Our Attention to Suffering*. Boston, MA: Beacon Press.

Spiegelman, Art. 1972. "The First Maus." *Funny Animals*.

Spinoza, Baruch. 1959. *Spinoza's Ethics. And on the Correction of the Understanding*. London, MA: Everyman's Library.

Spivak, Gayatri C. 1988. "Can the Subaltern Speak?" In *Marxism and the Interpretation of Cultur*e, edited by Cary Nelson and Lawrence Grossberg, 271–313. Basingstoke, UK: Macmillan Education.

Stead, Naomi. 2000. "The Ruins of History: Allegories of Destruction in Daniel Libeskind's Jewish Museum." *Open Museum Journal* 2: 1–13.

Stone, Philip. 2006. "A Dark Tourism Spectrum: Towards Typology of Death and Macabre Related Tourist Sites, Attractions and Exhibitions." *Tourism* 54 (2): 145–60.

Stone, Philip. 2009. "Dark Tourism: Mortality and New Moral Spaces." In *The Darker Side of Travel: The Theory and Practice of Dark Tourism*, edited by Richard Sharpley and Philip Stone, 56–74. Bristol, UK: Channel View Publications.

Stone, Philip, and Richard Sharpley. 2008. "Consuming Dark Tourism: A Thanatological Perspective." *Annals of Tourism Research* 35 (2): 574–95.

Strivale, Charles J. 1998. "Pragmatic/Machinic: Discussion with Félix Guattari (March 19, 1985)." In *The Two-Fold Thought of Deleuze and Guattari: Intersections and Animations*, edited by Charles J. Stivale 191–224. New York: Guilford Press.

Strongman, Kenneth T. 2003. *The Psychology of Emotion: From Everyday Life to Theory*. West Sussex, UK: Wiley and Sons.

Sturken, Marita. 1991. "The Wall, the Screen, and the Image: The Vietnam Veterans Memorial." *Representations* 35, Special Issue: Monumental Histories: 118–42.

Sturken, Marita. 1997. *Tangled Memories: The Vietnam War, the AIDS Epidemic, and the Politics of Remembering*. Berkeley, CA: University of California Press.

Stweart, Kathleen. 2007. *Ordinary Affect*. Durham, NC: Duke University Press.

Tenesini, Alessandra. 1999. "Feminism and 'Malestream' Epistemology." In *An Introduction to Feminist Epistemologies*, by Alessandra Tenesini, 38–65. Blackwell, UK: Oxford.

Thiele, Kathrin. 2014. "*Ethos* of Diffraction: New Paradigms for a (Post)humanist Ethics." *Parallax* 20 (3): 202–16.

Thrift, Nigel. 2004. "Intensities of Feeling: Towards a Spacial Politics of Affect." *Geografiska Annaler* 86: 57–78.

Thrift, Nigel. 2007. *Non-Representational Theory: Space, Politics, Affect*. London, UK: Routledge.

Till, Karen E. 2005. *The New Berlin: Memory, Politics, Place*. Minneapolis, MN: University of Minnesota Press.

Timothy, Dallen J., and Stephen W. Boyd. 2006. "Heritage Tourism in the 21st Century: Valued Traditions and New Perspectives." *Journal of Heritage Tourism* 1 (1): 1–16.

Tomkins, Silvan S. 1962. *Affect, Imagery, Consciousness: Volume I, The Positive Affects*. London, UK: Travistok.

Tomkins, Silvan S. 1963. *Affect, Imagery, Consciousness: Volume I, The Negative Affects*. London, UK: Travistok.

Tomlin, Adele. 2008. "Introduction. Contemplating the Undefinable." In *Aesthetic Experience*, edited by Richard Shusterman and Adele Tomlin, 1–13. New York and London: Routledge.

Trauer, Birgit. 2006. "Conceptualizing Special Interest Tourism—Frameworks for Analysis." *Tourism Management* 27: 183–200.

Trotta, James. 2006. "Grief Tourism Definition." Accessed September 22, 2013. http://www.grief-tourism.com/grief-tourism-definition/.

Tunbridge J. E., and G. J. Ashworth. 1996. *Dissonant Heritage. The Management of the Past as a Resource in Conflict*. Chichester: Wiley.

Uexküll, Jakob von. 2001. "The New Concept of Umwelt: A Link between Science and the Humanities." *Semiotica* 134 (1/4): 111–23.

Urry, John. 1999. "Sensing Leisure Spaces." In *Leisure/Tourism Geographies. Practices and Geographical Knowledge*, edited by David Crouch, 34–45. London and New York: Routledge.

Uzzell, David L. 1998. "Interpreting Our Heritage: A Theoretical Interpretation." In *Contemporary Issues in Heritage and Environmental Interpretation*, edited by David L. Uzzell and Roy Ballantyne, 11–25. London, UK: The Stationery Office.

Uzzell, David L., and Roy Ballantyne. 1998. "Heritage That Hurts: Interpretation in a Postmodern World." In *Contemporary Issues in Heritage and Environmental Interpretation*, edited by David L. Uzzell and Roy Ballantyne, 152–71. London, UK: The Stationery Office.

Van Alphen, Ernst. 1997. *Caught by History: Holocaust Effects in Contemporary Art, Literature and Theory*. Stanford, CA: Stanford University Press.

Van Alphen, Ernst. 2002. "Caught by Images: On the Role of Visual Imprints in Holocaust Testimonies." *Journal of Visual Culture* 1 (2): 205–21.

Van Alphen, Ernst. 2005. *Art in Mind: How Contemporary Images Shape Thought*. Chicago, IL: University of Chicago Press.

Van der Kolk, Bessel A., and Onno Van der Hart. 1995. "The Intrusive Past: The Flexibility of Memory and the Engraving of Trauma." In *Trauma: Explorations in Memory*, edited by Cathy Caruth, 158–82. Baltimore, MD: Johns Hopkins University Press.

van der Tuin, Iris. 2011. "'A Different Starting Point, a Different Metaphysics': Reading Bergson and Barad Diffractively." *Hypatia: A Journal of Feminist Philosophy* 26 (1): 22–42.

van der Tuin, Iris. 2014a. *Generational Feminism: New Materialist Introduction to a Generative Approach*. New York: Lexington Books.

van der Tuin, Iris. 2014b. "Diffraction as a Methodology for Feminist Onto-Epistemology: On Encountering Chantal Chawar and Posthuman Interpellation." *Parallax* 20 (3): 231–44.

van der Tuin, Iris. 2014c. "The Mode of Invention of Creative Research: Onto-Epistemology." In *Material Interventions. Applying Creative Arts Research*, edited by Estelle Barrett and Barbara Bolt, 257–72. London, UK: I.B. Tauris.

Violi, Patrizia. 2012. "Trauma Site Museums and Politics of Memory: Tuol Sleng, Villa Grimaldi and the Bologna Ustica Museum." *Theory, Culture & Society* 29: 36–75.

Walser, Martin. 1998. "Die Banalität des Guten" [The Banality of the Good]. *Frankfurter Allgemeine Zeitung*, October 12: 5.

Warf, Barney, and Santa Arias. 2014. *The Spatial Turn: Interdisciplinary Perspectives*. New York: Routledge.

Weinberg, Jeshajahu, and Rina Elieli. 1995. *The Holocaust Museum in Washington*. New York: Rizzoli International.

West, Patrick. 2004. *Conspicuous Compassion: Why Sometimes It Really Is Cruel to Be Kind*. London, UK: Civitas.

Westera, Wim. 2012. *The Digital Turn: How the Internet Transforms Our Existence*. London, UK: AuthorHouseUK.

Wetherell, Margaret. 1998. "Positioning and Interpretative Repertoires: Conversation Analysis and Post-Structuralism in Dialogue." *Discourse and Society* 9 (3): 431–56.

Wetherell, Margaret. 2012. *Affect and Emotion. A New Social Science Understanding*. London, UK: Sage.

Wetherell, Margaret. 2013. "Affect and Discourse—What's the Problem? From Affect as Excess to Affective/Discursive Practice." *Subjectivity* 6 (4): 349–68.

White, Goeffrey M. 1993. "Emotions Inside Out: The Anthropology of Affect." *Handbook of Emotions*, edited by Michael Lewis and Jeannette M. Haviland, 29–40. New York: Guildford Publications.

Whitehead, Alfred N. 1978. *Process and Reality*. New York: Free Press.

Wiesel, Elie. 1979. Report to the President. President's Commission of Holocaust. Accessed March 12, 2013. http://www.ushmm.org/m/pdfs/20050707-presidents-commission-holocaust.pdf.

Williams, Paul. 2004. "Witnessing Genocide: Vigilance and Remembrance at Tuol Sleng and Choeung Ek." *Holocaust and Genocide Studies* 18 (2): 234–55.

Williams, Paul. 2007. *Memorial Museums: The Global Rush to Commemorate Atrocities*. Oxford and New York: Berg.

Wojtaszek, Marek, and Dorota Golańska. 2009. "Seeing Differently: Towards an Affirmative Approach to Visual Culture." In *Teaching Visual Culture in an Interdisciplinary Classroom. Feminist (Re)Interpretations of the Field*, edited by Elżbieta H. Oleksy and Dorota Golańska 175–198. Utrecht: Uithof Drukkerijen.

Wolfreys, Julian. 2002. "Trauma, Testimony, Criticism: Witnessing, Memory and Responsibility." In *Introducing Criticism at the 21st Century*, edited by Julian Wolfreys, 126–48. Edinburgh: Edinburgh University Press.

Young, James E. 1992. The Counter-Monument: Memory against Itself in Germany Today. *Critical Inquiry* 18 (2): 267–96.

Young, James E. 1993. *The Texture of Memory: Holocaust Memorials and Meaning*. New Haven, CT: Yale University Press.

Young, James E. 2000. *At Memory's Edge: After-Images of the Holocaust in Contemporary Art and Architecture*. New Haven, CT, and London: Yale University Press.

Zelizer, Barbie. 1998. *Remembering to Forget: Holocaust Memory through the Camera's Eye*. Chicago, IL: University of Chicago Press.

Zerubavel, Yael. 1994. "The Death of Memory and the Memory of Death. Masada and the Holocaust as Historical Metaphors." *Representations* 45: 72–100.

Index

www.ingramcontent.com/pod-product-compliance
Ingram Content Group UK Ltd.
Pitfield, Milton Keynes, MK11 3LW, UK
UKHW041632031026
15587UKWH00001B/235